LONG LANCE

LONG LANCE
THE TRUE STORY OF AN IMPOSTOR

DONALD B. SMITH

MACMILLAN OF CANADA
A Division of Gage Publishing Limited

TORONTO, CANADA

A PEPPERMINT DESIGN © RICHARD MILLER

Canadian Cataloguing in Publication Data

Smith, Donald B., 1946-
Long Lance

Includes index.
ISBN 0-7715-9585-9

1. Buffalo Child Long Lance, Blood Indian Chief, d. 1932. 2. Indians of North America — Canada — Biography. 3. Impostors and imposture — Canada — Biography. I. Title.

E90.B9S65   970.004'97   C81-094843-5

The author wishes to thank Holt, Rinehart and Winston Ltd. of New York for permission to include several passages from *Long Lance*; *Cosmopolitan* magazine for the excerpts from Long Lance's article "My Trail Upward," published in their issue of June, 1926; the B. F. Goodrich Company of Akron, Ohio, for the two publicity items advertising the Chief Long Lance running shoe; and the estate of Jim Thorpe, for Thorpe's endorsement of the shoe.

Macmillan of Canada
A Division of Gage Publishing Limited

Printed in Canada

TO MY MOTHER
and in memory of my late father

CONTENTS

PREFACE

I FIRST BECAME INTERESTED in Chief Buffalo Child
Long Lance ten years ago. Rummaging in a second-
hand bookstore in Toronto, I noticed a small brown
volume, its title firmly imprinted on the spine: *Long
Lance*. Intrigued by what appeared to be an Indian's
autobiography, I pulled it down and turned to page one: "The
first thing in my life that I can remember is the exciting
aftermath of an Indian fight in northern Montana." I
bought the book, read it, and never forgot it.

My next encounter with Chief Long Lance came four
years later, this time in Calgary, in the heart of the Blackfoot's old hunting territory. In the fall of 1974, I began
teaching Canadian history at the University of Calgary;
fresh from eastern Canada, I knew little about the West. I
made several trips to the archives of the Glenbow-Alberta
Institute, a rich source of Western Canadiana, as well as
appropriate lecture material. There, one afternoon, I found
a sizeable carton full of letters, articles and newspaper
clippings about a Blackfoot warrior: Long Lance. The Glenbow materials had come from the estate of Canon S.H.
Middleton, Long Lance's executor, the recipient of many of
the Chief's possessions after his death. The articles and
letters told of his honors at the Carlisle Indian School in
Pennsylvania, of his appointment by President Woodrow
Wilson to West Point, of his distinguished service in the

Great War with the Canadian Army, of his years as a reporter in Western Canada, and of his incredible success in New York City as a writer, actor and aviator.

It was exciting material. Yet the file at Glenbow contained so many inconsistencies: for example, in an article published in the Los Angeles *Examiner* immediately after the Chief's death in 1932, I found a curious reference to his father — who had signed himself J.S. Long. That seemed strange; most Blackfoot Indians that I had read about usually had names like Crowfoot, Red Crow or Shot-Both-Sides. And there was another leading discrepancy. In the articles of the late 1920s, Long Lance was described as a young man of thirty-five. Yet in his autobiography, he claimed that he had hunted the buffalo in his youth, which, if he had been born in the early 1890s, was completely impossible.

All that winter of 1974/75, I sent out dozens of letters trying to discover Long Lance's true origins. Hugh Dempsey, the Director of History at the Glenbow-Alberta Institute, and Sheilagh Jameson, the Chief Archivist, had long been interested in the man. Both of them kindly put me in touch with several people who had known him in Alberta in the 1920s. In Calgary, I met Howard Kelly, Hugh Dann and George Gooderham, and on the Blood Reserve, Mike Eagle Speaker. At Waterton Park near the Alberta-Montana border, I contacted Sophie Allison, the daughter of Canon Middleton. All went out of their way to help me, supplying me with articles and letters written by and about Long Lance. (I have placed copies of all the materials collected from them in the archives of the Glenbow-Alberta Institute in Calgary.)

Having read in the article in the Los Angeles *Examiner* that Long Lance's father, "J.S. Long," claimed to live in Winston-Salem, North Carolina, I wrote to the city's public library in late February. In her reply, Ann Correll, the librarian in charge of the North Carolina Collection, provided the documentary proof of Long Lance's true origins. From his record of service in the Canadian army (filed at Glenbow) I already knew that he had enlisted as "Sylvester Long Lance." After I contacted her, the conscientious librarian checked through the Winston City directories for the early twentieth century. Yes, she wrote back on March 7, 1975, a Sylvester C. Long appeared in the directories from 1910 to 1913. Listed as a "student," his residence was given as 95 Brookstown Avenue, the home of Joseph S. and Sallie Long, and of Abraham and Walter Long. In the directories, Joseph S. Long was listed as colored. The librarian also enclosed an article written about Abraham "Abe" Long, "longtime manager of the old all-Negro balcony at the theater." In the *Winston-Salem Twin City Sentinel* on Saturday September 16, 1967, Abe had reminisced about the Carolina Theater of the old days. Three lines in that article especially struck me: "He is the last of the original Long family. A brother, Walter Long, a private detective, died here in 1941. Another brother, Sylvester, had died earlier in California." Chief Buffalo Child Long Lance had died in California. Sylvester Long of North Carolina and the famous Chief Buffalo Child had to be the same man.

In late June, 1975, I made the first of five trips to Winston-Salem. I made a few phone calls, met some relatives, and confirmed that Sylvester Long was not a full-blooded Indian. His father's ancestry was mixed: white and Indian. Joe Long himself had denied the possibility of any negro blood. Sylvester's mother was three-quarters white and one-quarter Croatan Indian. Each trip added to the information previously gathered. My research indicated that the man lionized as a Plains Indian by the North American press in the late 1920s was really an impostor. What made his story rather unique was this researcher's ability to document it, and the fact that the tale involved the continent's three major racial groupings: Indian, white, and black.

During my visits, it was fortunate that Joe Bradshaw, a distant cousin of Sylvester's, took such an interest in the project. He generously set aside many hours of his time, locating and then driving me to see Sylvester's relatives and childhood friends. Joe introduced me to Long Lance's first cousins: Charlie Carson and his sisters Daisy Blackburn, Jency Gaither, Mammie Patterson and Nannie Lewis. Lillian Doulin and her brother, Newman Dalton, allowed me to examine Abe Long's diaries and many of the Long family's photos. Joe Bradshaw showed me Long Lance's second scrapbook that Walter Long had brought back from Los Angeles. (This second scrapbook has since been donated by Mr. Bradshaw to the Glenbow-Alberta Institute. The first book is also there. After Long Lance's death, Clyde Fisher found it in the Chief's locker at the Explorers Club in New York and mailed it to Canon Middleton.)

In February, 1976, the *Canadian Magazine* published my two-part article on Chief Buffalo Child Long Lance. Thanks to the encouragement of the *Canadian*'s Alan Walker and David Cobb, who had helped me a great deal with the presentation of the articles, I decided to undertake a fuller treatment. Trips in Canada and the United States to interview those who had known Long Lance completed my research.

Since 1978, a number of people have read drafts of the book. My mother, Jean B. Smith, Ramsay Derry, and Lovat Dickson commented on the preliminary draft. Audrey Swaffield devoted long hours throughout 1978 and 1979 reading first and second versions. Working from the comments of Jan Walter of Macmillan, I prepared a third draft in 1980, which Judy Abel kindly read and criticized chapter by chapter. Both Professor Kenneth Porter of the University of Oregon, who has been interested in Long Lance since his graduate school days at Harvard, and filmmaker Alan King provided me with useful comments on this text. This, the final version of the story, owes much to the suggestions and improvements of my editor, Martin O'Malley. By coincidence, Martin's father, Fred O'Malley, worked with Long Lance at the Winnipeg *Tribune* in the early twenties. My thanks to all.

1

JANUARY 5, 1931

THAT MORNING IN NEW YORK, the fog was impenetrable, so thick an ocean liner had collided with a dredge in the harbor. Then came the winds and an unseasonable mist, and by the early evening, rain drenched the familiar thoroughfares of Manhattan, where a taxi carried two men to Pennsylvania Station. [1]

The cabbie might have recognized one of his passengers, an unusually handsome man with high cheekbones, copper skin and straight black hair. A tailored trench coat emphasized his trim athletic body and strong shoulders. He was Chief Buffalo Child Long Lance, the newest sensation in the city of sensations, and he knew his way around New York. He attended the best parties, courted actresses and gossiped with royalty—a charming, engaging, eloquent man and, somehow, self-effacing. His autobiography had been published three years earlier in 1928 and had become a critically acclaimed bestseller. More recently, he had starred in a film, *The Silent Enemy*, which had been shot in the wilds of northern Canada and premiered at the Criterion on Times Square in May, 1930. He was one of the most famous North American Indians of his day.

Newspapers and magazines hungered for stories about him, but never dug too deeply. The reporters reveled in his litany of achievements: athlete, war hero, journalist, Indian chief, author, actor, pilot. He once trained with Jim Thorpe;

1

he once sparred with Jack Dempsey. A president had granted him a special appointment to West Point; a grateful French nation had awarded him the Croix de Guerre. He was a man of wit and intelligence, and he was determined to have the best that life could offer.

The driver would not have recognized the other man, heavier, older, and dark-skinned. His name was Walter Long, a private detective from North Carolina, and to him New York was foreign and exotic territory.[2] Born in a log shanty near the Yadkin-Iredell county line in North Carolina, he lived in Winston-Salem, where the air hung heavy with the smell of licorice and tobacco. Walter Long grew up in but never broke through the stifling racial prerogatives of the South. When buying a pair of shoes, he had to be sure of his size; he would be allowed to try on only one pair. When whites approached on the sidewalk, he was expected to make way by stepping aside, even if it meant stepping into the gutter. As a "colored," Walter Long could not realize his boyhood ambition of joining the local police force; instead, he took his constabulary training in West Virginia, later returning home to start his own detective agency in the black community of Winston-Salem.

The taxi pushed through the wet streets of mid-Manhattan, past boarded-up stores and darkened restaurants, in this, the second full year of the Great Depression. Few people walked the streets; beggars foraged in garbage cans. From the glare of Times Square, the taxi entered the garment district and headed toward the ring of skyscraper-hotels surrounding the huge, two-block-long railway terminus at Seventh Avenue and Thirty-first Street.

The two men fidgeted. They barely spoke, for there was too much to speak about. The Indian in Long Lance knew about long silences and how they were not supposed to be awkward, for it is the way: *Don't speak unless you can improve the silence*.[3] The celebrated bon vivant also knew the other way, the social chit-chat, the meaningless small talk. Nothing worked for him this time, with this man. Walter Long was his brother.[4]

The taxi pulled up at the curb of the massive, columned entrance to Pennsylvania Station. Long Lance swung open the door, edged out and slammed the door behind him. He sprinted up the gray stone steps in the rain, not looking back, hurrying across the brightly lit entrance, then inside, where he disappeared into the crowd.

Walter followed him with his eyes, then paid the fare. They would never meet again.

2

ORGINS

SYLVESTER CLARK LONG was born on December 1, 1890,[1] soon after his family moved to Winston and to the little house on 4½ Street, behind the mansions of the rich whites on Fifth Street. R.J. Reynolds, the tobacco magnate, was a neighbor. In those days, before the automobile and the suburbs, black and white and rich and poor lived side by side, if not as equals at least in juxtaposition. The whites preferred to live close to downtown, with their black servants living nearby.

Sylvester's parents, Sallie and Joe Long, farmed at Carson Town in the early 1880s and were married there in 1879.[2] Carson Town, forty miles west of Winston, lay in Iredell County in the rolling foothills of western North Carolina. It was an area of tall, green forests and red clay. Winter came and stayed, but the summers were longer and hot. Sallie was born into slavery in the last months of the Civil War.[3] Joe came from a plantation in neighboring Yadkin County.[4]

Sallie and Joe Long maintained that they were white and Indian, and at this time in the South it was difficult to know and still more difficult to prove. Sallie's white grandfather, Robert Carson, was the son of the original plantation owner, Andrew Carson. She had seen his weathered gravestone in the cemetery just south of Carson Town: "Captain Andrew Carson. Born March 1, 1756. Died Jan'y 29, 1841. He was a soldier of the Revolutionary War."[5] Robert Carson's

4

tombstone stood in the Baptist Flat Rock Cemetery in Hamptonville, north of Carson Town.[6] Sallie rarely visited it, however, because the "colored" could not attend services there.

Robert Carson, or Bobby as he was known, was a wildcat in his young days. A slave-trader and a plantation owner, he was a reckless lover of many women,[7] practicing frequently on the slave women. He was considered a small-time slave-owner; the forty-six slaves he kept were not enough to warrant inclusion in the local records of the day.[8] He settled down after he bought a handsome Indian woman at a slave auction in South Carolina—Indians had been enslaved in the South in early colonial times and occasionally enslaved illegally as late as 1836[9]—and brought her to Carson Town, where he kept her as his concubine. She bore him twenty children.[10]

Sallie's mother, Adeline, one of the twenty children, was born in 1848[11] when Robert Carson was fifty-six years old. By law, as children of a slave, Adeline and her fair-skinned brothers and sisters also became slaves.[12] They grew up in one of ten tiny cabins near the big house[13] where Robert Carson lived, and they worked alongside his black field hands, planting and picking cotton, the prime crop of the area. Adeline felt it her duty to tell Sallie of her Indian past, as Adeline's mother had told her, and she repeated over and over that they were descended not from the black slaves, but from whites and Indians.

When Sallie was old enough, Adeline told her of her natural father, a man called Andrew Cowles of neighboring Hamptonville. It was her grandmother and Robert Carson all over again, the slave girl and the plantation owner. It was all part of being young and hot-blooded in the South, where a man's sexual appetites, if not skills, were whetted by the slave women. Andrew Cowles visited Robert Carson's plantation often, and there he bedded down with the more attractive slave women, fathering at least two children.[14] One of them was Sallie, born in January, 1865, when her mother, Adeline, was only sixteen.

As a girl, Sallie must have seen her father, the senator

from Yadkin County in the North Carolina Senate. [15] He was a handsome man, six feet, three inches tall, with black hair and brown eyes. [16] As a senator, his papers warranted inclusion in the records of the day, and among them was a pining letter he once wrote to a brother, in which he moaned about his solitude "in the language of one of our sentimental moonshine poets."

> No one to love, none to Caress,
> Wandering alone in this world's wilderness,
> Sad in my heart, Joy is unknown
> For in sorrow I'm weeping alone. [17]

When she shopped in Hamptonville, Sallie would walk by the old Cowles mansion, a three-storey building with an attached ballroom and a sunken garden on the grounds. [18] Always conscious of his image, the good senator never recognized Sallie, his fair-skinned daughter. [19]

Joe Long had been separated from his mother and sister at an early age, but after the Civil War he managed to find his sister in Carson Town, married to a cousin of Sallie. [20] It is a measure of his own tenacity and the racial imperatives of the South at the time that he never stopped looking for his mother. He eventually found her in a small town in Alabama, just before she died at the age of ninety. [21]

Soon after his birth in 1853, he was taken into the family of the Reverend Miles Long and given the family name. Joe Long's obituary says he was "a member of the Catawba tribe of Indians," [22] but he believed that his father was white and his mother a Cherokee slave. [23] Joe and Sallie both denied black ancestry, but they had no proof of Indian forebears, so they were "colored."

Joe and Sallie married in March, 1879, in one of the largest houses in Carson Town, owned by Joe's brother-in-law, Lee Carson. Joe was twenty-six and Sallie was fourteen. The "colored" Carsons had done well after emancipation. Segregation existed in and around Carson Town, but it was not nearly as rigid as it was in the more southerly cities. An outsider could not distinguish between "white" and "black"

among the Carson descendants, but the locals knew the
rules. Blacks could not attend the school for whites or the
Baptist Church at Hamptonville, though blacks and whites
still helped each other at harvest, and at the Carson Town
Church the blacks set a bench aside for the white farmers
and their families. Blacks and whites mixed easily and com-
fortably every October at the week-long religious festival
that they called the Big Meeting. [24]

Winston was more modern than Carson Town in every
way. When the Longs arrived in March, 1887,[25] drawn by
the prosperity of the city, Winston had telephones and soon
after electric street lights and a streetcar system.[26] Even its
segregation was more up-to-date than in Carson Town.
Two-thirds of the population was classified as "white" and
one-third as "black," and the lines were sharp and indelible.
There were no in-betweens. Blacks could not work as clerks
in stores or attend white schools. Whites stayed clear of
black churches. Blacks and whites never worked side by side
as equals. Blacks ate at their own restaurants, drank at their
own water fountains and relieved themselves in their own
rest rooms.[27]

Sallie's mother, Adeline, was devoutly religious. She mastered most of the memorable gospel songs when she lived in
her slave quarters, passing them on to Sallie. Adeline and
Sallie shared a strong Baptist faith and believed that their
rewards, if there were rewards, lay in the hereafter. It was
this attitude that Sallie and Joe sought to instill in their own
children, Abe and Walter, the two oldest sons, and Sylvester
and Katie, the youngest child and only daughter.[28]

With Sylvester, it did not "take." Something in him
resisted all attempts to teach him the rules of a racist society.
He could not swallow the platitudes, and he could not wait
for rewards in the hereafter. Doubtless he squirmed in his
seat when the black preacher spoke of the coloreds' place in
the world, when he rhapsodized about heaven and ter-
rorized about hell. His parents and his brothers explained
how he must show respect for the "white" folks, but their
admonitions only confused him. His mother, his brothers
and many of his Carson Town relatives all looked like white

folks. Still, the family persisted. Never talk back to the white folks. Always remove your hat in their presence. Step off the sidewalk to let them pass. When Sylvester reached adolescence, they added another rule: never look a white woman in the eye.[29]

Sylvester accompanied his family to Carson Town every October for the Big Meeting. It was at one of these gatherings that he first heard of his famous distant relative, Kit Carson, the trapper, guide, buffalo hunter and Indian fighter. Tradition held that Kit Carson had lived in Carson Town, but historians contend that he was born in 1809, more than a decade after his family left Carson Town for Kentucky. That did not stop the locals from telling — and inventing — stories about him. There was the time Kit Carson rode by and cut the top off a young oak in Carson Town. The oak grew to a huge height and outlasted Kit Carson by many years. It was always known as "the oak Kit Carson topped."[30] Sylvester hungered for this sort of a life, he fantasized about the West. One day he drew a simple sketch of a cowboy riding a bucking bronco in a scrapbook his mother kept. At the bottom of the drawing he carefully inscribed his initials, "SCL."[31]

There were no in-betweens in Winston, but the Longs were regarded as a special kind of negro because of their European features and Indian background. Joe worked as a clerk and later as a janitor at the whites' West End School.[32] Sallie was employed by white and black families as a nurse and midwife.[33] These were considered good jobs, and both Sallie and Joe could read and write,[34] a combination which made them aristocrats of the black community. But it did not make them white. If anything, especially for a high-spirited and adventurous boy like Sylvester, it probably heightened the confusion and frustration.

When he was six years old, Sylvester walked two miles to the Depot Street School for Negroes, even though the family then occupied a new home on Brookstown Avenue, only three blocks from West End School where his father worked as a janitor. He could help his father clean the school, but he could never hope to attend it as a student.[35]

He earned good marks at school,[36] and for a black in Winston he went far, obtaining his grade six before he left school at thirteen.[37] At school and on summer holidays, besides assisting his father, he worked with Felix Graves, his first cousin, doing odd jobs at O'Hanlon's Drug Store.[38] In 1904 he jumped at his first chance for adventure; he ran off with a circus.[39]

The turn of the century was the heyday of the American circus. Customers thrilled to gymnasts and trapezists, to the wild animal acts, and to sideshow freaks who would tear the heads off live chickens, and by the 1880s, as an extra attraction, to the Wild West Show. How could a boy like Sylvester resist? Doubtless he performed the menial chores, feeding the horses and carrying pails of water to the elephants, but he loved it. He met Arab tumblers, Mexican wire-walkers, Japanese acrobats, and American cowboys and Indians. There was little discrimination within the tight family of a traveling circus, though even here the blacks felt it somewhat, barred as they were from any of the major circus acts.[40] It did not affect Sylvester, however; with his straight black hair, high cheek bones and copper skin he was easily mistaken for an Indian. The experience changed him, forever.

When Sylvester returned home, he was lucky to get a job as the janitor at the new public library in Winston.[41] The months on the road with the circus, which took him throughout the South, ignited a curiosity that led him on to more discoveries. He used every break from floor-mopping at the library to pull down books from the shelves[42] and devour material on the world he had glimpsed from the tents and midways.

The daily humiliations now annoyed more than puzzled him. He did not want to be called "boy" the rest of his life. And it was not just riding at the back of the streetcar or watching movies high in the gallery that upset him; it was knowing that no matter what, the lowliest white would always be considered superior to even the most accomplished black. Sylvester was too ambitious to live with such fetters.

In October, 1908, with these frustrations bristling, Sylvester again rode out to Carson Town with his parents for another Big Meeting. [43] It was a crucial month for the young man, a turning point. He had quit his janitor's job at the library and returned to school to pick up his grade seven. [44] He had used his earnings to pay the enrollment fees at a small private school for blacks. All he might have hoped for then was to enter one of the South's colored colleges to prepare himself for a career as a lawyer, teacher or journalist in the black community, but it did not work out. The age gap between him and the other students was three or four years, and no doubt he found it embarrassing to be among so young a crowd. He dropped out just before the annual reunion at Carson Town.

The Big Meeting was held on the first Sunday of October, [45] when the cotton was ready for picking, the sugar cane was being ground, and the late corn was ready for husking. The Longs left early Saturday, taking the train to Statesville, where they rented a team of horses and a large wagon to carry them to Carson Town and the old houses strung out along the road to Hamptonville. The family rode over gently rolling ridges, past the ripe tobacco and corn fields and rich, uncut stands of tall oak and hickory in the browns, reds and rusts of autumn. The air was crisp, invigorating, and when they arrived in Carson Town their clothes were covered with fine red dust. There were seven Longs on the trip to the Big Meeting that year, for Abe had brought along his fetching young wife, Aurelia. [46]

Joe Long, now fifty-five, had straight black hair and his face was light brown, with finely chiseled features. Standing beside Aurelia, his dark daughter-in-law, he looked Portuguese, or Italian, or Greek. Sallie, now forty-three, was big-framed and milk-white. Their four children had the coloring of a marble cake, the darkest being Katie, nine. Sylvester looked Indian, and Abe, twenty-seven, and Walter, twenty-two, were fairer; like their father, they looked southern European.

Big Meeting week officially began with Sunday morning service at the Mt. Pleasant Church in Carson, followed that afternoon by a mammoth Sunday picnic. Most of the people stayed on for a week, but the industrious Longs had to return to Winston early—Joe to his janitorial job, Abe to Max Kobra's Saloon where he worked as bartender and Walter to his salesman's job. [47]

Sylvester was not as gregarious as his brothers, and as a boy he mostly kept to himself. [48] Besides, after the circus traveling and his disaffection when he returned to school, he was preoccupied with his future. His mind kept returning to the Wild West Show; it was his out, his trump card.

When they arrived at Carson Town, the men were working in the fields, but the women and children rushed out to meet them. Sylvester's observant eyes could not fail to notice the straight hair, blue eyes and otherwise white features of his relatives. He spotted a tall, slender, totally Caucasian woman, and when he recognized her as Adeline Carson, his grandmother, he ran to her. The Longs always stayed with Adeline in her little cottage close by the church, and it was she who told the old stories and filled in for Sylvester the gaps of the past.

The next day, Sunday, they arrived at the church in mule-drawn buggies and ox-carts. The men struggled into unfamiliar suits and ties and starched collars. The ladies wore Sunday bonnets, button shoes and dresses that swept the ground as they walked. From miles around came the famous colored preachers, the shouters, the hell-raisers and the healers. They exhorted all sinners to come to the center of the church, to the "mourners' bench," there to cleanse their immortal souls. Up walked big, strapping farmers trembling and weeping, to kneel at the tiny bench. There were the hymns and the wailing, mournful spirituals, and Sallie Long usually led the singing of "Go Down Moses," "Swing Low, Sweet Chariot" and "Steal Away to Jesus." [49]

One can imagine the thoughts that passed through young Sylvester's mind as he sat on the hard wooden bench, brooding. All around him burst those ecstatic, rhythmic exclamations of "Yes, God!" and "Jee-sus!" and "Bless the Lord!" What did he feel? Disgust? Pity? Boredom? All the evidence suggests he was terrified—terrified of becoming one of

them, terrified of the religious half-life and the deadening
slave mentality of his relatives with all its distant, hereafter
adventures and rewards. He had broken away, briefly, had
tasted what the other life offered, and he did not want to
have to die to taste it again.

When the church service ended, the picnic began, and for
an afternoon at least the rewards plainly were in the here
and now: baked country hams, fried chicken, deviled eggs,
home-baked bread, homemade pickles, orange sponge cake,
pound cake and great stacks of apple pies still warm from the
oven. When all this was wolfed down and when all the games
had been played and pleasantries exchanged, the Longs
loaded their wagon and said goodbye for another year. They
reached the train station in two hours, then rattled along for
another hour in the Jim Crow car to Winston.

Sylvester never stopped thinking of the future for very
long, and by the time he was back in Winston his thoughts
had coalesced into a word: Carlisle. It was the only way. The
Carlisle Indian Residential School in Carlisle, Pennsylvania,
was the most famous Indian school in the United States.
Every year it accepted a thousand children from ninety
different tribes across the country and provided them with a
basic trade school education. The boys were trained to be
carpenters, shoemakers, tailors and printers; the girls
learned homemaking skills. Carlisle also had a national reputation as a hotbed of sports, and by 1909 the Carlisle football
team was known throughout the continent. In 1907, led by
the mighty Jim Thorpe, one of the greatest athletes in the
United States, the Carlisle Redskins defeated Chicago and
Harvard. In 1908, the Redskins won ten games, lost only
two and tied one. [50] The more Sylvester read about Carlisle,
and he read everything he could get his hands on, the more
he knew he had to go there. But first he took off again with
the circus and the Wild West Show.

It was with Robinson's Circus, once more passing easily as
an Indian, that he worked with the horses and learned to
ride so well some thought he had been born on a ranch. [51] He
became friends with Allen Whipporwill, a registered East-

ern Cherokee, ten years his senior. [52] From this long-haired, full-blooded Indian with a name that evoked the mysteries of the bush and the plains, Sylvester picked up some useful, if rudimentary, Cherokee — the names of the months, the days of the week, the numbers up to ten. At night he memorized simple words and phrases — *si yu* (hello) and *o gi na li i* (my friend). [53] Eager and bright, and determined, Sylvester soon mastered a workable vocabulary that helped to solidify his Indian persona.

He returned to Winston in the summer of 1909, when the air was redolent of tobacco, thickest downtown by the warehouses and red-brick factories. Blacks from the surrounding areas flocked to Winston ("The Tobacco Center of North Carolina") to work in the newly mechanized tobacco plants. In ten years, Winston's population grew from 10,000 to nearly 17,000, [54] but Sylvester wanted no part of it, nor did he want a career in the black community as a teacher or lawyer or doctor. His dreams now embraced much more than that, more than Winston itself, more than the entire state of North Carolina and the whole of the South. He sent for and received an application from Carlisle.

Sylvester first heard of Carlisle in one of those critical boyhood incidents that could have gone either way. One day when he was eighteen, he borrowed the keys to the white West End School where his father worked as the janitor and slipped into the main office, there to whack away on the typewriter. The principal caught him, but instead of calling the police, he summoned Sylvester's father. If your son is so anxious to learn typing that he would risk reform school, he told Joe Long, then he deserves more schooling. Aware of the family's Indian background, the principal suggested that he apply for Sylvester's entry to Carlisle. [55]

On August 10, 1909, Sylvester applied for admission, committing his first serious deception. The Carlisle form clearly stated that candidates be within the preferred age of "fourteen to eighteen." To pass as eighteen, rather than nineteen, which he would be on his next birthday, Sylvester chopped off a full year, making his birthdate December 1,

1891.[56] His parents supported him, anxious as they were to see one of their children escape the strait jacket of segregation.

The application asked that the candidate's parents state their tribal affiliations, a near impossible task for the tens of thousands of people of mixed origins on the eastern seaboard. Tribal groups along the Atlantic coast had been splintered beyond recognition after the massive arrival of Europeans. Smallpox and typhus, against which North American Indians had no hereditary protection, cut terrible swaths in the native population. The epidemics, and the slave hunts, reduced entire tribes to insignificant pockets, and by the early twentieth century only two discernible Indian groups remained in North Carolina: the Cherokees and the Croatans.[57]

Sallie Long identified with the Croatans. After the Europeans moved in and nearly obliterated the tribes on the coast of the Carolinas, many of the survivors intermingled with the first settlers, losing their ancient languages and customs. The descendants adopted the tribal name Croatan to embrace all such peoples. Joe Long regarded himself as a descendant of the Eastern Cherokee, a tribe which suffered horribly at the hands of white settlers. In 1838, federal and state governments removed at gunpoint twenty thousand Cherokees from Alabama, Georgia, Tennessee and North Carolina. The governments wanted the rich Indian land and sent the Cherokees west of the Mississippi on a forced march known as the "Trail of Tears." Four thousand Cherokees died on the way. A small group known today as the Eastern Cherokee escaped by hiding in the mountains of western North Carolina. In the late nineteenth century, federal and state authorities recognized their right to remain and allowed them to settle in the southwestern section of the state, several hundred miles west of Winston. Joe Long had no proof of his mother's Cherokee origins, and the Cherokees themselves owned slaves, so it could be charged that she was one of them. To be a recognized Cherokee, Joe Long would have had to be registered on the Eastern Cherokee tribal rolls.

This did not deter him from writing on the Carlisle application that Sylvester was "half Indian of the Cherokee Tribe located at Cherokee County, NC." For his wife, Sallie, he said she was "half Indian of the Croatan Tribe located at Robeson Co., NC." In fact, Sallie was one-quarter Indian, as her mother, Adeline, was half-white. These distortions lifted Sylvester well above Carlisle's stipulation that candidates be "at least one-fourth Indian, preferably full Indian."

The application asked for vouchers from two "disinterested persons" testifying that the applicant "is known and recognized in the community in which he lives as an Indian." The Longs decided to solicit vouchers from a black and a white. G. Hamilton Willis, the black principal of the private school Sylvester attended for a month in September, 1908, signed one voucher and wrote: "I am acquainted with Sylvester Long; that he is known and recognized in the community in which he lives as an Indian; that in my opinion he cannot receive proper and adequate schooling at home for the reason that the public schools do not now receive pupils of Indian blood and parentage."[58]

Obtaining the endorsement of a member of the white community was trickier. Joe Long approached John Wesley Harrison, a friendly white merchant who had founded and operated the Winston Clothing Company. Harrison knew Joe from childhood days in Yadkin County, and he had heard stories of Joe's mother being a Cherokee. Harrison's name was respected; he taught at the Men's Bible Class at the North Winston Presbyterian Church. He signed the voucher.[59]

The Longs appeared before a notary to testify to the accuracy of the information, then mailed the application. In the last week of August, Sylvester was officially invited to visit Carlisle. Undoubtedly, his family and his girlfriend, Lovie Galloway,[60] would have gathered at the railway platform to see him off. Lovie Galloway was pretty and bright and devoted to Sylvester. If he had been less ambitious, less determined to break out, perhaps he would have married her, but he left Winston and by all accounts never saw her again. In his relationships with women, this would be the pattern he would follow the rest of his life.

After kissing his mother and Lovie goodbye, Sylvester climbed aboard the Jim Crow car, and the train pulled away in the stifling ninety-degree heat. The train passed through Virginia and Maryland, leaving behind the dank smell of the decaying vegetation. He liked the cooler weather, and felt invigorated by it and the old euphoria of travel. On the hoardings he studied posters in German, Russian and Italian, all part of the rapid industrialization of the northern states in the first decade of the new century, when more than seven million immigrants arrived to find work.[61] The white-skinned foreigners were encouraged to come, and made welcome, while he, the grandson of a North Carolina senator, had to lie about his own ancestry.

All went well at Carlisle — for a while. The two vouchers signed by the black principal and the white merchant showed that he was accepted as an Indian in Winston, but alone they were not enough. Linguistic proof of his Cherokee heritage was required. James Henderson, one of the Carlisle teachers examining the three hundred incoming students that fall, suspected that Sylvester was not what he claimed to be, and he challenged him to speak a few words in his native tongue. No doubt Sylvester initially froze. But then it all rushed back, and he spoke in phrases and sentences, confidently, coherently. Allen Whipporwill's circus lessons had paid off. Sylvester also absorbed another lesson, that the burden of proof is always on the accuser. It was too late for any teacher to travel three hundred miles back to North Carolina to investigate his vague tribal origins. Carlisle's admissions committee accepted him.[62]

3

A WHITE MAN'S CHANCE

THE CARLISLE INDIAN RESIDENTIAL SCHOOL was a school with a purpose, and the purpose was to give the Indian "a white man's chance." Those were the words of Moses Friedman, a thin-faced man with a goatee who was superintendent of Carlisle when Sylvester Long arrived in the fall of 1909.[1] For the young men and women who sought that opportunity, Carlisle was hugely successful, and it mattered not if, for Sylvester Long, it also worked to give him an Indian's chance in a white man's world.

Early in October that first year, Superintendent Friedman called the new students to an assembly and told them about hard work and perseverance, using the unlikely example of the Netherlands to inspire them. Through industry and determination, he declared, the people of the Netherlands transformed a barren, marshy wasteland into a country of opportunity and prosperity. He exhorted them to stick to the rules, to resist temptation and to overcome hardships, frustrations and homesickness. "Waste neither your time nor your opportunities," he urged them.[2]

Carlisle, founded in 1879 by Richard Henry Pratt, an idealistic American army officer, operated on rigid military discipline. Every morning Sylvester rose at five-thirty, ate breakfast at six-fifteen, then spent half a day at studies and half a day working in the shops. The military regimen was

17

designed as much to wean the students off a lackadaisical "Indian time" as to toughen them physically and mentally.

Pratt's contact with Indians began just after the Civil War when his unit, the 10th United States Cavalry, was posted to the West. In Texas he commanded his regiment's Indian scouts in fierce clashes with the Kiowa, Comanche, Cheyenne and Arapahoe. When, after seven years of fighting, the 10th Cavalry captured the Indian leaders, the army entrusted them to Pratt. He took them to Fort Marion in St. Augustine, Florida, and set about to reform them. His methods proved so successful in "lifting up" and "civilizing" the Indians that he dedicated his life to the task.

When his Indian prisoners' terms expired, Pratt managed to convince twenty-one of them to stay in the East for further education. In 1878, he enrolled them in Virginia's Hampton Institute, an elementary school founded a decade earlier by former slaves. Later that same year, fearing that association with blacks would bring the southern color bar down on his Indians, Pratt asked the army for a new home for the school. To his joy, he was given the century-old Carlisle Barracks in the Cumberland Valley, a lush farming region in southeastern Pennsylvania, just north of the site of the historic Battle of Gettysburg.[3]

Pratt ran Carlisle like a military outpost for twenty-five years, until he retired in 1904. Besides the unyielding discipline, he put great emphasis on the mastery of English. Only English was allowed in classrooms, no tribal mumbo-jumbo. He assigned students of different tribes and languages as roommates in the dormitories so they would have to speak English to communicate. Once they learned the basics of the language, the students studied a trade. Carlisle taught boys carpentry, blacksmithing, printing, harness making, wagon making, painting and plastering. They also kept the school in good repair, cleaning the grounds and tending the furnaces. The girls were trained in general household duties such as washing, ironing, sewing and needlework. They kept the dining room in order and helped to prepare the meals.

All Indian names were replaced with Anglo-Saxon Christian names, the first step in giving them "a white man's chance." Upon arrival at Carlisle, they were scrubbed, their hair was cut, and they were issued the mandatory uniforms. They were soon made aware that their Indian identity was something they would have to overcome, along with frustrations and homesickness. They marched in companies to the classrooms, to the shops, to meals, to chapel and back to the dormitories. [4] The Carlisle Indian Residential School gained an international reputation, and other schools in the United States and Canada were modeled on it. [5] But after Pratt retired in 1904, his influence slowly waned. Carlisle continued fourteen years beyond Pratt, and it was still very much inspired by him when Sylvester Long was a student between 1909 and 1912, but it closed forever in 1918.

Sylvester's first months at Carlisle were exciting and challenging, and he immersed himself in the experience, but he had it tougher than the others. He sensed hostility from some of the students, and for the reason he most feared: they suspected he was black. In the dining hall, classrooms and shops the tension was palpable.

The Western Cherokees from Oklahoma were anti-black, and they were not subtle about it. A number of their families had been slave-holders, had mixed racially with whites, and even fought on the side of the Confederacy in the Civil War. When the Eastern Cherokees at Carlisle told them that they had never heard of Sylvester Long, or his family, suspicion mounted, and the rumors became uglier. One day a delegation of Cherokees confronted the superintendent to protest against Sylvester's enrollment as an Eastern Cherokee. One of them called him a "Cherokee nigger." [6]

Sylvester refused to be intimidated. Acceptance at Carlisle was his ticket out, his escape, and so he fought back by working hard and winning approval from his instructors. One of the stories, which may be apocryphal, is that a sympathetic instructor tried to make him fit in more easily by calling him "Long Lance" on the drill hall floor. In any event, within a year of his graduation from Carlisle, he was calling himself Long Lance, or, more properly, Sylvester Chahuska Long Lance. The "Clark" was simply dropped, never to appear again. [7]

His first close friend at the school was Emma Newashe, a Sac and Fox girl from Oklahoma. Her mother had carried her on a brightly decorated papoose board, taught her the tribal customs and raised her to speak the native language. Her parents died when she was nine. Three years later, as an orphan, she was sent to Carlisle from a Quaker-run school in Oklahoma. She came to enjoy the school, but, like Sylvester, found the early months difficult. She applied herself to her studies with the same vigor, learning English, history, art and music.

Emma noticed how shy and self-contained Sylvester was when he arrived at Carlisle, and she thought it unusual, even for an Indian. When she came to know him, however, she found "there was no limit to his loyalty." She admired his sense of honor, his sincerity, and she loved his sense of fun. [8] He amused her by imitating bird calls. He was strong, even as a young man at Carlisle, and took it upon himself to protect weaker, slower classmates against the bullies and hecklers. [9]

Sylvester stood by his claims of Cherokee and Croatan ancestry, and, with the instincts of an athlete, he knew the best defense was a good offense. He contributed articles to *The Carlisle Arrow*, and in one of them, published in November, 1910, under the title "Origin of Names Among the Cherokees," he told how the Cherokees named their children after birds and animals. The school authorities liked it enough to include it in *The Red Man*, the school magazine that was circulated all across the country. [10] The next year, *The Carlisle Arrow* carried another Sylvester Long by-line, this time an account of "Virginia Dare, or the White Fawn," a Croatan tale of the first English child born in North America. [11]

Eventually he won acceptance by dint of what Superintendent Friedman called hard work and perseverance. In time, the other students regarded him as the son of a Cherokee father and a Croatan mother. A prominent

Cherokee, a female student named Iva Miller—she later became Jim Thorpe's first wife—accepted him without question as a member of her tribe. The Carlisle students kept "character books," listings of classmates' names, tribes and pet expressions, and in Sylvester's book Iva Miller identified her tribe fondly as "same as yours." [12]

Still, rumors persisted, [13] and even if Sylvester was regarded as part-Cherokee, his part-Croatan ancestry laid him open to suspicion of black blood. Barely two months after he entered Carlisle, *The Carlisle Arrow* published an article on the Croatans. Fannie Keokuk, a Sac and Fox Indian, wrote that the Croatans were "a mixed race" in eastern North Carolina, where they had "separate schools and churches and are given privileges which are not granted to the negroes." She said they were "a peculiar people," descended from native tribes, white sailors, early settlers— and blacks. [14]

All his life, from Carlisle on, Sylvester reacted badly to this sort of talk. If he did not always openly deny it, his behavior served to put him squarely on the side of the Indians, or even the whites, and some evidence suggests he may have acquiesced in anti-black bigotry and even taken the initiative. It is certain that he had a quick temper, and that temper could be easily ignited by accusations that he was black.

Edgar Miller, the school printer, doubted Sylvester's Indian background, and years later said quite openly that he was "a half-blood," by which he meant half-black. Miller then softened his opinion by adding that all Indians from the area around Winston "look more or less that way and I may be mistaken on that point." [15]

Miller's attitude doubtless disturbed Sylvester, but he would not shrink in the face of innuendo; indeed, he selected printing as his trade, with Miller as his instructor. He worked with forty other students printing the *Arrow* and the *Red Man*, as well as various printing jobs for the school. Miller recognized his skills and came to rely on him heavily. On his first report, he noted that Sylvester's conduct was excellent and that he was "a promising student." Within two years, Sylvester had so impressed Miller that the teacher put him in charge of all the printing machinery. [16]

Carlisle was mainly an elementary school, with two years of high school for senior students. [17] Sylvester entered grade six on his arrival in the fall of 1909, but the teachers quickly accelerated him when they saw evidence of his abilities. He had no problems with English or in motivating himself, and he meticulously completed all his assignments. He excelled in the classroom, particularly in English and history, and in the fall of 1911 he entered the tenth and final grade, with Mrs. Emma Foster as his English teacher.

Mrs. Foster was one of Carlisle's best educators. She had been at Carlisle for ten years and before that had taught at Indian schools in the West. She knew how to use imaginative techniques to get her lessons across. If she sensed the students were confused about, say, Shakespeare, she stopped everything and asked them to try to interpret the more obscure passages in everyday English. She encouraged them to ask questions, to probe, to search for meanings in Robert Louis Stevenson and Longfellow and Mark Twain. More important, she cared, and the students knew it. [18]

Emma Foster found Sylvester to be energetic and sensitive, the type of student a teacher treasures. He did more than was expected of him, submitting extra book reviews and assignments for her comments. Years later, she could still recall the day, in one of those impromptu classroom exercises, when Sylvester played Shylock in *The Merchant of Venice*. "Shylock reminds me of the Indian race," he told her after. "When cornered, he showed only his worst side to a world that misunderstood and misjudged him cruelly." Mrs. Foster thought it an unusually perceptive remark. Sylvester read all that was expected, and much more, reading to improve himself, to develop his vocabulary. He found especially rewarding Benjamin Franklin's *Autobiography*, soaking up all the great man had to say about pulling oneself up by the bootstraps, about rising from obscurity to "a state of affluence and some degree of celebrity in the world." [19]

Only when he realized that he was not the only shy and awkward one at Carlisle did he begin to relax and extend

himself. He found the Indians from Alaska even more
hidebound and anti-social, doubtless intimidated by the foreign surroundings of the south. He noticed the peculiar
tribal animosities that kept students apart and alienated
from one another, such as those between the Sioux and the
Chippewa. There were Carlisle students from such isolated,
backward settlements that they never handled English with
any confidence, and signs in the printing shop sometimes
catered to a backwoods mentality: DO NOT SPIT ON THE
FLOOR.[20] He felt the outsider. At first everyone looked the
same in his eyes, but gradually he perceived the differences,
and learned. At Carlisle, there were sons of Iroquois steel-
workers, daughters of wealthy Indian farmers, awkward
rustics from isolated settlements, dandies who knew about
clothes and style, and gentle people like Emma Newashe,
the orphan who befriended him.

In his first year, Sylvester joined the "Invincibles," the
boys' debating society, and by December had been elected
secretary. In his second year, he was winning debates. He
joined the Carlisle YMCA, and his experience at the Carson
Town "Big Meetings" prepared him for the religious
activities. In a fine bass voice he sang the old hymns, "Rock
of Ages" and "What a Friend We Have in Jesus," at the Bible
study meetings.[21] He sent postcards home, and in 1911 no
doubt reported a singular honor. He had been elected president of the Carlisle YMCA.[22]

He also joined the Carlisle school band, proudly donning
the blue and red uniform for concerts at special school days
and in the town of Carlisle when the band performed in the
public square. Sylvester played the E-flat clarinet, a
treacherous little instrument.[23] Carlisle students spent
their summers living with white families in central Pennsylvania, learning household duties, farm chores and practicing
the skills they learned in the school shops. In the summer of
1912, Sylvester worked in a printing office and played his
E-flat clarinet in the Pennsylvania Railroad Band at Tyrone,
a thriving railroad town one hundred miles west of the town
of Carlisle.[24]

Sylvester never made the famous varsity football team at

Carlisle, the one led by Jim Thorpe, but he did play on the intramural football teams. His best sport was long-distance running and he made the school's track team—no mean feat, for the competition was stiff. Thorpe, everyone's all-round athlete, was also on the track team, and he recognized Sylvester's talent, choosing him as a training partner. In the 1912 Olympics at Stockholm, Thorpe won the decathlon and pentathlon, and when he returned home he was hailed as nothing less than "the world's greatest athlete." Jim Thorpe and Sylvester Long remained lifelong friends. Among Sylvester's treasured souvenirs was a picture of Thorpe wearing a New York Giants baseball uniform, bearing an inscription in Thorpe's hand: "Remember the mile runs, was great training for the Olympics."[25]

Sylvester learned as much from friends and classmates at Carlisle as he learned from his teachers. Besides Thorpe and Emma Newashe, there was Joe Ross, a Pueblo from Cubero, New Mexico, who played with him in the band. Sylvester listened intently to the legends, customs and folklore of his new acquaintances. Wesley Two Moons, son of Chief Two Moons who had commanded the Cheyennes in the fight with Sitting Bull at Little Big Horn, told him of the battle. From the Sioux he learned the details of Wounded Knee, the massacre in December, 1890—almost to the day of Sylvester's birth—when the U.S. cavalry killed hundreds of defenseless Indians. All around him at Carlisle were the sons of the great chiefs, such as Robert Geronimo, who arrived at the school in 1911.[26] As many of the others struggled to shed their Indian identity, Sylvester tried to retrieve and somehow incorporate their cast-off traits, and become all that they were being taught to deny.

He was not above a little grandstanding. In late May, 1911, there was a hunt for a four-year-old girl lost in the Tuscarora Mountains, some thirty miles north of Carlisle. Sylvester joined the search party and reveled in the attention he garnered as a "genuine Indian." He told Robert Gorman, a reporter for the Harrisburg *Telegraph*, that he arrived at Carlisle "from the plains and forests of the West."[27] His words were quoted in the subsequent news-

paper reports, just as he had told them, and he discovered
how easy it was to bamboozle the press. He cut out the most
complimentary stories and pasted them in his scrapbook. It
seemed he could be anything he wanted to be, sometimes
merely by saying so.

As one of the top students in his graduating class, Sylvester was chosen by Superintendent Friedman to address the
school at its commencement exercises in the spring of 1912.
He stood at the podium in the Carlisle gymnasium in front of
a thousand Indian students and three thousand guests.[28]
Sylvester, now twenty-one and self-assured, cleared his
voice and began: "Ladies and gentlemen, fellow students,
and instructors. . . . " Like any cocky, self-assured valedicto-
rian, he reviewed the years at school, looked to the future
and peppered his talk with the usual "culminations" and
"pleasant memories" and "proud moments."

But, he had something else to say.

"When we have gone through, for the last time as students, the brick portals of this institution, into the great
world of competition, we do not wish to be designated as
Cherokees, Sioux or Pawnees, but we wish to be known as
Carlisle Indians, belonging to that great universal tribe of
North American Indians, speaking the same language and
having the same chief—the great White Father at Washington. . . . "[29] He talked of the goals of "true character" and
"fully developed manhood," and his presence at the podium
was testimony to what a half-blood or a quarter-blood could
achieve through hard work and perseverance, and just the
right amount of bravado to pull it off.

There was no turning back now, and so, accepting his
teachers' suggestions, Sylvester applied to the preparatory
school of Dickinson College in Carlisle. If Lovie Galloway or
anybody else were waiting for him, they would have to wait
a while longer.

4

THE OLDEST FRESHMAN

S FAR BACK as Sylvester could remember, a Republican had been president of the United States. When he attended the Depot Street School for Negroes in Winston, it was McKinley, next, Roosevelt, then, during his years at Carlisle, Taft. In November, 1912, when Sylvester was at Conway Hall, the preparatory school for Dickinson College, Woodrow Wilson came to power.

Wilson was a Democrat, a Virginian and a former president of Princeton University. Throughout his campaign, he championed a "New Freedom" and talked of returning the government to the people and introducing in Congress tariff reform and anti-trust legislation. The change could hardly have been symbolized more vividly than at the 1913 inaugural ceremony when Taft and Wilson stood side by side. There was Taft—all three hundred pounds of him—representing the old order of well-fed, unresponsive Republicans, and beside him, Wilson—tall, lean, scholarly—the embodiment of the hungry reformer.

During Sylvester's boyhood, the United States had moved from a rural, farming nation to an industrial world power. Railways snaked across the country, tying together its disparate regions, opening new markets and encouraging the standardization of products that could be mass-produced. At the time of Sylvester's birth in 1890, the Union's population was sixty-five million, most of it on farms and in villages. By

1913, the population neared one hundred million, and nearly half of the nation's citizens lived in cities. For twenty years the new wealth had been monopolized by a privileged few who were protected by the Republicans.

President Wilson introduced many progressive reforms. The Underwood Tariff, passed in October, 1913, instituted the lowest tariffs since the Civil War. Another progressive measure provided for a graduated federal income tax, designed to lift the tax burden from the back of the common man.

The "New Freedom" had its limits, however, and along with the reforms, President Wilson pushed for formal and official segregation. During his first months in office, the federal government extended segregation in Washington to nearly all departments. In the Bureau of Census, the Post Office and the Bureau of Printing and Engraving, workers were segregated in offices, shops, rest rooms and restaurants. Anyone opposed was fired. Widespread downgrading and firing of black postal and Treasury employees followed in the South. Thirty-five blacks were discharged in Atlanta, and the Collector of Internal Revenue in Georgia declared: "There are no government positions for Negroes in the South. A Negro's place is in the cornfield." [1]

Southerners took over in Washington, and their racial policies gained ascendency in congress, which heightened public service segregation in all quarters. But Sylvester managed to escape the tide. He was at Carlisle, and he was safe in his new identity as an Indian.

Sylvester was twenty-two when he registered at Conway Hall on October 14, 1912. [2] Though his adventures were not as wild as he imagined them, certainly they surpassed the experiences of his contemporaries. He knew poverty, had traveled with a circus as far as Cuba,[3] understood what hard work and bluff could do, had felt the sting of being called "nigger," and knew the lynch-mob fear felt by anyone not entirely white in the South.

On registering, he rearranged his birth date again, this time stating the truth—December 1, 1890—but he shifted his place of birth from Winston to Cherokee County, 150 miles to the west, where he knew some Eastern Cherokees lived.

He felt old and world-weary. The juvenile atmosphere at Conway Hall embarrassed him, and he hated it. He had to abide by the freshman rules, which meant enduring the customary small indignities: meeting visiting athletic teams and carrying their bags from the railway station; wearing a derby hat on Sundays; observing a ban on colored socks.[4] The freshman rules reminded him of the strictures that prevailed in Winston—stepping off the sidewalk for the white folks, never looking a white woman in the eye.

He did not see himself this way anymore. In one of many fanciful stories about his young days, one catches a glimpse of his fantasies. He wrote a story for *Cosmopolitan* that appeared in June, 1926, under the title "My Trail Upward."

> Since the day back in Wyoming when I had lost my temper and popped poor old Curly on the head, I had had two dangerous fights, both before I entered school. In one of them a friend had knocked me senseless with a six-shooter to prevent me from driving a knife into a fellow being on whose chest I sat. Two weeks later a six-shooter leveled at this same fellow being was knocked out of my hand just as I was pulling the trigger. It was only necessary to say that a feud existed between us, and he had sworn to get me.[5]

The tale was pure fiction, and Conway Hall was no match for this sort of imagination. Sylvester could not wait to get out.

Nevertheless, he did well academically in what today would be the equivalent of grade ten, his best subjects English and ancient history. He joined the W.A. Hutchinson Literary Society, made the Conway Hall track team, and to everyone concerned he appeared to fit in well, but we know he was unhappy.[6] When the school year ended, he worked another summer with the railroad band at Tyrone.[7]

That summer of 1913 found Sylvester again agonizing over choices. He knew he did not want to return to Conway Hall, but he knew also he did not want to launch a railroad career, working sixty hours a week in the yard office at

Tyrone with only the band concerts as a weekly diversion. That summer he made friends with E.A. Wall, who once played in John Philip Sousa's band. It was Wall who suggested that Sylvester apply for a band scholarship to St. John's Military Academy, one of the most exclusive military schools in New York State.

Sylvester mailed the application forms early in the summer, and, on July 9, the director of the St. John's Cadet Band wrote to Moses Friedman, the superintendent at Carlisle, asking for a letter of reference on Sylvester's behalf. Friedman replied that Sylvester was "a splendid young man in every way" with an entirely satisfactory record at Carlisle. When St. John's Military Academy approved Sylvester's application, *The Carlisle Arrow* rejoiced. "We know he will be successful," the newspaper editorialized, "as he has the energy, stick-to-it-iveness and character."[8]

By 1913, St. John's had been under the strong hand of General William Verbeck for twenty-five years. General Verbeck possessed the stern, slope-browed face of a man born to be a headmaster, and under his aegis St. John's had become one of the country's top military schools. He spent the first seventeen years of his life in Japan, where his parents were missionaries, and there, growing up with Japanese boys, he learned something of the Samurai tradition and its code of honor. He was unusually open-minded on racial questions at a time when bigotry was the norm at other northern schools and universities. (Blacks were not permitted in the dormitories at Harvard until the late 1920s.[9]) Students at St. John's came from far and wide, from all across the United States and from Canada, Mexico, and occasionally even from Cuba. General Verbeck patterned St. John's on the great English schools of Harrow, Rugby and Winchester, even borrowing Winchester's ancient motto: "Manners makyth man."[10]

It was at St. John's that Sylvester acquired some of the polish he later displayed to good effect in drawing rooms and on the lecture circuits. He managed to rid himself of the gawky mannerisms of his upbringing; he learned how to start a meal with the fork on the outside and work in, how to break the roll into pieces, then butter it. He learned proper enunciation, biting off the syllables, pronouncing each vowel distinctly and correctly. Discipline at St. John's was much stricter than at Carlisle, where the older boys had frequently slipped into the town of Carlisle to meet women and visit the bars.[11] Sylvester, with the others at St. John's, woke up to reveille at six-thirty, ate breakfast at seven, said his prayers at seven-thirty, attended school from eight to one o'clock in the afternoon, ate lunch at one, attended guard mounting at two, military drill at two-thirty, recreation at three-thirty, parade at five-forty-five, supper at six, prayers again at six-thirty, study from seven to nine-fifteen, military tattoo at nine-thirty, and taps at nine-forty-five. Bugle calls regulated Sylvester's life for three years at St. John's Military Academy.

He usually stood third or fourth in class, in what today would be roughly equivalent to grades eleven and twelve. He was the only Indian at the Academy, and soon was nicknamed "Chief." He joined the dramatic society (the Punchinello Club), and again made the school track team. In return for board and tuition, he played clarinet in the band, under principal musician Edmund Wall, E.A. Wall's oldest son.[12]

Edmund Wall met Long Lance when he arrived in the fall of 1913. He rated him "acceptable, moderately good" on the clarinet. Unlike his classmates at Carlisle, the St. John's students warmed to Long Lance immediately. One day, Ed Wall's brother discovered that his clarinet had been stolen from the school's rehearsal room. At the same time, one of the workers at the school quit. Long Lance obtained a pass a few days later, went into Syracuse and, by chance, happened to encounter the former worker. He chased after him, dodging passing cars, grabbed him in the middle of a street and had him arrested. Long Lance told the police to search the man's home. They did not find the clarinet,[13] but the incident bolstered Long Lance's reputation as a loyal friend.

Long Lance, though at first shy and quiet, loved attention, and always had an instinct for center stage. There was a Circus Day at St. John's on June 9, 1914, and Long Lance prepared for it, using all the tricks he had picked up while traveling with the circus. Nearly seven hundred people from Manlius and Syracuse converged on the St. John's football field that day to watch the military academy's Wild West Show, complete with cowboys, Indians, soldiers and clowns.

Long Lance, now "The Chief," stole the show, wearing flaming red blankets and a headdress, leading a party of Indians through a war dance, then running into the bushes to lie in wait for the unsuspecting palefaces. At the propitious moment, out he leaped with his whooping followers, surprising a wagon train—according to a report in *The Syracuse Journal*—"in true professional style."[14]

Long Lance enjoyed St. John's. Barely two months after he enrolled, he wrote Superintendent Friedman at Carlisle to say: "The instruction both military and academic is of the highest quality. Both cadets and instructors are in uniform at all times, and the regulation army rules are carried out in detail. The discipline that they have here is remarkable for its realness."[15] But, soon enough, he was back to agonizing over the future. What next? What to do in the spring of 1915 with what would amount to a high school diploma? He wanted to continue his studies, but he thrived in the quasimilitary atmosphere of St. John's. In March, 1915, he settled on a plan that was simple and audacious. He would write a letter to the president himself, to Woodrow Wilson, requesting an appointment to the United States Military Academy at West Point.

There was a major hurdle, however: West Point candidates must be at least seventeen years of age but not yet twenty-two.[16] In 1915, Sylvester Chahuska Long Lance was twenty-four. He would have to lie again, this time to President Wilson. It was a bold move, not merely because he was lying to the president, but also because West Point was not known for its enlightened racial policies; in fact, between 1802 and 1915 only three blacks had graduated from the academy, the last in 1889.[17] After much writing and rewriting, Long Lance sent the letter, telling President Wilson:

I am graduating from St. John's Military Academy this spring, and am desirous of entering West Point next fall. . . .

Knowing that you have the power of appointing a limited
number of students to this institution each year, I wish to ask
your assistance in securing an appointment for me this
year. . . .

He reviewed his achievements at Carlisle and St. John's,
then, screwing up his courage, came to the part about Indian
ancestry and age. By now, Long Lance had lied enough to be
inured to it. It was becoming a habit; indeed, he was close to
being a compulsive liar, daring fate to catch him at the game.
Sometimes it seemed almost a challenge. And so he wrote
the president of the United States:

I am of Indian ancestry, being a member of the Eastern
Cherokee tribe. I shall be twenty-one the first day of next
December. I stand five feet, nine inches in my stocking-feet
and weigh one hundred and sixty-eight pounds in the same
condition. . . .[18]

President Wilson probably never saw Long Lance's application, but the adjutant general of the War Department
certainly did. Upon receiving this engaging request—an
Indian for West Point?—he immediately conducted an
inquiry. On March 18, he wrote Oscar H. Lipps, Carlisle's
new superintendent, enclosing Long Lance's letter, requesting information about him. Lipps replied the next day that
he had been an excellent student, and said that on his application to Carlisle, Long Lance stated that his father was
half-Cherokee and his mother half-Croatan.

After mailing his letter to President Wilson, Long Lance
spoke to General Verbeck at St. John's, telling him of his
plans and asking for a letter of reference, which he knew
would carry much weight. General Verbeck was always
taken seriously on these matters, for he had a considerable
reputation, having served as a brigadier-general in the New
York National Guard and as one of the first three commissioners of the newly formed Boy Scouts of America. The
general was only too pleased to help: he encouraged his best
students to apply to West Point. On March 31, he also sent a

letter to President Wilson, recommending Long Lance's appointment in the highest terms. He reported that he had been an excellent student and a fine soldier and "has all the essential qualities to make an officer in the Army."

In early May, the War Department contacted Long Lance with the happy news that he had been granted the appointment, meaning he could enter the competitive exam the following spring for one of the vacancies at West Point. Long Lance wrote another letter to President Wilson, thanking him for the honor and assuring him he would "strive earnestly to justify it."[19]

When the press heard of the appointment in June, it treated it as a major story, especially welcome in the troubled world of the time. The previous summer, Franz Ferdinand, the Austrian Archduke, had been murdered in the obscure Balkan town of Sarajevo, plunging Europe into war. Earlier in the year, Germany unleashed unrestricted submarine warfare in the North Atlantic. On May 7, about the time Long Lance's appointment was approved, a U-boat sank the liner *Lusitania* off the coast of Ireland, killing twelve hundred, including 124 Americans. The incident nearly brought the United States into the war, just as Long Lance was completing his final exams at St. John's.

Newspapers across the country picked up the fascinating story of the handsome Indian boy selected by the president to attend West Point. it was too good to ignore. On June 16, 1915, *The Washington Post* commented in an editorial: "The appointment by the president of a full-blooded Cherokee to a West Point cadetship comes as a recognition of educational qualifications in the appointee that promise to do further honor not only to his own race, but to the country as well. Sylvester Long Lance has already attained a high mark in a long course of scholastic training, besides having a record in athletics. True to the hint contained in his name—and a name means much with an Indian—he early determined in favor of a military career, which the kind offices of the president have now made possible."

Other big dailies carried the story, and it eventually filtered down to the hinterland and Long Lance's own home town. On June 24, 1915, it reached Winston-Salem, and the *Twin City Daily Sentinel* carried a photograph of "Sylvester C. Long-Lance" on the front page under a headline that read: "Full-blooded Cherokee to Enter West Point." The caption for the photograph added: "He is a full-blooded Cherokee Indian, and the first of his race to become a student at West Point."[20]

If anybody in Winston-Salem knew otherwise, and some obviously did, nobody betrayed the native son. Young Sylvester Long, the boy from 4½ Street, had somehow escaped and was doing well on the outside. More power to him.

Sylvester regularly mailed home letters, postcards and clippings during his first years at school.[21] Although her letters have not survived, one can be certain that Sallie wrote to him frequently in her large-letter script, telling him about his father, his sister and brothers, and the state of affairs around Winston-Salem. The Longs still were officially "colored," and Sylvester's success did nothing to alter the family's status. He could not go home, of course, for that would undermine all that he made himself out to be. The family was proud of him, but protected him with silence. Joe still worked as a janitor in the white school system. Walter married his black girlfriend. Abe and Aurelia had a daughter, Vivian, who turned five during Sylvester's last year at St. John's Military Academy. Abe ran a small smoke shop for blacks in the city. Walter sold newspapers at a downtown newsstand.[22] Lovie Galloway, Sylvester's girlfriend in Winston six years earlier, had attended the Hampton Institute, become a teacher and married a black druggist.[23]

On July 3, 1915, the adjutant general of the War Department wrote again to Oscar Lipps at Carlisle, this time to request more information about the candidate's "alleged Indian ancestry." All that Lipps could do was forward a copy of Sylvester Long's original application, saying in his reply of July 6 that it was "all the information they had on his Indian ancestry." James Henderson, who had left Carlisle in late 1912 to become the superintendent of the Cherokee Indian School at Cherokee, North Carolina, was then asked to investigate Sylvester's family background among the Eastern Cherokees. When Henderson's search at Cherokee proved fruitless[24] the investigation apparently ended. Joe and Sallie Long were never contacted, were never asked to answer any questions about their son.

5

FIGHTING FOR CANADA

ALL WINTER, while the war raged in Europe, Sylvester prepared for the West Point examinations. He took special courses in algebra, plane geometry and military science at St. John's Military Academy, where his instructors were anxious for him to succeed. He chose to write the tests at the examination center nearest to St. John's, which was Fort Slocum, a large army recruiting depot on David's Island, off New Rochelle, New York.

Early on the morning of March 21, he took an army ferry across to the island under a dark, overcast sky that threatened snow. He read in the morning newspaper that the French had checked the German offensive at Verdun, and that American troops had advanced deeper into Mexico in pursuit of the elusive border-raider, Pancho Villa. Forty thousand American suffragists planned to demonstrate at the national Republican and Democratic Party conventions in June in support of the vote for women.[1]

He headed for the examination center across an immense parade ground on David's Island, and on the way he noticed a group of black recruits for the regular army. They were assigned to a separate company, lived in their own segregated barracks, and all their noncommissioned officers at Fort Slocum were white.[2]

There were two parts to the West Point examination, the physical and the mental. Sylvester was in excellent shape,

36

with a rugged, medium build, and a solid twenty pounds heavier than when he entered Carlisle seven years earlier. He passed the physical easily. Then came the written exams in algebra, plane geometry, English grammar, English composition and literature, geography and history. The six papers were to be written over a three-day period, each paper four hours long, with the exception of plane geometry, which was only three.[3]

The unthinkable happened; he failed. He scored only forty-five in algebra and, incredibly, only thirty-seven in geometry. At St. John's that winter, he showed he could master both subjects, scoring averages of ninety-five. And for all his reading and love of the written word, he managed only a disappointing fifty-five in English composition and literature.[4] Had he panicked under the pressure of the examination schedule? Was the preparation at St. John's simply not up to the standards of West Point? One hardly would think so, as St. John's had established an enviable reputation for standards across the country, and he had been one of the school's top students. What happened on David's Island?

A clue might be found in the autobiographical story he later wrote for *Cosmopolitan*, in which he described bashing poor Curly on the head and nearly driving a knife into a fellow being. He explained in the article why he enlisted with the Canadian forces in the Great War. In the story he said that he "purposely 'flunked'" the entrance examinations at Fort Slocum, having "decided that the best place for a chap who could not keep from disgracing himself and his friends was fighting under the colors of an army that was upholding a world cause."[5] Perhaps, but why, if that was how he felt, did he not simply refuse to take the examinations and announce he was going to Canada to join the army to uphold a great world cause? Why bother even to write the exams, and why bother spending most of a winter preparing for them? He could have done all he intended to do, without the stigma of failure.

A likelier explanation is that he deliberately scored poorly on the exams, not because of a desire to fight for a larger cause, but because he was, for the first time, in fear of discovery. All along, Sylvester had kept in touch with his former teachers at Carlisle,[6] and he must have known of the War Department's investigation into his "alleged Indian ancestry." If Sylvester had learned of James Henderson's enquiries,[7] it could also have unnerved him. By then he prized his identity as an Indian more than any future stature as a West Point graduate. Possibly, Sylvester also realized that if the War Department received a copy of his application to Carlisle, it would reveal he had lied about his age which was now three years over the maximum age for West Point.

Whatever the reason, he failed three of the six tests, and he was out. And he was in no great hurry to head north to Canada and join the army. He waited nearly five months to do that, spending most of the time in New York, which he found as exciting as the circus days of his boyhood. Doubtless he wandered all over Manhattan, visiting Chinatown, the Fulton Fish Market, the Jewish East Side and Little Italy. He marveled at how the well-dressed and well-fed mingled so easily with the poor and depraved: the hookers, dope peddlers and gangsters.

To make some money, he entered wrestling matches at the athletic clubs, and did quite well, putting to good use his training at St. John's. Sylvester was not easily intimidated, and one day he took on a brute named Frank Leavitt, who called himself "Man Mountain," and who outweighed Sylvester by a good seventy pounds.[8] After the bout, Leavitt gave his picture to Sylvester, and it was faithfully pasted in the scrapbook.

How and when he decided to enlist with the Canadian armed forces is not known, though it is reasonably certain that Long Lance would have admired the Canadian war effort, as did his alma mater, St. John's. The school newspaper, *The Windmill*, praised Canadians for their bravery in the face of the chlorine gas attacks at Ypres in late April. An editorial in May, 1915, declared, "Canadian soldiers at the front have set the real Canada before the eyes of the world, and we Americans, your neighbors, are proud of you." The adventure of war, the appeal of a cause, and the

glamor of the military would all have conspired to attract
Long Lance. Since the odd wrestling bout did not bring in
much money, he would find the security of army pay quite
tempting.

In early August he took the train north to Canada, and in
less than a day arrived in Montreal, then Canada's largest
city, with a population of five hundred thousand, most of
them French-speaking. He asked for the nearest recruiting
station and was directed to an office on Sainte Catherine
Street. There he enlisted[9] and, as he explained later in the
Cosmopolitan article, "three weeks after I had coughed and
said 'Ahh' for the medical officer, I was on my way to
France...."[10]

The Canadians were glad to see him, for the casualties at
the front had been staggering. Canadians distinguished
themselves at Sanctuary Wood, but in that bloody twelve-
day battle eight thousand Canadians were killed. The supply
of recruits was drying up, having fallen from thirty thousand in January to a mere eight thousand in July. Canada
lowered the medical qualifications, no longer insisting that a
married man must have his wife's consent to enlist.[11]

French Canadians were hardly enthusiastic about the war
effort. They did not see the war as their struggle, and they
resisted serving in English-speaking regiments, under
English-speaking officers. And just when French Canadians
were being asked to fight in Europe, the provincial government in Ontario was eliminating French-language instruction in its schools, a controversy that excited the Quebec
press more than distant heroics in Flanders.[12]

Long Lance enlisted on August 4, 1916, two years to the
day that Britain had declared war on Germany for invading
neutral Belgium. Britain's declaration brought Canada into
the conflict. At his enlistment, Long Lance gave his father
as his next-of-kin and listed him as "Joseph Long-Lance."
He provided his family's correct address in Winston-Salem,
95 Brookstown Avenue, but then he allowed his imagination
to run rampant. He lied again about his birthdate, stating
that it was December 1, 1891. He listed West Point in the
space marked "previous military experience." His height

was measured at five feet, eight and a half inches, his chest
at thirty-six inches breathing out and forty-one inches
breathing in. The form mentions his complexion ("dark"),
eyes ("dark brown"), and hair ("black"). It also noted a
tattoo on his right forearm, a tattoo of his initials on his right
hand, and a scar on his back.[13]

In his first month in the Canadian Expeditionary Force,
Long Lance belonged to the 237th Battalion of the American
Legion, a unit comprising American enlistees. Later, he was
transferred to the 97th Battalion, crossed the Atlantic on
the troopship *Olympic*, and arrived in England on September 25, 1916. Immediately, his unit headed for the Shorn-
cliffe training camp near Folkestone and Dover, on the
English Channel. In October Long Lance learned the basics:
route marching, entrenching, musket practice, grenade
throwing, bayonet fighting. In his company of green,
untrained recruits, he was a man of considerable experience, having participated at St. John's in mock battles that
included assaults on trenches protected by barbed-wire
entanglement and wooden abatis. He also won respect as an
Indian, for hundreds of other Indians in the Canadian army
already had shown great skill as snipers. (One Indian sniper,
a lance-corporal from northern Alberta, was credited with
115 observed "hits."[14])

His superiors quickly promoted Long Lance to acting
corporal on October 6, then to acting sergeant on October
22. Three days later, however, he sprained his right knee in
training, preventing any speedy departure to the battle-
fields of Europe. He recovered in hospital for two weeks,
then was transferred to the Royal Canadian Regiment and
the crack Princess Patricia's Canadian Light Infantry Depot
at Seaford, near Brighton, fifty miles to the east. There he
remained for three months.

While waiting for the call to France, Long Lance could not
resist the opportunity to impress old friends back in
America. He mailed a Christmas card to his Carlisle
acquaintances, including the superintendent. Under the
message, "Kind Remembrance and Best Wishes for the

New Year," he included a poem of sorts, in which he promoted himself to lieutenant and talked of life in the trenches.

> I've just come out of the trenches
> Where we made the Germans dance,
> And I'm sending this Greeting to let you know
> That he is still alive, Yours Truly, Lieut. Long-Lance;
>
> Alive and fit as fit can be,
> Though fighting's not all sport,
> And manners "made in Germany"
> Aren't quite what you and I were taught.[15]

The poem was a hit at home. One of the teachers at Carlisle, sensing good publicity for the school, and with the United States relentlessly moving toward war, sent the Christmas card to the press. For the second time in less than a year, Long Lance made the papers. "American Indian is Fighting for Allies," the headline in the New York *Sun* read on February 12, 1917. "Lieut. Long Lance of Carlisle Surprises Teacher with Note from Trenches." The day the story appeared, Long Lance and the 38th Battalion at last shipped out for the front. On arrival, he reverted to the ranks, and remained a private for all of his four months in France.

For two years, Allied and German armies had been locked in battle along the Western Front, which stretched from the North Sea to Switzerland. By early 1917, the war had deteriorated into an endurance test. Who would crack first? Millions of men had died in suicidal attacks trying to dislodge the enemy. In the four-month Somme offensive of 1916, British forces suffered 420,000 casualties (including nearly 25,000 Canadians), and the French more than 200,000, all for a gain of some seven miles.[16]

The Allies wanted to capture a strongly fortified escarpment four miles long, commanding the flat plains around Arras. The Canadian Corps had been withdrawn in October from the Somme area to take over part of the Vimy Ridge front. Considering the ridge as a menace to the Allies' posi-

tion in northern France, Sir Douglas Haig, commander of
the British forces, ordered the four Canadian divisions to
take it.

Once he was at the front, Long Lance's enthusiasm for the
war quickly waned. The winter of 1916–17 was brutally cold,
the cruelest in twenty-two years. The trenches at least were
dry, but when the Canadians lined up for their food, the
temperatures were so low that by the time they ate, the hot
rations had frozen at the edges of their mess tins. Long
Lance endured lice—"itchie-coos," the soldiers called them
—and the enormous rats that ate on the human remains
littering the battlefield. And, always, he lived with the din of
artillery, mine charges and machine gun fire.

After extensive preparations, the attack on Vimy Ridge
began at four o'clock, Easter Monday, April 9. Every battalion was in place, some not more than a hundred yards from
the enemy. All night it had rained, and now the rain had
turned to sleet and snow. From dugouts, shell holes, and
trenches, the Canadians surged forward. Amidst a heavy
artillery barrage, the infantrymen rushed up the sleet-
drenched hillside. All around, gun flashes lit up the sky. The
38th had a particularly difficult time. The ground they had to
cross was so pocked and scarred by continuous shell fire that
the men could not keep up with the artillery barrage. Some
of the wounded drowned after falling into water-filled shell
holes.

Vimy's German defenders emerged at unexpected places
and put up a spirited resistance. But by the morning of the
tenth, the summit had been cleared. On the eleventh, the
Germans pulled back two miles to a defensive line outside
the western suburbs of Lens.[17] The Canadians had scored a
striking victory. The French gratefully termed the feat, "an
Easter gift from Canada to France."[18]

Long Lance emerged from Vimy unscathed, but, as he
later wrote, accustomed to seeing men "gutted and lacer-
ated day in and day out," choked with the stench of blood,
iodine, cordite, burnt flares and mud. He got hit a month
later, on May 22, and from a field bed in France he wrote: "I
am in a field hospital, convalescing from a wound in the head

received a couple of weeks ago. Nothing serious; only a piece of shrapnel in the back part of the head and a broken nose — the latter sustained in falling on my face, I presume. I came through [Vimy Ridge] without a scratch . . . only to get hit a month later on one of the quietest days. . . . Such is war!"[19]

He was hospitalized two weeks and rejoined his unit on June 4. Three weeks later, he was hit again in an attack on Lens, and this time shrapnel in both thighs put him out of the war and back in England. He rested a month at a military hospital in Oxford and several weeks more at the Canadian Convalescent Hospital at Woodcote Park, Epsom, south of London. Only his excellent physical condition, he felt, saved him from having both legs amputated.[20]

When he was in hospital in England, he read another story about himself. An American reporter had interviewed him at the front and in mid-July, 1917, newspapers across the United States carried a long, illustrated article on "The American Full-Blooded Indian Who Fought at Vimy Ridge." This time the hyperbole ran wild, as a glance at only the captions of the New York *World* article reveals:

Fenimore Cooper's Romances Have Nothing on the Real Life Story of This Full-Blooded Cherokee From Kit Carson's Country — Trick Rider, Fistic "Meeter of all Comers," All-Round College Athlete, Prize Debater and Literary Essayist, Musician . . . Carlisle and St. John's Graduate, President Wilson's Appointee to West Point Cadetship. He Now Turns Up as First Lieutenant of Princess Pat's Crack Canadian Regiment.[21]

Following his release from hospital, Long Lance was posted as a clerk to the headquarters of the Overseas Military Forces of Canada in Argyll House on Regent Street in London. Appointed acting staff sergeant, he served from April, 1918, to April, 1919, in the Intelligence Section of the Canadian General Staff. He sailed for Canada on July 3, and as his point of discharge he asked for the last Canadian province to be settled, distant Alberta and the Rocky Mountains of Western Canada. Alberta seemed ideal for the man, removed as it was in time and distance from his origins and all that he was trying to deny and escape.

Reports on racial troubles in the United States were carried in Canadian newspapers. Thirty-eight blacks were lynched in 1917, when he was fighting in Europe. Fifty-eight more were hanged in 1918, when the Great War ended. Seventy blacks were lynched in 1919, the year Long Lance arrived in Canada.[22]

With the war over and thousands of southern blacks heading to the northern cities for work, more racial violence threatened. In the "red summer" of 1919, twenty-five race riots erupted in American cities, and the year before that even Winston-Salem was not spared. In November, 1918, a mob of two thousand whites stormed the city jail in Winston-Salem, trying to get at a black man who was charged with raping a white woman. The home guard fought back with fire hoses, then shooting broke out. Five whites were killed and estimates of the number of blacks killed ranged as high as fifty. The black prisoner was later found to be innocent.[23]

Sylvester Chahuska Long Lance boarded a train at Halifax and headed west across a wide, rough country to Alberta, where he would start all over. Again.

S.C. LONG LANCE, REPORTER

T HE TROOP TRAIN pulled into Calgary on Friday, July 18, 1919. [1] For the soldiers who stepped off the train and into the arms of loved ones, that was the moment when the war ended. They marched one last time, ten blocks to Mewata Barracks, there to pick up their discharge papers and back pay, and then they were civilians again.

Calgary was a young, vibrant boom town. In just ten years its population had grown to sixty thousand from six thousand. New buildings stood in fields inaccessible by road, everybody had a deal going and profit was the operative word. [2] Calgary was as keen and ambitious as Long Lance, and nearly as young, having been founded only fifteen years before he was born. There were biases and prejudices, to be sure, but Long Lance did not feel the weight of them as he did in the South. The brash young city felt as exhilarating as the mountain air.

Nobody rushed to greet him at the train station. After the backslaps and farewells, he was on his own, and he must have missed the high-spirited camaraderie of the train trip. He loved to be the center of attention, and rattling across the country in a train packed with soldiers, ready to believe anything, Long Lance was in his element. Without much prompting, he could tell them about his friend Jim Thorpe, the man he had trained with in preparation for the 1912 Olympics, and who was hitting .411 for the Boston Braves in the major leagues that season.[3] He knew boxing, too, and could describe in graphic detail how Jack Dempsey had won the heavyweight championship two weeks earlier in Ohio, beating Jess Willard, who outweighed Dempsey by fifty-five pounds. Long Lance liked to act out these bouts, and he especially liked Dempsey's crouching, aggressive style and his vicious, compact, eight-inch punches. Long Lance looked like a boxer, and he even sported the broken nose that goes with the territory. He was not a braggart, not loud, but he was not the unresponsive, monosyllabic Indian the Canadian soldiers were accustomed to. He laughed easily.

If asked why he chose Alberta, he could answer that his spirit needed a frontier. By now he had moved his birth place to eastern Oklahoma, some fifteen hundred miles from North Carolina, and he could complain that he wanted something less settled, less predictable, less rooted. The past was like a child's slate board, and anytime he felt like it he could erase his history and start clean again, becoming anything he wanted to be.

Long Lance left the barracks with his back pay and set out to find a room. Certainly he could not afford the big new hotels, such as the gleaming Palliser, next to the Canadian Pacific Railway station, which by Alberta standards in 1919 was a skyscraper at nine storeys. He walked by the new Alexandra Hotel and the Royal George Hotel on Ninth Avenue and probably settled for a cheap, fleabag hotel further to the east, one in which the tap in the washbasin leaked, the drapes were soiled, and a bare light bulb hung over the bed. He was not fussy about where he stayed.

While strolling about the city he would occasionally see brown faces like his own: at the train station perhaps a woman in an ankle-length, shapeless dress and a head scarf, and with a papoose on her back; beside her a man with braided hair, wearing rumpled white man's clothing. One can imagine Long Lance nodding at them, and walking on. Three or four Indians rattled by on an old buckboard wagon with firewood from the Sarcee Reserve to sell to whites who lived in frame houses with wood stoves in the poorer residential areas.

He found his way around the city easily, for all the streets ran north and south and all the avenues east and west. After New York and London, Calgary was small and manageable, but colorful: cowboys in ranch gear, Chinese in quilted satin jackets, Englishmen in tweed caps and knickerbockers, and hundreds of soldiers in khaki. The women looked sassy and boyish in the styles of the day, their arms and legs bare, and Long Lance watched the young ones hurrying by on their lunch hours. He looked them in the eye and heard no thunderclaps from the heavens.

He stopped at a clothing store and bought a lightweight Palm Beach suit,[4] one that sat well on his body, then selected a fine soft Panama hat. Outside, on the sidewalks again, he could see the foothills in the distance, and beyond them the great saw-toothed, snow-capped Rockies eighty miles away. The Blackfoot Indians called them "the backbone of the world."[5]

The streets were jammed as the next day, Saturday, July 19, was Peace Day, when the entire country would celebrate the end of hostilities. Prohibition had been in effect since 1916, however, and there was not a bar or saloon to be found. By nightfall, Calgary's Eighth Avenue and Centre Street became as congested as Piccadilly Circus in London, with streetcars clanging and the automobile horns ooga-ooga-ing. He dodged the ubiquitous Model-Ts and the Maxwells, the McLaughlins and the Hudsons. Men and women walked arm in arm in the evening under the electric lights downtown, some going to a theater on Eighth Avenue to see Charlie Chaplin in *Charlie's Recreation*, to be followed by Lou Newman in *Smiles*, all scored by the theater's pianist.[6]

The next day, Long Lance spotted an old army friend in the crowd: Major Carlyle William MacInnis, one of his officers overseas. Long Lance rushed to him, pumped the major's hand, and was delighted to find him as chipper as ever despite wounds suffered in France. MacInnis was secretary and treasurer of Alberta's Great War Veterans' Association.

"What are you going to do now, Chief?" he asked Long Lance.

Sylvester told him he planned to get a job in Calgary.

The major laughed and poked him under the arm. "I'll give you one year to go back to the blanket, Chief," MacInnis told him. "You may think you are going to stick it out in this civilized life, but you're not. I know you better than you know yourself. You're going back to the blanket—a squaw and a papoose."

It was a challenge Long Lance could hardly resist.

"I'll bet you $100 you're wrong," he shot back.

"Taken," MacInnis said, then walked away, chuckling.[7]

Long Lance searched for work all summer. At times he must have felt that he was back in the South, but despite rejections, he recognized a difference. Many whites despised the local Sarcee Indians and regarded them as dirty and lazy. Sales clerks usually served white customers before they served him. He learned that farmers paid Indians $2.50 a day for harvest work, while European immigrants were offered $4 a day.[8] And yet when he had a chance to speak in his clear, concise English, and when he mentioned his service record, he won respect. He also noticed that the prejudice here was not insurmountable, not as indelible as back home. There was Lady Lougheed, the wife of Senator Sir James Lougheed, and she was of mixed blood. Brigadier-General H.F. MacDonald, Commanding Officer of the Alberta Military District, had Indian ancestry. In the adjacent province of Saskatchewan, James McKay, a judge of the Supreme Court, was part Indian.[9]

Before moving on to another town, Long Lance left his name with the Soldiers Civil Re-establishment Office on the first floor of the Lancaster Building on Eighth Avenue, in case something turned up.[10] He may have tried his luck elsewhere, or he may have holed up somewhere in or around Calgary—there are inexplicable gaps—but he did say in the piece he did for *Cosmopolitan* in 1926 that he spent some time chasing a dream in Los Angeles about this time. His "autobiographical" articles, even if fanciful, say much about what he wanted to do, or at least what he thought he could do.

With the war over, eventually I was sent home and demobilized as a captain. And then I had to begin all over again. At twenty-five, I had adopted the white man's customs, comforts and ways of thinking — and yet I had no way to earn a living commensurate with these newly acquired tastes.

Some friend suggested I go to Los Angeles, where two professions might open for me — moving picture acting or professional boxing. In France, I had been Canadian light-heavyweight champion, and I had been told that I could go to the very top of the heap if I continued fighting.

Almost immediately after I landed in California, I was offered $500 to fight — and the heavy barred doors into the movies were opening to me.

Then, according to the *Cosmopolitan* story, he received two offers: a two-year army scholarship to study journalism, and a reporter's job on the *Calgary Herald*. "That night," he wrote, "I wired the *Herald* to hold that thirty-dollar-a-week job."

That was six years ago — and never for a day have I regretted my choice. Had I taken a different road, I might have been light-heavyweight champion of the world — Jack Dempsey told me he would make me that in six months — and I might have been a movie star.[11]

One fact is certain. By October, he was in Calgary.[12] Charlie Hayden, managing editor of the *Herald*, was impressed by the application which the Soldiers Civil Re-establishment Office had forwarded to him. He hired Long Lance as a reporter, and for the next year he constantly encouraged him. Long Lance's first by-line appeared after an unusually long preamble to the story. Unfortunately, Long Lance himself supplied the information, and, given that freedom, did what he loved to do best: invent. The preamble said that Long Lance, "an officer on the intelligence staff of General Plumer's forces in Italy during the latter part of the war," enlisted as a private in the Canadian Expeditionary Force early in 1916. It continued: "Although an American citizen, born in Oklahoma and educated at St. John's Military Institute, Carlisle University and West Point, the famous military academy of the United States, he came to Canada during the war and signed on for overseas service. He served in the field as a private and N.C.O., receiving the Croix de Guerre for bravery when a sergeant, and afterwards being promoted to the rank of lieutenant. He also served in France as an officer before being elevated to a staff appointment in Italy. Captain Long Lance was wounded twice in the course of his war service. When the Canadian forces were demobilized, he returned to the United States, and after a brief stay there came to Western Canada and joined the staff of the *Calgary Herald*. In both his college and army careers, Captain Long Lance has been noted as an athlete and is well known as a boxer, wrestler, footballer and all-round track man."[13]

It was an astounding example of reckless lying, lying for the sake of lying, lying-as-adventure. Any of his "facts" could easily have been checked. He never fought in Italy, nor was he born in Oklahoma. He was never a lieutenant or a captain. Carlisle was not a university. He did not attend West Point. He did not win the Croix de Guerre. No matter; the next day it was all there in print for everyone to see, while he sat at his desk in the newsroom behind a bulky Remington: Long Lance was assuming the role of a living legend.

Long Lance's best friend in the newsroom was Howard Kelly, who, at twenty, was one of the youngest sports editors on a daily newspaper in Canada. Both men were sports-minded and attended all the football, baseball and boxing matches, and they kicked up their heels at the local dances. Kelly's mother cooked meals for Long Lance, or "the Chief," as he once again became known. Howard Kelly and other members of the *Herald* liked Long Lance's sense of humor. The younger staffers hero-worshipped him.[14]

For nearly three years, Long Lance worked at the *Herald*, covering every beat from sports to city politics. He learned how to write fast, how to write running copy, and he rarely worked only eight-hour days. Colonel Woods, the editor, ran a tight ship and expected mileage from his reporters. He refused to allow reporters to use taxis in the city, and once ruled that pencil stubs be saved and joined together as an economy measure.[15] The *Herald* made money. And Long Lance was a natural. The words seemed to flow from his typewriter, though he was a stylist and worked hard at it, finding that the harder he worked, the more effortless the writing appeared.

He boarded with the Vahey family on Sixth Avenue, only two blocks from the *Herald*. The large white frame house with the white picket fence and the veranda where everyone gathered on warm afternoons and evenings was a comfortable retreat. "The spirits were friendly," Long Lance liked to say of the Vahey place. He lingered after many dinners, telling them of his travels, Carlisle, West Point and the war. Long Lance was the perfect boarder (he did not smoke or drink then), but he could be a prankster. One evening while the family was sitting down to dinner, the door to the dining room slowly creaked open and a hand holding a gun appeared, then a masked face with grotesque false teeth. "Hold up!" the intruder shouted to the startled group. Then Long Lance pulled off his disguise and the laughter bounced off the walls.[16]

It is probable that he was as relaxed with himself and the world in Calgary, especially during his time with the Vaheys, as he ever had been before or would be again. He had a job with a future, close friends, a home and youth— which he thought important, for about this time he lopped three years off his age, making his birth date 1893.[17] He started to date women, white women, and invariably he selected the most beautiful and vivacious. He liked the way women laughed and the way they responded to his flirtations, and he certainly had no difficulty winning their attention or affections.

Long Lance shunned the baggy, unkempt look which was popular then among the unpressed gentlemen of the press. He abhorred sloppiness and usually stood ramrod straight, shoulders back, chin up, hands at his side or clasped behind his back. He knew the difference between fashion and style. He preferred clothes that accentuated his body, and in a lithe, animal way, his Indian identity. He knew how to dress for women the way some women know how to dress for men

—and it worked. Ralph Wilson, a fellow reporter, remembers him as "a dashing, handsome Indian who always ended up with the most beautiful girl."[18]

About this time he became involved, briefly but thoroughly, with a wealthy married woman who arrived in Calgary in one of the first Rolls-Royces ever seen in the city. They picnicked in the countryside, drove everywhere in the cushioned Rolls, and generally enacted their own Scott and Zelda romance in the best, high-rolling style of what soon would be known as the Jazz Age.[19]

Long Lance realized that in race-conscious Calgary there were limits beyond which he could not go. He knew he could never marry the women he courted, and sometimes he confided in Howard Kelly and Hugh Dann, another Calgary friend, about his predicament. They could only suggest that he travel to Oklahoma and seek out and marry an educated Cherokee girl. Such well-intentioned advice merely heightened his inner frustration, for he was neither a Cherokee nor an Oklahoman.[20]

He immersed himself in the life of the city, officiating at amateur boxing bouts, joining the militia and signing up with the local Elks' Lodge. When Bill Strother, the renowned "Human Fly," came to Calgary and climbed the nine-storey Palliser Hotel—blindfolded—Long Lance somehow managed to greet him on the roof, while fifteen thousand Calgarians whooped and cheered on the street below. He often went flying with Fred McCall, one of the great aces of the war, and in 1921 the two men edited an 85-page aviation manual titled *Devoted to Flying in Alberta*. He coached football for the Calgary Canucks Football Club and was elected to the executive.[21]

No matter how late he stayed up the previous night, he always rose at six o'clock the next morning and did an hour's calisthenics and gymnastics,[22] a regime which paid off when the rough-faced "Manassa Mauler" Jack Dempsey, the heavyweight champion, visited Calgary on March 23, 1921. Dempsey was on a cross-country tour of the Pantages Vaudeville Circuit, making some extra money. He had been a copper mine mucker, lumberjack and dance hall bouncer and, though he went on in the next twelve years to earn $4 million in the ring, he had pocketed only $21.50 from his first professional bout in 1915.[23]

When Dempsey was in Calgary, Harry Wills, a black contender, had challenged him for the heavyweight title. In boxing circles, this was an explosive issue. Doc Kearns, Dempsey's manager, advised his man to ignore the challenge, and so, in the Calgary *Albertan*, the champ was quoted as saying, "I will never accept a challenge from a colored man. I absolutely draw the colored line."[24] Wills would have to wait, but Long Lance, as an Indian, would not. He showed up with his press credentials the next day to watch Dempsey perform, and observe a demonstration with a sparring partner of how Dempsey defeated Willard to win the championship. After this, Long Lance showed his pass and was allowed to visit Dempsey in his dressing room. The fighter's mother had some Cherokee blood, and the two men got along well. They met for breakfast the next day at the Palliser, then sparred a few rounds at the Pantages. The next morning they met again, boxed and wrestled and went for a swim at the YMCA. Dempsey was a few inches taller than Long Lance, and twenty-five pounds heavier, but they resembled each other in many remarkable ways. Both had taut, well-muscled bodies, broad facial features and dark skin. Dempsey later remembered Long Lance as fast and "light on his feet."[25]

Any reference to his Indian background pleased Long Lance. One of his friends on the newspaper, and a fellow militia officer, was Lieutenant Douglas Cunnington, who worked in the *Herald*'s advertising department. During the war he had won the Military Cross for capturing a machine gun nest. In the officers' mess one day, Cunnington said to Long Lance: "Chief, there is one thing I always admired about you. Though for years I have seen you mingle with every rank of officer from general down, I have never seen you try to be anything but an Indian." Long Lance wrote in one of his later articles that this was his "most appreciated compliment,"[26] and he went out of his way to link his own name with Indian subjects.

In June, 1920, Long Lance met Ormer Locklear, an American stunt flyer who performed every day at the Calgary Exhibition. Before crowds of thousands, the Texan pilot changed biplanes in mid-air, and executed other thrilling maneuvers. He stayed in Calgary a short time, and he was very popular. Calgarians were shocked to learn, a month later, that Locklear had crashed to his death near Los Angeles. In the obituary that Long Lance wrote for the *Herald,* he included this story:

Few, if any in Calgary or elsewhere, knew that Locklear was a quarter-breed Indian, of the Croatan Tribe, the oldest known tribe in the southwestern United States. . . . This story was brought forth when the *Herald* representative asked him if he were any relation of an Ormer Locklear from North Carolina, with whom he had attended college. Locklear recognized him as a cousin on the instant for he knew that his grandfather's brother in North Carolina also bore his Christian name. [27]

Long Lance doubtless winced at the "nigger jokes" that were heard in the city. Calgary had only a few black citizens, and they were seldom seen away from the shoeshine stands and the railways. The respected *Beaver* magazine, published by the Hudson's Bay Company in Winnipeg, included in the March, 1926, issue several such barbs. One was titled "Genealogy."

Two negroes were standing on the corner discussing family trees.
   "Yes, suh, man," said Ambrose, "Ah kin trace mah relations back to a family tree."
   "Chase 'em back to a family tree?" said Mose.
   "No, man! Trace 'em! Not chase 'em."
   "Well, dey ain't but two kinds of things dat lives in trees— birds and monkeys—and yo' sho' ain't got no feathers on yo'." [28]

Long Lance hated to be mistaken for a black, and there is evidence that he went along with the humor when it served to take the heat off him. He could be pushed only so far, however, and one night in Calgary he reached his breaking point. Fred Kennedy, a popular Calgary columnist, was covering a regimental dinner at the Palliser Hotel and sat at a table with Long Lance. After dinner, Kennedy, Long Lance and two other companions walked across the street to McCrohan's Restaurant and sat at the horseshoe counter. Ten minutes later, two men entered, and when the waitress motioned them to the stools next to Kennedy's group, they moved forward, then abruptly stopped. "I am not sitting alongside any nigger," one of the men told the waitress. Long Lance ignored the remark, so the same man repeated it, louder. "I am not sitting alongside any nigger!"

Long Lance politely excused himself, turned to the man who by now was glowering at him, and asked: "Were you addressing me, sir?"

"I sure as hell was," the man said.

The way Kennedy remembers it, "Long Lance's left didn't seem to travel any more than eight inches, but when it connected with the man's jaw, he went out like a light." [29]

7

INDIAN STORIES

O N THE MORNING OF May 27, 1921, when a late frost
had covered the green lawns of Calgary with a haze
of frozen dew, [1] Long Lance headed off by train on
his first out-of-town story. He enjoyed the ride
eastward, through the small station stops with grain
elevators marked Indus, Dalemead, West Carseland and
Carseland. It was Long Lance's assignment to go to
Gleichen, sixty miles east of Calgary, to report on the Blackfoot Indian Reserve.

As he stared out the coach window, it would have been
easy to imagine the prairie land covered with tall grass,
buffalo and mounted Blackfoot hunters. And he had time to
scribble a letter or postcard to his family. He wondered
about them often when he was alone. Over the past year he
had mailed many letters and photographs from Calgary,
each photograph bearing a carefully typed caption on the
back: the big parade in honor of the 250th anniversary of the
founding of the Hudson's Bay Company, Long Lance climbing out of the cockpit of a biplane, Long Lance with Howard
Kelly and other white friends on a prairie picnic, the national
parks at Banff and Jasper. One of the most recent snapshots
was a picture of himself in his militia uniform, which he
inscribed "To Mother and Dad." [2]

At Gleichen the train jolted to a stop. One can imagine
what he might have seen that morning on his walk to the

reserve. Gleichen was a busy little distribution center, with four grain elevators. There were buckboards at the station, and a few cars, and Long Lance observed the ranchers and homesteaders, and some distinctively dressed men in dark suits and black hats, and accompanied by women in bonnets and plain dresses. These were the Dunkards, the German Baptist Brethren, who were much like the Amish of southeastern Pennsylvania near Carlisle. The Dunkards lived close to Arrowwood, just south of town beyond the Blackfoot Reserve. [3]

He walked from the station toward a cluster of white frame buildings on the reserve side of the tracks. On a fence post he saw a meadowlark; its song reminded him of spring, despite the cold weather. He moved quickly to keep warm and soon came upon the Indian agent's office, where a few Indians loitered on the steps, chatting among themselves, and using expressive hand gestures as they talked. The men wore their hair in braids, some with wide-brimmed "Indian Joe" hats, colorful handkerchiefs tied under their chins, buckskin coats, and store-bought shirts and trousers. The women were clad in blankets with bright handkerchiefs over their heads.

Long Lance approached them and said hello in English. The men stopped talking; the women did not look up. The response did not surprise him, for he knew from Carlisle how wary Plains Indians were of strangers and how the old-timers would treat other Indians with the same glacial reserve they would whites.

Inside the building a fire burned, and one of the clerks directed Long Lance to the largest office where he saw a man about his own age, dressed in a jacket and tie, working at his desk. The agent, George Gooderham, looked up, listened to Long Lance explain his assignment, then suggested he come back after lunch. "You can join Corporal Harper of the Mounted Police and myself on an inspection of the western end of the reserve," he said.

In the early afternoon, Long Lance returned, and soon the three men rattled off in Gooderham's new black Ford, dust billowing behind them. At the first stop, the Anglican

Residential School, Gooderham read out the Truant Act, warning the children that they must attend school. (The year before, the federal Department of Indian Affairs had made school attendance compulsory on all reserves in Canada.) If they did not attend, he continued, with some exaggeration to make his point stick, they could be thrown in jail.

Driving around the reserve, Gooderham instructed Long Lance on what to write about, what points to include. The Indians were having great difficulty adjusting to white society, he emphasized. Only forty-five years ago they had lived off the buffalo, and since the great herds no longer roamed the prairies, the Indians were in distress. After ten thousand years of nomadic life, they could not be expected to settle down easily in a single generation. Gooderham spoke to the reporter as if he had never seen an Indian before. Long Lance grew restless and soon put away his notebook.

As they bumped over roads that were little more than wagon ruts, the men could see through the windshield flocks of migrating birds of every size and color flying to their nesting grounds in the north. On the green hillsides, they saw cattle, thin from the long winter, moving out to pasture with the calves. They saw small herds of Indian ponies, cayuses. All along, Gooderham continued his narrative, explaining that the Indians first obtained the cayuse after the arrival of the Spaniards. Runaways were traded north from Mexico and had reached the Blackfoot some two hundred years earlier.

Finally, Long Lance could take no more. "I am a Cherokee from Oklahoma and a graduate of Carlisle Indian School," he told Gooderham, who had been too preoccupied to read Long Lance's references. He assumed, from the stranger's dark complexion, that he was West Indian. It was an awkward introduction, but Gooderham and Long Lance quickly warmed to each other. Long Lance did the talking now, telling the agent about the Cherokee, the Carlisle Indian School and his friend, the great Jim Thorpe. As they passed some Indian women on the road, Long Lance asked Gooderham to stop. He tried some of his own rustic Cherokee on the Blackfoot women, who seemed startled and baffled. They could not understand a word Long Lance spoke. [4]

The party visited several farms after the tour of the reserve. At the 160-acre operation of Harry Red Gun, they found the proprietor in his field with a team of horses, busily plowing and seeding. Long Lance always traveled with a camera, and he snapped a picture of Harry to accompany his article. Gooderham explained how the Indians with cattle worked from sunup to sundown, branding the animals in the spring, castrating the males, segregating the dry cows. Long Lance knew enough about the operation from his trips to Carson Town to make pleasant conversation.

The Indian agent wielded immense power under Canada's Indian Act, the federal legislation that governed all aspects of a native's life. Even to leave the reserve, an Indian had to obtain a pass from the agent, stating where he was going and the purpose of the trip. Gooderham and his staff of about a dozen looked after the Blackfoot's land sales and leasing, housing, health, livestock—everything and anything from bookkeeping to directing the sowing of the crops. The Blackfoot Reserve, Gooderham explained, was the richest in Canada, about a third of its 450 square miles having been sold to the federal government in 1910. Money from the sale enabled the Blackfoot to buy plows, reapers, binders and harrows. [5]

Gooderham and Long Lance talked about the war, too. Gooderham had joined the Imperial Army in Britain, and as a lieutenant had commanded a battery in 1918 on the Passchendaele front in 1918. Long Lance told him he was a captain and described Vimy Ridge and Lens. Long Lance and Gooderham became friends, and over the next five years Long Lance came to know the Gooderham family well. George's wife, Mary, was the first woman to attend the School of Practical Science and study architecture at the University of Toronto.

Gooderham's father had been an Indian agent in Saskatchewan and later among the Blackfoot in Alberta. His family belonged to the temperance branch of the Gooderham family; the other branch owned Gooderham and Worts, the old Ontario distilling firm. George was born in 1889 on Poor

Man's Reserve in central Saskatchewan, and since he grew up there and later at neighboring Piapot's Reserve, his first friends were Indian children. He learned Cree from them, and often ate in their rough log huts along the flats of the Qu'Appelle River. His friends' mothers fed him bannock, and, as a treat, tea. He observed Indian rituals and ceremonies, such as the Feast of the White Dog and the Sun Dance, including the self-torture ritual of the Sun Dance that was later outlawed by the Department of Indian Affairs.

His parents sent him east to Ontario for his education, but he always returned to the plains in summer. While visiting the Blackfoot at Gleichen after the war, his father suffered a sudden and fatal heart attack. Pressed by his father's friends, George applied for the position of Indian agent in January, 1920. When Long Lance arrived in Gleichen, Gooderham had been the agent only for a year and a half,[6] yet his early years among the Indians gave him an air of maturity and long experience.

George and Mary Gooderham were much impressed with Long Lance. Mary remarked that Long Lance's vocabulary and turn of phrase were infinitely better than most white men in the neighborhood. From the first meeting, they saw in Long Lance a man with a "burning ambition to make a name for himself."[7]

Long Lance also called on Canon Stocken, the resident Anglican missionary with the Blackfoot, whose rectory was not far from Gooderham's office. Stocken had come to the reserve from England in 1885 as a young man of twenty-seven, and had served nearly forty years in Indian missions in southern Alberta.[8] He was able to tell Long Lance what the reserve had looked like in the mid-1880s. The Indians' large skin tepees were gone. Their clothing was no better than cotton sacking from the ration house. In 1879 the last of the great buffalo herds had been exterminated on the Canadian side of the border and, four years later, on the American side as well. The Indians were deprived of the mainstay of their way of life, and were trying to adjust both to poverty and to the confinements of the reserve. They had also to cope with tuberculosis and scrofula that ran rampant.[9]

Long Lance wrote down what he was told by the missionary uncritically, which doubtless reflected a lack of confidence in his own observations and judgments. At the Carlisle Indian School, he had been taught to respect the pious, unselfish character of the white missionaries, and the humanitarianism of the Indian agents. In his first article, he praised the "broad educational system" of the Anglican church and the work of the "paleface missionary" that he predicted "will always be a perpetual monument of self-sacrifice." He described Canon Stocken as "the most honored and respected white known to the Blackfoot of Canada," and he referred to Canada's Indian policy as "clearsighted" and administered by "a group of self-sacrificing employees."[10] He tried to please everyone, and the result also pleased the city editor at the *Herald*, who thought the article was uplifting and asked Long Lance for another, this time on the Sarcee.

A June provincial election prevented Long Lance from visiting the reserves for a while. For several years, the farmers of Alberta had felt themselves the victims of an eastern Canadian oligarchy, one that sold them high-priced farm machinery and at the same time allowed the railways to charge excessively high freight rates, all of which conspired to keep the farmers impoverished. A growing resentment against old party lines nourished a backlash against the Liberal party in Alberta. On June 17, a new agrarian party, the United Farmers of Alberta, pledged to liberating the province from "eastern domination," won a resounding victory. Long Lance had exercised his franchise since he joined the Canadian army,[11] and he voted this time, but we do not know for whom.

With the election over, Long Lance headed off on his next out-of-town assignment, to the Sarcee Reserve south of Calgary. He enjoyed these excursions, seeing new places and meeting new people, escaping the routine and the predictable in the city. His boredom threshold was low. Thanks to Canon Stocken of the Blackfoot Reserve, he had a contact with the Sarcees, Archdeacon John Tims, who had been the first Anglican missionary with the Blackfoot, from 1883 to 1895, and the resident missionary at the Sarcee Reserve

since 1895. Tims was the father of Anglican Indian missions
in the Calgary area in the late nineteenth century. A strict
and efficient administrator, he had acted for years as the
secretary-treasurer for all Anglican schools and missions in
the diocese. [12]

Long Lance borrowed a friend's roadster this time for the
short trip—ten miles south of the city—up 14th Street, past
the large elevated water tank, across Weasel Head Bridge.
It was a bone-dry summer, with the green grass of May now
burnt and brown, and the mid-day heat reminded Long
Lance of North Carolina. Over a rough gravel road, he
approached a cluster of houses, barns, cattle sheds and
granaries surrounding a church, mission house, hospital and
school. Each Sarcee family, like the Blackfoot, sited their
stables a hundred yards behind their homes. In all directions
he saw the small frame houses of the Sarcee, painted white
with red trim, dotting the rolling upland around the mission. [13] He parked the roadster and walked to the rectory,
where Archdeacon Tims greeted him at the door. An elderly
man who always wore his clerical collar, the archdeacon had
lost most of his accent, but none of his formally polite English manner. He invited the young reporter into the parlor.

Long Lance studied the room and made notes he thought
would be helpful. He noticed dozens of silver cups standing
on the mantelpiece, each one dutifully inscribed. When
asked, Archdeacon Tims gladly told of his rowing days in
England, where he had won his first silver cup at the age of
eight for coxing the winning four in the Oxford Royal
Regatta of 1865. He won other silver cups for rowing, canoe-
ing, coxing and boating of every description.

Immigrant missionaries were not the exception in Canada. (Many Canadian-born clergy shunned the Indian missions, preferring instead to travel to distant corners of the
world.) Numerous French and Belgian Oblate Fathers
served in the Roman Catholic stations and self-sacrificing,
middle-class Englishmen, like Stocken and Tims, in the
Anglican missions.

Archdeacon Tims originally intended to work in Uganda,
where Anglican missionary work had just begun, but there

was an urgent appeal for missionaries in the northwest, and in 1883 he was sent to establish an Anglican mission to the Blackfoot. At age twenty-five, he sailed from England to New York, took the Northern Pacific Railway to Helena, Montana Territory, then a stage to Fort Benton, Montana, and finally an express wagon to Blackfoot country on the Bow River at Blackfoot Crossing. He arrived just weeks before the Canadian Pacific Railway construction crews, and found the Indians in a pitiable condition. "The buffalo had disappeared and they were just settling down to reserve life," he said. "They did nothing except dance and attend the ration house. Morally, they had descended to the depths of iniquity. Gambling, thieving, lying and adultery were common." The young missionary watched his first Sun Dance that July, and wondered what, in God's name, he was doing here. "The fantastic costumes of the people, the paint and feathers, the... foreign tongue made my heart sink within me, and if ever I felt the hopelessness of a task... it was then."

He suffered a nervous breakdown, and two attempts were made on his life, the last in 1895, which resulted in his departure from the Blackfoot mission and his replacement by Canon Stocken. When Long Lance arrived to interview him, however, great progress had been made and Archdeacon Tims was in good spirits and fine health, as his burly frame and barrel chest attested. "Our adherents are not all of them what we would wish," he admitted, "but comparing them with the average white congregation, I think their attendance at Divine Service and on the means of grace generally is good." Their material lives, too, had improved. "Many of the natives have good floors and good roofs overhead, whilst their walls are covered with pictures and ornaments, clocks stand on shelves, cupboards hold crockery and tables, chairs and cooking ranges are found in nearly all."[14]

The archdeacon's daughter, Winnifred Tims, was a teacher at the Sarcee Anglican School; at her father's suggestion, she took Long Lance on a tour of the school. Long Lance also met Doctor Thomas F. Murray, a friendly twenty-eight-year-old Indian agent and medical doctor who

had recently arrived from London, Ontario. Dr. Murray told
him of the terrible mortality rate among the Sarcees. Three
out of four died before reaching the age of twenty. The
Sarcee population had fallen from more than three hundred
when the treaty was made in 1877 to 155 at the beginning of
1921. To combat tuberculosis, Dr. Murray explained that the
Anglican school itself would become a sanitarium and government school later that year. [15]

Long Lance's article on the Sarcees was much tougher
than the puffery he wrote about the Blackfoot. The thought
that kept running through his head was that the Indians had
surrendered their land in return for tuberculosis. "The
plight of the Sarcee is a real tragedy," Long Lance wrote.
"Little do the people of Calgary realize that they are daily
witnessing the passing of a nation as dramatically as any
that have been depicted by the pen of J. Fenimore Cooper."

Through Archdeacon Tims, Long Lance met Jim Starlight, the Sarcee chief. Chief Starlight, known as a progressive, owned the reserve's largest farm, on which he raised
wheat and oats and some of the best stock. He was educated
at the mission school, spoke excellent English and played a
strong game of chess. Long Lance and Chief Starlight liked
each other from the start. Three years later, the chief would
loan Long Lance his white buckskin costume for the Calgary
Stampede. [16]

Long Lance did not attempt any in-depth investigation of
the Sarcee. He talked to the missionary and the agent,
toured the school and talked with the chief, then hurried
back to Calgary to write his story. Another visitor to the
same reserve that summer worked much differently, and
Long Lance happened to mention him indirectly in his story,
published in late July. Describing the Thunder Dance performed by the "pagans" in the spring, Long Lance wrote: "A
government ethnologist has just bought the tribe's entire
outfit for the pipe dance, to be kept in the government
museum as a historic relic of the aborigines of this country."
The government ethnologist was Diamond Jenness, soon to
become one of Canada's best-known anthropologists.

Jenness spent two months on the Sarcee reserve, arriving

each day by horse and saddle to talk to some of the older Indians, to learn of the early organization and history of the tribe. He was a government employee, determined to gather as much knowledge as possible about the Indian people at a time when they were rapidly dying off. Using skills he acquired in field work in New Guinea and the Arctic, Jenness cross-checked all the facts given him through his interpreter. Their paths might have crossed the day Long Lance visited the reserve.

There were similarities between Jenness and Long Lance. Both were of medium height, strong and wiry, and nearly the same age. They were recent immigrants to Canada, Jenness coming from New Zealand and England, Long Lance from the United States. Each man wrote extensively in the 1920s on Canada's Indians. [17] But here the likeness ends. Long Lance wrote in a light, breezy style, capable of such things as, "Buffalo was to the Indian what roast beef is to the white man." Jenness confined himself to strict, balanced, academic prose. Long Lance brightened his writing with anecdotes, and never shied from using himself in his stories if it helped to move the story along. In his article on the Sarcees, he told of Chief Bull's Head, who had been a great Sarcee warrior in his youth, and who had gone on many war parties against the Crees to the north. One day Chief Bull's Head unexpectedly encountered a Cree chief whom he had fought years earlier. The Cree simply poked his head into Chief Bull's Head's tepee, and the old Sarcee, as Long Lance put it, "almost jumped out of his skin."

"I thought I left you dead on the battlefield," Chief Bull's Head exclaimed.

"You thought so, but you didn't," the Cree replied, smiling.

The next Sunday, according to Long Lance's account, the two old warriors attended church together at the suggestion of Archdeacon Tims. Long Lance remarked in his article that the incident reminded him of an event he had witnessed at Carlisle (which he called in his story an Indian "university"). This was the meeting at Carlisle of the famous Nez Percé, Chief Joseph, and the elderly American Army general who had chased him for thousands of miles in the Nez Percé War of 1877. On the commencement platform, Long Lance wrote, the two men met for the first time since the war. "The one-armed general and the blind chief stood motionless for a moment; then they grasped each other's hands and turned and faced the audience." They could not speak, these "two men of iron, who had maimed each other in a terrible massacre years before." For the remainder of the commencement, Long Lance concluded, the two men stayed close by each other "and the general became the blind chief's guide."

It all made for a nice, well-rounded tale, and Long Lance became better at this through the years, but it was not the sort of account one might expect from someone as exacting as Diamond Jenness. Chief Joseph and General O.O. Howard did meet at Carlisle, but Long Lance could not possibly have been there. The encounter occurred at the commencement of 1903,[18] when Long Lance was at his desk at the Depot Street School for Negroes in Winston.

George Gooderham, the agent with the Blackfoot, recognized that Long Lance knew little of the Plains Indians, but he also perceived the man's talent for conveying the sense of a story and writing it in a way that would appeal to the whites.[19] He encouraged him to write more stories on the Indians, as did his editor at the *Herald*. Long Lance's next assignment was the Blood Indians, who lived one hundred miles south of Calgary. Here Long Lance met another Anglican missionary, the Rev. S.H. Middleton, who would teach him more about Indians than he ever expected to know.

8

BUFFALO CHILD

SAMUEL HENRY MIDDLETON, or "S.H." as he was known, met Long Lance at the train station in Macleod and drove him to St. Paul's Blood Indian School, located on Big Island in the middle of Belly River, fifteen miles south of Macleod.

The Blood Indian Reserve was beautiful and easily the largest in Canada, some fifty miles long and thirty miles wide, just north of the Montana border. All around him Long Lance saw fields under cultivation, hundreds of thousands of acres, as far as the eye could see. The Indians were horse and cattle ranchers as well, and they built their own homes on the grasslands. With the money they made, they purchased the newest, most efficient farm implements, and the reserve thrived.

Middleton liked what he saw in Long Lance, and what he saw was his model of the ideal Indian, one who could measure up to any white man. On the drive to the school, the two men talked politics, discussing Arthur Meighen, who had just replaced Robert Borden as prime minister of Canada, and the new American president, Warren Harding. They touched on sports, as the Anglican missionary, though considerably slighter and less robust than Long Lance, loved to hike, ride, climb mountains and indulge himself in soccer. Long Lance was also drawn to Middleton. He listened for hours to stories of the Blood language and legends. Unlike

Archdeacon Tims, who was appalled at the brutality of the
Sun Dance, Middleton explained that in fact the Sun Dance
grew out of a longstanding worship of the Great Spirit,
whom the Indians believed to be identical to the Christian
God. If Long Lance was to be Middleton's vision of the
Indian-made-good, then Middleton was to be Long Lance's
patient tutor and life-long friend.

All his life, Samuel Middleton had fantasized about the
"Red Indians." He was an orphan and a romantic. He lived
with his grandparents in Burton-on-Trent, a crowded English industrial town in the western Midlands and, like thousands of English boys, he thought of North American
Indians as brave and noble savages who roamed never-
ending plains and brandished tomahawks against their
enemies. Children's books and magazines, the penny dread-
fuls, were crammed with stories of Indians and the Wild
West. At the turn of the century, Buffalo Bill stirred up
great excitement in Britain when he brought his ex-
travaganza to the land of Shakespeare.

When Middleton graduated with a Bachelor of Science
degree in agriculture from Kingston College in 1904, he
declined an offer from his grandfather to join the family firm
of carriage-makers in Derbyshire, and decided instead to go
to Canada for the challenge and the adventure. He set off for
Brocket in the Canadian northwest and the North Peigan
Reserve in early 1905.[1] The North Peigan were the smallest
of three Blackfoot-speaking tribes in Canada (the Blackfoot,
Blood and Peigan). About five hundred North Peigan lived
north of the forty-ninth parallel, while some three thousand
resided in the United States, where they were called the
Blackfeet.[2]

Young Middleton bought a small ranch near Brocket,
some work horses and fifty head of cattle. He hired Indians
to help him put up fences and buildings, and he came to know
them well. There were terrible blizzards that first winter,
and in summer hailstorms pelted his crops. During the fall of
1907 half his stock froze to death.

The Peigan ranchers did not have it any easier. They were
confused and demoralized, suffering through what later

anthropologists would call "culture shock." The former buffalo hunters and their sons failed at farming, and now their attempts at ranching were floundering. Few could read or write or understand English. Middleton volunteered his services to the Anglican Diocese of Calgary, offering to help in any way to bring the Indians into the twentieth century.

These were boom years in Western Canada, and the Anglican bishop in Calgary needed all the help he could get. As the Indian population dropped, white sodbusters increased a hundredfold. In 1895, the District of Alberta had thirty thousand inhabitants; by 1905, the new province of Alberta boasted nearly two hundred thousand inhabitants; by 1911, the population had doubled to four hundred thousand.[3] The bishop asked Middleton if he would work as a lay reader for the Rev. R.W. Haynes, an Anglican missionary at the Peigan Reserve. Middleton agreed, and loved the work. Two years later, the bishop asked him to give up his ranch to become the principal of the St. Paul's Boarding School on the reserve. In 1909, he sold the ranch and his stock and, like the early Jesuit missionaries who worked and lived among the Hurons and Iroquois in Eastern Canada, devoted his life to the service of the Indians.

Middleton spent his first days with the Bloods, patiently traveling by saddlehorse over the vast open grasslands of their reserve. Thousands of horses and cattle grazed on the unbroken prairie, and scattered along the streams and in isolated spots in the uplands, he found small family groups of Bloods. He loved to visit the old Indians in their tepees and crude log homes, smoking with them the *kinnikinic*, an Indian tobacco made from the bark and leaves of sumac and willow.

To the west, the imposing Rockies were always in view, and in particular a lone citadel of rock that stood apart from the rest like a fortress. The Blackfoot called this peak, which rose nearly a mile above the surrounding plains, *Ninaistoko* (Chief Mountain) because it stood out like a brave leader. When Middleton lived near the North Peigans at Brocket, the Indians honored him by calling him by the same name.

He started to learn the Blackfoot language that winter

during his free hours at St. Paul's. He studied Archdeacon Tims's and Canon Stocken's translations of the gospel, and from his students' parents he learned rudimentary pronunciation. Soon he managed a basic vocabulary and acquired a rough command of the language's sound and intonation. For Christmas, 1909, he attempted to preach in Blackfoot, and from then on he held a regular Sunday service in the language of his congregation. The Blackfoot admired his courage — all his predecessors had used translators for their sermons — and encouraged him to continue. He began putting prayers and hymns into Blackfoot, and the congregation grew.[4]

The center of Middleton's life now was Big Island. He repaired the dilapidated buildings, as much as the mission's small budget allowed. For eleven years he pleaded with the Department of Indian Affairs for new quarters, but to no avail. The response was always the same: "The Government will consider your proposals and you will be favored with an answer in due course."[5] He found that a fresh coat of white paint could make the mission look as if it had had a complete face-lift, at least from a distance.

Progress was slow but steady. At the entrance to the school campus, on the left of the driveway, stood the hospital and gymnasium. On the right was the girls' dormitory, which also served as the school's dining room and kitchen. Further on was the boys' residence, the rectory, the church (used as a schoolroom on weekdays), stables, a granary and outbuildings. It was a problem to obtain enough firewood for the hot-air furnace, and Middleton worried that the use of so many coal oil lamps for lighting posed a fire hazard to the old frame buildings. He installed additional fire extinguishers, axes and fire pails, then worried that he had overextended himself and the school's budget for the sake of fire safety.

When Middleton became principal, St. Paul's had thirty students, from six to eighteen years of age. The enrollment rose to fifty in a few years, and to sixty-five by 1917. He believed that agriculture was the salvation of the Bloods, and he modified the school program to emphasize it. The boys worked on the farm in the morning and spent the afternoons in the classroom, following the government-approved curriculum for Alberta's public schools. Middleton conducted a special evening class on modern methods of farming and care of livestock. The boys farmed forty acres and cultivated a four-acre kitchen garden. It proved such a success that within a few years the school sold surplus farm produce to white neighbors. While the boys worked in the fields, the girls learned cooking, needlework and general housekeeping. Middleton insisted that only English could be spoken in the classrooms and on the school grounds. Indian music and dancing were forbidden. [6] He reasoned that however cruel the regulations seemed, they were necessary if the Bloods were to compete with their white neighbors. He also included an hour of daily religious instruction, and every morning and evening he led the students in prayer.

It was hard to attract good teachers to the school, for the church could pay them only half of what the best city school board offered. [7] When Middleton arrived at St. Paul's, he met Katherine Underwood, a teacher he regarded as a perfect candidate. She was a young woman missionary from Norwich, England, who had come to St. Paul's to teach in 1905. She was quiet, hard-working and greatly respected by the Bloods, who named her *Sipistaki* (Owl Woman) because she kept such a good watch over their girls. In time, Middleton and Miss Underwood fell in love, and on April 19, 1911, Archdeacon Tims officiated at their marriage. They had four children, but even with family duties, Katherine continued to work as the school nurse. [8]

Bishop Pinkham ordained Middleton a minister in 1913, and he dropped his first name, "Sam," in favor of the initials "S.H.," which he thought was more befitting a minister and a school principal. Every week, S.H. instructed the advanced students for half an hour on "the duties of British citizenship" and strongly encouraged patriotism among the Bloods. Portraits of King George V and Queen Mary were hung in the school's big dining room, and the Union Jack was flown every Sunday. S.H. even taught his students to eat as they did in the "Old Country." "Stay with your British teaching," he told them. "The fork is a left-hand instru-

ment." He organized St. Paul's like his old grammar school
at Ashby-de-la-Zouch in England, with school uniforms, a
prefect system and an Old Boys' Association. [9]

Early on, Middleton tried to establish a Boy Scout troop,
but the boys showed little interest. Appealing to the Bloods'
old warrior spirit, he then organized a cadet corps, which
was welcomed with great enthusiasm by the sons and grand-
sons of the last great plains warriors. In no time, Corps
Commander Rev. S.H. Middleton had his unit in competitive
trim, and in 1920 it won the R.B. Bennett Shield Trophy for
the best all-round cadet corps in Alberta, beating sixty
white units in the province. [10] Middleton made no secret of
his admiration for the Carlisle Indian Residential School
that Long Lance had attended. He tried to duplicate it,
albeit on a very reduced budget and considerably smaller
scale. He especially admired General Pratt, the founder of
Carlisle, and in a letter to Pratt's daughter in 1935, he
admitted that "for years I have eulogized his memory, and
quoted him time and again." [11]

What infuriated him was the government's stingy financial support. By treaty, the Dominion of Canada promised
the Blackfoot a white man's education, then failed to provide
it by making inadequate grants to the churches to cover the
expense of teachers and school facilities. When Long Lance
arrived in August, 1921, Middleton bitterly poured out all
his grievances.

Long Lance's published story championed the Bloods, and
took on the government, much to Middleton's delight. He
wrote that the Bloods were the most progressive tribe in
Alberta. [12] The Blackfoot had sold more than a third of their
reserve, and the Sarcee leased a third of their land to the
government, all to obtain the necessary farm equipment and
housing that the Department of Indian Affairs had refused
to provide. The Bloods, however, held on to every acre that
was theirs. Without government money, they built their
own houses and bought the farm equipment they needed.
Somehow, Long Lance wrote, "they seemed to have
acquired a desirable kick in their make-up that is not
enjoyed to the same degree by their two brother bands."

The Bloods refused "to lie in the feathered nests that most Indians like to wallow in, under the protecting wings of the government."

Long Lance described the Indians out haying, "hundreds of them, old and young...working silently on immense stacks of the golden stems, mowing and cutting, or turning over the summer fallow." The rye crop, even though the harvest was several weeks away, already reached one's chest. Long Lance knew about horses from his days with the Wild West Show, and he was impressed by the quality of the animals he found on the Blood Reserve. He noticed a few pintos, but "none of the ordinary cayuses, so commonly owned by Indians."

He gave Middleton most of the credit for the success of the Bloods, calling him "a powerful stimulant to character building among the younger Indians...a remarkable power for good among this tribe." He had scribbled his notes furiously while talking to Middleton, and the inevitable errors crept in. Middleton told him of an old Blood warrior, Mountain Horse, and Long Lance recorded that he was the head chief of all the Bloods and not just one of the minor chiefs. Long Lance also ignored, in his enthusiasm for Middleton and the Anglican operation, the work of the Roman Catholic mission on the reserve. The Roman Catholic residential boarding school for the Bloods had roughly the same enrollment as St. Paul's.

When Long Lance's article appeared in the *Herald* on August 27, Middleton read it carefully. He was fascinated and puzzled by the man. It surprised him that Long Lance referred to a young Indian as a "buck" and quite bizarrely described a group of St. Paul's girls he met at Waterton Park as "a group of dusky daughters of the plains, not yet one generation away from savagery...." He considered Long Lance extraordinary, but also, at times, demonstrably non-Indian—his ease with strangers, his command of English, his firm handshake, the smartly tailored suit. He reconciled this with the fact that, as a Cherokee, Long Lance indeed had been "civilized" for more than a century and easily a couple of generations ahead of the Canadian Plains Indians.

Still, the conundrum remained. Years later, Middleton would write of Long Lance: "He was an interesting personality, sometimes Indian, ofttimes white, but the two together—never. They did not blend. He was inwardly torn by strange conflicting emotions."[13]

Long Lance sent thirty copies of his story to St. Paul's and warmly thanked Middleton for his help.[14] A few months later, Middleton wrote Long Lance to invite him to speak at the annual school reunion in mid-February, a big event that was attended by the graduates and friends of St. Paul's.[15] Long Lance accepted, and in a cheery note on January 15 he thanked Middleton "for the boosting which you have given me." He added, "I hope the Bloods will not be disappointed when they see what sort of an article you have been praising."

He arrived in Macleod for the second time on the noon train from Calgary on Saturday, February 11. Middleton met him at the depot and drove him to the mission on Big Island. This time the prairie was covered with drifts of snow.

All day the following Monday, St. Paul's prepared feverishly for the 9th Annual Re-Union of the Old Boys' and Girls' Association, which was to commence at six-thirty that evening. The girls cooked roasts in the kitchen and cut up potatoes, carrots, turnips and onions by the sackful. They baked fresh bread and prepared pies and cakes. The boys hauled in dry wood for the fires and scrubbed and decorated the school dining hall, then set freshly laundered sheets on the tables.

At dusk, the wagons, drawn by frost-covered ponies, began to pull up at the school. The visitors thawed out in the hall, removed their coats, and greeted one another. As the hall filled, Mr. and Mrs. Middleton entered, with the five teachers and instructors, and the distinguished visitor, Long Lance. They took their places at the head table directly under a huge Union Jack flanked by the portraits of King George V and Queen Mary. Throughout the dinner, the older people, like Mountain Horse, spoke Blackfoot, but the younger Bloods talked among themselves in English.[16] A generation of buffalo hunters and a generation of modern, progressive farmers sat side by side in the dining hall, enjoying the feast.

When the dishes were cleared and tea served, Middleton tapped his water glass, cleared his throat, and in a deep, commanding voice proposed a toast to His Majesty, King George V. Then, with everyone seated, he introduced the honored guest, "Captain Sylvester Chahuska Long Lance, Cherokee Indian... brilliant student and athlete at Carlisle, war hero in the Great War, distinguished journalist.... all male students at St. Paul's would do well to try to imitate his outstanding career." Long Lance stood, resplendent in his blue Carlisle uniform, and proposed a toast to the former pupils of St. Paul's.[17] Then he spoke.

"The average Indian walks daily among worlds unrealized. He sees the pleasures and advantages of the white world in a sort of haze that forever denies them to him." Echoing General Pratt, he emphasized the message that "the pleasures and advantages of the white man [are] with a dash of initiative, grit and determination... as available to you as they are to him."[18] One of the St. Paul's graduates who had served overseas, Mike Mountain Horse, replied to the toast.[19]

Mike Mountain Horse's father, the old Mountain Horse, a man in his mid-sixties, was given a quick translation of Long Lance's speech. He probably did not agree with everything Long Lance said, especially when he exhorted the Bloods to adopt the ways of the white man, but as an old warrior and as the father of three sons who had seen action with the Canadian Expeditionary Force, he admired courage. For his generation, courage was still the most valued quality of a man's character, and he knew of Long Lance's war record.

Middleton hoped to present Long Lance as a role model for the young Bloods, and recalled that old Mountain Horse had helped with the ceremony by which Edward, Prince of Wales, was adopted by the Bloods during his Royal Tour of Canada in 1919.[20] Middleton asked Old Mountain Horse to give Long Lance, the Cherokee war hero, a Blackfoot name, and he gladly consented.

When the toasts and speeches ended, Mountain Horse

motioned Long Lance to step forward and kneel with him on
a buffalo robe in the center of the dining room, where the
wooden benches and long tables had been pushed back.
Long Lance came forward with his usual assurance, then the
Indians surrounded them. Mountain Horse, wearing an
eagle-plume headdress, began the ceremony by taking from
one of his sons a long, forked stick which held a hot coal. He
placed it on a metal pan and covered it with sweet grass. A
pleasant fragrance quickly wafted over the room. Mountain
Horse held his hands in the smoke of the sweet grass, then
stroked his arms and his chest as if to purify himself with its
essence.

After a Blackfoot prayer, Mountain Horse took red clay
from a buckskin bag and carefully painted Long Lance's face
with the sacred paint, which the Blackfoot believed had the
power to ward off sickness and bring long life. As Long
Lance knelt before him, the old Indian daubed his forehead,
chin and both cheeks, to represent the sun's daily course
through the heavens, the forehead signifying the rising and
the left cheek the setting sun. [21] After this, Mountain Horse
raised Long Lance to his feet, then he prayed again. Long
Lance was most likely aware of what was happening, for
Middleton had no doubt described to him how the Prince of
Wales had been adopted as a member of the Blood tribe. In
the old Indian mission building, two thousand miles from his
home, his wildest dreams were being made real: spiritually,
he was being reborn a Plains Indian. To him, this ritual was
deadly serious.

Mountain Horse placed his war bonnet on Long Lance's
head, then he and his wife chanted the war song of "Buffalo
Child," the Blackfoot gutturals giving the war cry a fero-
cious sound. The new Buffalo Child was to sing this song at
all times of danger.

The ceremony over, Mountain Horse turned Long Lance
around, and abruptly pushed him away. In Indian society, all
stand at the same level. Having honored one with an adoption, the Bloods, aware of the perils of vanity, quickly cut
him down to the status of every other warrior. [22]

Middleton explained later the exact words Mountain

Horse had used when he gave Long Lance his new name:
"Buffalo Child's bravery is talked of daily among the Blackfoot, Blood and Peigan Indians of these plains, and as you
must henceforth be known by this honorable name among
these tribes, you must ever endeavor to be the great Indian
whose spirit now comes back to earth and enters your
body."[23] Among the Bloods, Long Lance now replaced the
warrior Buffalo Child.[24]

The rest of the evening was given over to fun, with a
"white" dance following the speeches and ceremonies. Long
Lance loved to dance, and he sat out few of the waltzes,
polkas and fox trots that night. St. Paul's Old Boys and Girls
rhythmically stepped around the newly adopted Blood and
he reveled in their attention. Before he left the next morning, he asked Middleton to photograph him in a Blood war
bonnet and a Hudson's Bay Company blanket.[25]

FREELANCING

B Y THE END OF the winter of 1922, Long Lance was ready to move on. Calgary had served its purpose. In all likelihood he had remained in the city as long as he had only to fulfill his need for a period of stability after the uprootings and adventures of war. Perhaps he stayed because he was satisfied and happy, perhaps too satisfied and too happy for his own ambition.

He was getting started as a journalist, and his writing improved markedly from one feature story to another. He had men and women friends, and with the Vaheys the facsimile of a family. He liked the sunshine and the clarity of the air in southern Alberta, which he later described in an article for *McClure's* as a "mild intoxicant," called by the locals "Alberta pep." He might have been tempted to linger, but he knew the danger of putting down roots. His relationship with Calgary was something like a man's relationship with a saucy young woman when it has gone on one day too long and he knows, as if by instinct, that from here on it can only go badly—or worse, get serious. That is when a man begins to look for ways to extricate himself from the situation.

By March of 1922, Long Lance was restless, even a little bored. For months he had been assigned to City Hall, trying to find some challenge in yet another debate on mill rates, snow removal or storm sewers. He was reckless enough to decide to try to liven things up. On the morning of March 29, Long Lance left his rooming house carrying a large paper bag containing a mask, matches and a fuse. When he arrived at City Hall, he went straight to the city engineer's office, where he was known, and without any trouble managed to obtain a gas inspector's bag and a large pressure gauge, which he took to the men's washroom on the main floor.

He spread out his utensils on a wash basin, removed the pressure gauge from its leather satchel, attached it to one of two leather handles on the outside, then attached the fuse to the gas inspector's bag. He stuffed all this back into the paper bag and walked upstairs to the mayor's office. From the anteroom, he heard Mayor Sam Adams and the commissioners heatedly discussing what Long Lance had come to regard as "the totally unexciting question of city finances."[1]

Long Lance pulled the gas mask from his bag, slipped it over his face, then ignited the fuse to his homemade "bomb" and opened the door to the meeting. He dropped the package just inside the doorway. Mayor Adams, facing the door, yelled, and ran from the room, colliding with his secretary on the way out. One commissioner dove under the conference table, while another, watching the fuse burn down, clenched his fists and smashed through three layers of glass in one of the office's west windows. He plunged ten feet to the ground, his feet running before he landed.

It was the biggest prank in Calgary in years, and two days later, the rival *Albertan* printed a poem to honor "the scheme of Lance's."

> Come, gather round my trusty friends
> And hear the ghastly tale;
> Whilst the world in laughter bends,
> The city hall doth wail. . . .[2]

"Tellum Bigley," the *Albertan*'s resident humorist, loved it. "Commissioner Samis wasn't scared when he saw the bomb," he wrote. "He merely ducked under the table so as to give the rest of the crowd room to get to the door."[3]

Colonel Woods, the *Herald*'s strict, Victorian editor, was

not amused, and knowing that Charlie Hayden, the kind-hearted city editor, would not give Long Lance the punishment he deserved, he called in C.O. Smith to act as hatchet-man. When Long Lance arrived in the newsroom, Smith motioned him to his office, where he delivered a tongue lashing and a stern lecture on the proprieties and responsibilities of a *Herald* reporter. Long Lance had disgraced his newspaper and insulted the city's elected officials. Abruptly, and coldly, Smith fired him.

In that evening's edition, Colonel Woods and C.O. Smith apologized for the prank. "The Herald deeply regrets this occurrence and that this indignity to His Worship Mayor Adams and to the commissioners and other officers of the city was suffered by them through the act of a member of its staff, and tenders its sincere apologies to Mayor Adams and to the other City Hall officials affected by his conduct." Long Lance had already apologized to Mayor Adams, and the mayor was good-spirited enough to see the fun of the joke. The mayor refused to accept the newspaper's apology, and intervened on Long Lance's behalf,[4] but Colonel Woods would not relent. Long Lance was out.

He left Calgary in April and went by train to Vancouver, where he was welcomed by the mild, nearly summer weather of the Pacific Coast. Vancouver, with a population of two hundred thousand, was three times the size of Calgary, and the bustling city excited Long Lance. Downtown Vancouver was built at the base of a short peninsula that ended in the city's famous Stanley Park. To the northeast lay the section of Burrard Inlet known as Vancouver Harbour, protected by Stanley Park from the Gulf of Georgia. Three small Squamish Indian reserves — Capilano, Mission and Seymour Creek — faced the harbor on the mountainous North Shore.

Long Lance took a room at 906 Howe Street,[5] a block from busy Granville, one of the major shopping districts. Immediately south of his rooming house lay the industrial area of False Creek, and beyond it the residential areas of Kitsilano, Point Grey and Shaughnessy. The tall burners of nearly a hundred sawmills on the north shore of False Creek and Burrard Inlet belched smelly pollution into the Vancouver sky.

Vancouver was not yet forty years old, and owed its prosperity to its selection as the western terminus of the Canadian Pacific Railway in 1886. A second transcontinental line was built to the year-round, ice-free port just before World War I.[6] The local newspapers had shared in the boom times, swelling on weekends to fifty and more pages. In 1922, the leading paper was the evening *Province*, with a circulation of sixty thousand, about three times that of the younger, morning *Sun*.[7]

Long Lance decided, rightly, that the more sensationalist *Sun* would likely be interested in his Indian stories. He went to see Bert Stein, the city editor,[8] and brought out his portfolio of articles on the Blackfoot, Sarcee and Blood Indians. He impressed Stein with his stories and dazzled him with all that Chief Buffalo Child Long Lance — which was how he introduced himself when he arrived in Vancouver — had accomplished. The *Sun* agreed to buy a series of stories on the Indians of British Columbia for their Sunday edition.

The editor glowingly introduced Long Lance's first story which appeared in the *Sun* on May 7:

> Here's a regular story from a regular Indian. It was written by
> Chief Buffalo Child Long Lance of Calgary. He is one of the
> few outstanding figures of his race. He is a graduate of Carlisle
> Indian School and of St. John's Military Academy of Manlius,
> New York. He is the only Indian to be appointed to West Point,
> the United States Military Academy, by a president of the
> United States. Appointed by President Wilson in 1914.
> Relinquished this appointment one year later to go overseas
> with the Canadian troops. Went overseas as a private, was
> commissioned and rose to the rank of captain. Twice wounded
> and decorated with the Croix de Guerre.

Long Lance's warm reception in Vancouver was unusual, especially as it was afforded by the *Sun*, which had been fueling the fire of racism for months. The sly reference to

Long Lance being "one of the few outstanding figures of his race" was indicative of their attitude. A wave of "yellow peril" fear had washed over the province about this time. One out of fourteen of British Columbia's five hundred thousand inhabitants was of Chinese or Japanese descent. As if to sound the alarm, the *Sun* published *The Writing on the Wall* in August, 1921, a tract urging white British Columbians to be vigilant against the Chinese and Japanese. To believe the author, Mrs. Glynn-Ward, the Chinese were repulsive characters, opium smokers who lived in filth, and the Japanese were agents of Imperial Japan, who were furiously buying up property at strategic locations on the coast. After the book appeared, the *Sun* praised the work as serving "to awaken those unbelievers in eastern Canada who still wonder why the West is crying out on its knees for new immigration legislation."[9]

Diamond Jenness, who regularly traveled throughout British Columbia after World War I, observed the ugly racial situation on the Pacific Coast. Jenness found that British Columbia Indians suffered the same invective as the Chinese and Japanese. The whites, he wrote, "spoke of the native population as 'Siwashes' and, for good measure, they occasionally added the epithet 'dirty.' " He wrote that everywhere on the coast, whether they worked as stevedores, fishermen or cannery workers "it was said that the Indians were shiftless and unreliable." Jenness noted that in the interior of the province, one or two villages even enforced their own Jim Crow system. In the town of Hazelton, for example, which had a population of three hundred whites and four hundred Indians, "no Indian might walk beside a white man or woman, or sit on the same side in the village church."[10] It was all too familiar to Long Lance.

Racial hate existed on the Indian side as well. In 1922, many Indians refused to speak to journalists in British Columbia. Franz Boas, the distinguished American anthropologist, discovered this animosity to whites when he made his first field trip there in 1886. As one Cowichan Indian on Vancouver Island told him, "Whites look upon the Indians not as humans but as dogs." As a result, the Indian said his people "did not want to explain their culture to outsiders, as they might laugh at things that were their laws, such as painted houses, and articles used for celebrating their festivals."[11]

Long Lance, as an Indian journalist with splendid credentials, was able to break through this barrier of distrust. One of his first contacts was Andy Paull, an articulate, thirty-six-year-old Squamish Indian leader who knew the cultures of white and Indian intimately. He had attended a Roman Catholic residential school for six years on his home reserve of Mission. Paull also spent two years learning the traditional ways of his elders in the Squamish settlements on Burrard Inlet and Howe Sound. The elders encouraged him to study the white man's legal system, and from 1907 to 1911, Paull worked in the law office of Hugh St. Quentin Cayley in Vancouver. The young Indian had a fine, retentive mind, and he acquired a good general knowledge of Canadian law and legal procedures, and memorized substantial sections of the statutes relating to Indian affairs in British Columbia.[12]

When Paull was growing up, British Columbia Indians were beginning to realize the weight of the provincial government's injustices against them. In Ontario and the prairie provinces, British and, later, Canadian authorities claimed absolute sovereignty over all the land, but still recognized that the Indians had certain rights to tribal lands on the principle of prior occupancy. Through the numbered treaties on the prairies, the Crown officially "extinguished" native title by an exchange: the Crown promised the Indians reserves varying from one-quarter to one square mile per family of five, and specified trapping, fishing or farming equipment, annual treaty payments and schools. In return, the Indians gave up their land claims, retaining only their fishing and hunting rights in the surrendered territory.

In the 1850s, the Indians on Vancouver Island were approached to cede lands, but when the economy-minded colonial legislature refused to make any further payments after 1859, the surrenders ceased. Successive British Columbia governments (even after the province entered Confederation in 1871) have held to a simple premise: the

Indians have no justifiable land rights. Without negotiation, the provincial government, on its own authority, took Indian lands and then assigned small tracts to the respective bands as their reserves.[13]

The Indians' small numbers enabled the British Columbia government to proceed as it wished in the late nineteenth century. At the moment of white contact, about a third of all Canada's native people lived along the Pacific coastline and along the major western rivers flowing through it. Here the climate was mild, with rich and easily available food resources. The natives had no agriculture and depended on the abundant wild roots and berries and the salmon, halibut and eulachon (candlefish, prized for its oil) as their staples. White settlement of the area forced them from their traditional lands, however, and, as happened on the plains, diseases against which they had no natural immunity devastated the tribes, reducing their numbers by as much as ninety per cent.[14] As the nineteenth century ended, many lost hope and self-respect. They could not speak English and had no grasp of the British legal system. The government could ignore them.

Long Lance met Andy Paull ten years after the young Squamish had returned from his four years of study with Hugh Cayley, the Vancouver lawyer. On his first visit, Long Lance took the ferry across to North Vancouver, then walked to Mission. He could see in the distance the silver-painted towers of the reserve's Roman Catholic church. Soon, he reached the white picket fence that set off the thirty acres left by the provincial government to a band of about one hundred Indians. He walked along a graveled street lined with small houses, and in the yards he noticed the Squamish's dugout racing canoes. Finally he reached the small, frame building that was Andy Paull's house.[15]

Paull was smaller than the average Blackfoot. The Pacific Coast Indians had the dark eyes and black hair of the Plains Indians, but they were built entirely differently, more compact and powerful, with large shoulders and small legs. Their physique, it was said, came from centuries in canoes.[16] At school, Paull was nicknamed "white boy" for the way he

Left: Sallie Long's mother, Adeline Carson. (Daisy Carson Blackburn)

Below left: Sylvester Long's mother, Sallie Long. (Newman Dalton) *Below:* Sylvester Long's father, Joe Long. (Newman Dalton)

Sylvester's drawing of a bucking bronco, found in his mother's clipping book, speaks of his boyhood fantasies. (Lillian Doulin)

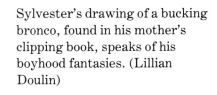

Below left: Abe Long, janitor at the North Winston School, 1902. He was then twenty-one years old. (Newman Dalton) *Below:* Sylvester Long, left, and his brother Walter, taken shortly before Sylvester left Winston for Carlisle. (Newman Dalton)

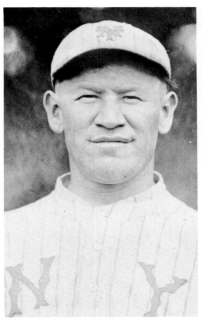

Above: Jim Thorpe's gift to his friend reads, "High Chief— Remember the mile runs, was great training for the Olympics." (Joe Bradshaw) *Above right:* Long Lance in uniform, taken while he was with the 38th Battalion, Canadian Expeditionary Force, 1917. (Newman Dalton) *Right:* "To:— Mother and Dad", the photo Sylvester sent his parents from Calgary, showing him in his Canadian Militia uniform. (Newman Dalton)

Above: Long Lance, second from the left, with Howard Kelly, bottom left, and friends in Calgary. (Howard Kelly)

Left: George Gooderham, Indian agent to the Blackfoot, speaking to Boy Chief at Brooks, Alberta, early 1930s. (Glenbow-Alberta Institute)

Right: The Rev. S. H. Middleton, around 1920. (Sophie Allison)

Below: At the Dempsey-Gibbons fight, Shelby, Montana. Long Lance is in the center, Howard Kelly is on the immediate left, and C. O. Smith of the *Calgary Herald* is on the immediate right. Smith was the man who had fired Long Lance from the *Herald* in late March, 1922; nevertheless, they remained friends. (Hugh Dann)

Given by Long Lance to his "old friend", Fred O'Malley, of the *Winnipeg Tribune*. (Mrs. H. O'Malley)

Long Lance at the Calgary Stampede of 1923. (Glenbow-Alberta Institute)

Mike Eagle Speaker as a young man. (Mike Eagle Speaker)

Always impeccably dressed, Long Lance travelled across the continent many times in the mid-1920s. (Glenbow-Alberta Institute, Canon Middleton Collection)

Long Lance at the Logan Elm, Circleville, Ohio, October 5, 1924,
wearing the romantic garb of the Indian spokesman.
(Glenbow-Alberta Institute, Canon Middleton Collection)

easily mingled and sometimes imitated those of the dominant white society around him. He was an extrovert and,
like Long Lance, loved sports. He played and coached
baseball, lacrosse, boxing and canoe racing.[17] Long Lance
talked of his days at the *Calgary Herald*, and Paull would
have remembered the name of the newspaper. Cayley, the
lawyer he worked for in Vancouver, had been one of the
Herald's first editors, during the time of the Riel Rebellion
of 1885.[18]

Long Lance wrote to his friend the Rev. S. H. Middleton and
described Paull as "one of the smartest Indians I have ever
met."[19] He was impressed by Paull's familiarity with the
legal aspects of the Indian situation in British Columbia, and
he was intrigued by the political organization of the British
Columbia Indians, for which Paull was the provincial secretary. In 1915, the coastal tribes under the leadership of Paull
and the Rev. Peter Kelly, a Haida minister, established the
first province-wide native organization, calling it the Allied
Tribes.[20] In his letter to Middleton, Long Lance expressed
surprise at finding so much life among the British Columbia
Indians. "You can tell the young fellows there that they are
way ahead of us on the plains. "[21]

On Sunday, May 21, the *Sun* carried Long Lance's story
on the Squamish. Long Lance had relied on Paull, Chief
Mathias of the Capilano Reserve, and what he called "representative members" of the tribe. Paull strongly distrusted
Indian agents and the Department of Indian Affairs, and
greatly influenced Long Lance, who a short year earlier had
written that Canadian Indian policy was "clear-sighted."
This time, Long Lance gently criticized the federal Department of Indian Affairs, questioning such actions as the out-
lawing of the Indian "potlatch."

For years the Department of Indian Affairs, and the
missionaries, had tried to destroy Indian society and culture. The missionaries spoke against totem poles and traditional carvings. They wanted Indians to work, dress and
pray like the white man. Then, in the 1880s, they attacked
the famous potlatch ceremony of the Pacific Coast Indians.
The potlatch was a great event at which the host gave away

huge amounts of food and valuable gifts to all his guests. In its various forms, the potlatch validated the transfer of property, recognized the change from adolescence to adulthood, recorded marriage arrangements or settled personal quarrels. The government, and the missionaries, disapproved of this "wasteful, heathen" custom, and in time the holding of and attendance at a potlatch was made a criminal offense. Since November, 1921, a number of indictments had been secured against Indians for participating in potlatches. In early May, 1922, twenty-three of those convicted, including a grandmother, were serving prison sentences of not less than two months each in the Oakalla Prison. [22]

Paull and other Squamish Indians explained the age-old potlatch custom to Long Lance, and in his story for the *Sun* Long Lance wrote: "The potlatch does not entail the giving away of anything. The Indian who holds it is either paying a debt to his guests for some material kindness which they have rendered him or for a similar potlatch rendered to him in the past, or is simply giving away what he knows he will get back." [23]

During Long Lance's first month in Vancouver, the Methodist Church was fighting a campaign to convince a local service club, the Gyro Club, to drop the word potlatch as the name of its week-long summer carnival. In defense of both the name and "the respected custom," Long Lance wrote a forceful article that appeared in the *Sun* on Friday, May 19. He argued that "the law governing the Potlatch is at once oppressive and antagonising." The law was so loosely worded, he wrote, that "an agricultural show or an exhibition may be held as a Potlatch in the eyes of the law." He asked why the Indian was "compelled to throw aside every native custom that formerly gave him self-respect. . . . why cannot he be allowed to remain a decent Indian instead of being forced into a ragged nondescript?"

The whole potlatch issue and his association with Andy Paull led Long Lance to reassess his views of the Indians' future. Until that summer, he usually repeated General Pratt's assimilationist goals, a philosophy that had been thoroughly drummed into his mind at the Carlisle Indian

School. A month in British Columbia and he began to see things differently — from the Indians' perspective.

It must have been Paull who supplied him with names and addresses and the necessary contacts. From May to July, by steamer and train, Long Lance traveled hundreds of miles visiting bands along the coast. He produced feature stories for the *Sun* every Sunday, and they read well. He knew how to collect information quickly, how to use a telling anecdote, and how to make the story vivid and appealing to his readers. When he interviewed old Indians who spoke little or no English, he used young graduates of the Indian residential schools as interpreters. He did his homework, too, reading all the standard books available, including John McLean's *The Indians of Canada* (1889) and *Canadian Savage Folk: The Native Tribes of Canada* (1896), and a recent study by Franz Boas, the American anthropologist. [24]

On June 4, the *Sun* carried Long Lance's account of the Nanaimo Indians on Vancouver Island. The next week it featured his story on the natives of the Lower Fraser Valley ("Chilliwack Indians Possess Richest Store of Folklore"). On June 18, he reported on the Haidas, the Indians of the Queen Charlotte Islands to the north of Vancouver Island ("Name of Haida Struck Panic to Indian Heart"). In late June and July, he sent in stories from the interior of British Columbia on the history, legends and current state of the Kootenays, Lillooets, Thompsons and Shuswap. [25]

As he traveled throughout the province, Long Lance increasingly became aware of the untenable position in which the Indians of British Columbia found themselves. On the mainland, there had been few attempts to buy Indian land. Even their rights to the small land areas arbitrarily allotted them were not always respected. When Long Lance visited the Shuswap Reserve at Kamloops, he reported to S. H. Middleton that "the Western Canadian Ranching Company [is] pumping water right off the reserve, while the Indians' crops are literally burning up for lack of moisture." And, he added, "I meet many cases of this sort every day."[26]

At Nanaimo, Long Lance met the most influential native leader in British Columbia, Peter Kelly, chairman of the

Allied Tribes. Kelly was born in 1885 in a Haida longhouse on the Queen Charlotte Islands. His parents, of noble Haida lineage — and by 1885 both Christian converts — sent him to Coqualeetza Institute, the Methodist boarding school for Indians at Sardis, just outside Chilliwack, sixty miles east of Vancouver. At Coqualeetza, he attended an elementary school, then became a teacher among his own people at Skidegate in the Queen Charlottes. He was the first Indian teacher among the Haida. Gifted, energetic and determined to succeed, Kelly studied long and intensely. Through home study, he qualified for entrance to the Methodist Columbian College at New Westminster. Here, with four white students, he took instruction for three years, and upon his graduation in 1916, he was ordained as the first full-blooded Indian clergyman of any denomination on the Pacific Coast.

Kelly became known among his people as *Klee-Als* (the Orator) and as the driving force behind the Allied Tribes. He proved himself a capable and popular minister both to the Nanaimo Reserve and to the neighboring white settlements of Cassidy, Cedar, Extension, Chase River and South Wellington. Both Indians and whites respected him.[27]

Long Lance described Kelly in the *Sun* as "a man of commanding appearance.... Barely more than thirty, he possesses the strong, athletic build of the Haida, plus their strong facial characteristics...."[28] He found Kelly more restrained and aristocratic than Andy Paull, who was immensely likeable and down-to-earth.

In the summer of 1922, Long Lance had an opportunity to see Kelly and Paull in action. The Allied Tribes staged an important meeting in Vancouver, where fifty chiefs met with Charles Stewart, Mackenzie King's Minister of the Interior and of Mines and Superintendent General of Indian Affairs, and Duncan Campbell Scott, the Deputy Superintendent General and the most senior civil servant in the Department of Indian Affairs. The seven-hour meeting took place on July 23 in the Vancouver Post Office Building. As Long Lance reported in the *Sun*, the Allied Tribes asked for "full title to their reserve lands, as enjoyed by the other tribes of the Dominion, and for better education facilities and medical attention for the natives of this province."[29] To Long Lance's delight, Stewart and his cohorts met the most spirited delegation of Indians they had ever seen. "There were no folded-arm, dignified speeches by ex-warriors and chiefs," he wrote to S. H. Middleton, "but instead, there was a superb firing line of brainy, quick-witted young men who knew the Indian Act and all its tangents as well as the Honourable Dunk [Duncan Campbell Scott] himself."[30]

Long Lance's association with the *Sun* ended with his final submission in late July. He had never intended to stay long in British Columbia, the agreement with the newspaper having been only for the weekly series. In May, when he was in the midst of his travels throughout the province, he had written to Middleton to tell him of his next project. "If things work out right," he wrote on May 11, "I am planning to go from here to Regina and write up the Saskatchewan Indians for the *Leader*, and on to Winnipeg, for the Manitobans — and so on down the line, finishing up with a book."

10

ON TO SASKATCHEWAN

A FEW DAYS before Long Lance arrived in Regina, the capital of the province of Saskatchewan, hundreds of local citizens had gathered at the City Hall to hear their city's first radio broadcast, which beamed a quavering "Rule Britannia" to the city of only thirty-five thousand people. The wireless came to Regina months after it arrived in Calgary and Vancouver, but as Long Lance's train pulled into the station, the locals were still thrilled at the prospect of turning a knob and magically being entertained by a distant play, or jazz, or a sportscast.[1]

He checked his bags and, as in the other cities, walked first to the local newspaper office, that of the Regina *Leader*. As was often the case, he needed money. Long Lance was not one to hoard his hard-won income; he spent it on clothes, food, entertainment, women and travel. He liked to live well.

He produced again a fat portfolio of articles on the Sarcee, Squamish, Haida and a dozen other tribes for the managing editor, who was suitably impressed. Journeymen reporters with this flair for feature writing did not come by often, and Long Lance's ability to handle a story was quickly apparent. He was no cub reporter anymore, but an experienced professional who knew how to read unfamiliar situations, how to ingratiate himself, how to get the "goods" and how to make sense of it all—and he knew what editors wanted.

The managing editor of the *Leader* sensed immediately the news value of a series of articles on the Indians of Saskatchewan, especially after studying what Long Lance had produced in British Columbia. He told him that in Regina one hardly ever saw Indians,[2] yet they were all over, out there, in isolated corners of the province. He told Long Lance the *Leader* would be happy to buy four feature articles for the Saturday edition.

But, where to go in this strange, huge province that started in the south at the American border and pushed all the way up to the sub-Arctic? Saskatchewan had sixty-eight Indian reserves[3] and Long Lance could not visit all of them, not in a province this big and this sparsely populated. He went to see Bill Graham, the Indian Commissioner for Western Canada, who worked out of an office in the Canada Life Building. Graham, a short man in his mid-fifties, was a pudgy fellow with a peg leg, the result of a boyhood accident, but he was an energetic, no-nonsense administrator. He joined the Indian Department when he was eighteen, and by 1922 he had served thirty-eight years, rising from a lowly agency clerk in Manitoba to the Indian agent of the File Hills Band in Saskatchewan in 1896, to inspector of all the Indian agents in southern Saskatchewan in 1904, and finally, in 1918, to Indian Commissioner for Western Canada. During the war he organized white farmers to work twenty-one thousand acres of reserve land, under what was known as the Great Production Movement, and he nearly doubled the acreage under cultivation by the Indians themselves.[4]

Graham's secretary was his wife's cousin, Alice Tye,[5] an attractive woman who took to Long Lance immediately. She had never encountered an Indian quite like him, never one quite so sophisticated and well-spoken. He seemed to have been everywhere and to have done everything, and yet, somehow, he managed this engaging modesty — unlike most white men she knew. He could tell her about his presidential appointment to West Point, he could mention his rise to the rank of captain on the battlefield, he could let drop that he had won the Croix de Guerre in France — and all the time his tone would imply that these were the quite ordinary accomplishments of an everyday sort of hero. He knew how to impress women as easily as he knew how to impress managing editors.

Commissioner Graham got down to business with Long Lance in short order, starting with his two favorite subjects: Indian education and Indian farming. For twenty years, he had worked to develop a model Indian agricultural settlement in the File Hills, about sixty miles northeast of Regina. With help from the principals of the neighboring Protestant and Roman Catholic residential schools, he had personally selected Indian graduates for the program at the Peepeewesis Reserve. If the young men agreed to join the agricultural colony, he had them placed on their own individual farms. The Indian Department laid out roads running north and south every half mile, and east and west every mile. The young Indians built their own houses of whitewashed hewed logs and covered the one-and-a-half-storey buildings with red painted shingle roofs. Within ten years, twenty-five heads of families lived in the colony.

File Hills was Commissioner Graham's answer to "the Indian problem," he proudly informed Long Lance. He believed that Indian graduates, under strong management and control, could become good farmers. At File Hills, he constantly brought in agricultural experts to lecture on new techniques. During the first year or two of an ex-pupil's life on the reserve, the white farm instructor visited him nearly every day. Commissioner Graham boasted that he ruled File Hills with an iron hand; fiddle dances, pow-wows and all tribal ceremonies that he considered to be a hindrance to progress were forbidden. [6]

Long Lance listened politely, but he must have been appalled. Peepeewesis sounded more like an Indian prison camp than a new native paradise on earth. Always curious, he announced that he would like to see File Hills first. On August 8, suitcase in hand, Long Lance set off by train for Balcarres to visit the four File Hills reserves — Little Black Bear, Star Blanket, Okanese and Commissioner Graham's beloved Peepeewesis. He enjoyed traveling through the rolling country, interspersed with beautiful small lakes and groves of cottonwood trees.

At File Hills, Long Lance could see for himself that Graham's claims were exaggerated, if not false. And he claimed to have uncovered a scandal, the story of how Graham had "pulled the wool over" the eyes of Charles Stewart, Superintendent General of Indian Affairs. On his way back to Ottawa in mid-summer, just days before Long Lance's visit, the influential federal minister had stopped in Saskatchewan to check out Commissioner Graham's show-piece operation. Graham, anxious to impress the new Liberal appointee, went out of his way to convince Stewart that all was well on the western reserves. On September 10, Long Lance wrote to S. H. Middleton:

> The agent had received instructions from powers above, situated not far from here, to keep the fact that the minister was to come through, from all Indians. Hence, when the royal car rolled through, the Indians, the few who happened to see it along the trail, thought it was a party of tourists. The route of the car naturally led through a beautifully "prepared" route; that is, one which had been planted very carefully with wheat and oats — and to add the desired kick of nonchalance, nice little patches of summer fallow were very studiously perfected here and there along the chosen trail. All of which goes to show what a great, self-supporting man we have made out of the Indian during the past few years. . . .

Commissioner Graham's decoy worked, and his job — Graham was a Conservative appointee — was safe. Stewart returned to Ottawa convinced of the "splendid results" achieved at File Hills. He told the House of Commons that he found young Indian people "were making as great a success of farming as were their white brothers in the surrounding territory."[7] For the next eight years, Stewart continued to cite File Hills as a great success story, heaping most of the credit on Commissioner Graham.

Of all his portfolios, which included Interior, Mines and Immigration, the Indian Department seemed the least of Stewart's worries. In his own province of Alberta, the Indian population had fallen from about eighteen thousand in the 1870s to less than six thousand by the 1920s.[8] The federal government's own experts, the Oxford-trained anthropologists Diamond Jenness and Marius Barbeau, confirmed that the Indians were a vanishing people. In 1931, Barbeau wrote: "At present the indications point convincingly to the extinction of the race."[9] The following year, Jenness commented in his *Indians of Canada*: "Doubtless all the tribes will disappear. Some will endure only a few years longer, others, like the Eskimo, may last several centuries." Duncan Campbell Scott, the Indian Department's senior civil servant, questioned the expenditure of monies to provide medical and social services to a "dying race" of one hundred thousand people, who constituted only one per cent of Canada's population.[10]

Long Lance liked Stewart, a plain man brought up under pioneer conditions in Alberta, who earned a reputation as one who brought good horse sense to the solution of public problems.[11] In a letter to Middleton, however, Long Lance astutely observed: "I think he is sincere and that he is a darned sight better specimen than many who are under him. But — I am afraid that these underlings are going to succeed so completely in pulling the wool over his eyes as he goes about, that, in the end, all of his apparent pep and good intentions are going to be dissipated by much misunderstanding of true facts."[12]

Commissioner Graham was one of these underlings, and Duncan Campbell Scott was another and by far the more damaging and dangerous of the two. Scott, the distinguished poet and intellectual,[13] was the tactician, always searching for answers to the "Indian problem." In 1919, Scott enthusiastically identified what he saw as "the millennium of those engaged in Indian work":

> ...when all the quaint old customs, the weird and picturesque ceremonies, and the sun dance and the potlatch and even the musical and poetic native languages shall be as obsolete as the buffalo and the tomahawk, and the last tepee of the northern wilds give place to a model farmhouse. In other words, the Indian shall become one with his neighbour in his speech, life and habits, thus conforming to that worldwide tendency

towards universal standardization which would appear to be the essential underlying purport of all modern social evolution. [14]

Long Lance's prediction that the underlings would succeed in pulling the wool over Stewart's eyes proved entirely correct. In 1927, the government denied the native claim to British Columbia, and further expanded the Department of Indian Affairs' restrictive controls. In 1930, in the House of Commons, Charles Stewart energetically defended the "poolroom amendment" to the Indian Act, a law which made an Indian liable to a fine of up to $25 or imprisonment of up to thirty days merely for frequenting a poolroom. [15]

All his life, Long Lance had been taught the superiority of the white race and the need for the white man to direct and guide the "lower" groups. Yet now he wanted the Plains Indians to fight back, to resist their subjugation. He traveled from File Hills to other reserves in the Qu'Appelle Valley: Piapot, Muscowpetung, Pasquah, Standing Buffalo. He visited the Assiniboine Reserve at Sintaluta. He tried to spread the idea that the Plains Indians must organize to protect themselves against the likes of the underlings, Graham and Scott.

As Long Lance visited the Plains Cree, Sioux and Assiniboine reserves, he must have compared their past and present conditions. Half a century earlier, they enjoyed the greatest independence perhaps known to man; now the government controlled all aspects of their lives. In some respects, and nobody was more aware of it than Long Lance, it was worse to be an Indian in Canada than a "colored" in the South. A band member required the Indian agent's permission to travel off the reserve. Before he could sell his hay, grain or livestock, he needed a permit. Even to hold a traditional Indian dance required the agent's consent. Writing in 1923, the Rev. Edward Ahenakew, a Plains Cree minister, summed up the situation: "We have been brought up as children, treated as children, made to act according to rules and regulations that are not our own, and at the command of officials whom we do not always respect." [16]

Traveling throughout Saskatchewan, Long Lance became convinced of the need for the Indians to do something. He pointed to the Treaty promises and showed how the government had reneged by not providing adequate education and medical care. From Muscowpetung Reserve, just north of Regina, he wrote S. H. Middleton on September 10: "I am getting each chief and each leading young man on every reserve in touch with the secretary of the Allied Tribes of B.C., so that he can explain the workings of their organization and help them out in details of a more intricate nature. In other words I am trying to get everybody in touch with each other."

Long Lance was becoming a seasoned political agitator. Commissioner Graham had no idea what he was doing on his travels about the province; he did not think Long Lance needed to be consulted or given any special guidance. And when he met Commissioner Graham, Long Lance knew enough not to volunteer any information concerning his political work with the Indians. He used Graham's office as a mail drop, swapping jokes with him and using Miss Tye's typewriter to type up his articles.[17] He worked silently, confiding only to Middleton, and possibly to George Gooderham of the Blackfoot Reserve, who likewise regarded Commissioner Graham as "dictatorial."[18]

At the reserves in southern Saskatchewan, Long Lance ate bannock with the Indians in their homes and smoked kinnikinic with the old men. On every visit, he picked up more stories of resentment against the white man. On the Piapot Reserve in the Qu'Appelle Valley, the older Cree told him of their bitter disappointment at the white man's failure to enact the provisions of the treaties.[19]

Probably the most articulate of the Indian leaders that Long Lance met was Dan Kennedy, or Ochankugahe, "the Pathmaker." He belonged to the Assiniboine Band at Carry-the-Kettle's Reserve, about fifty miles east of Regina. Born in 1874, Kennedy had known the last days of the Assiniboine's free way of life before they settled on their reserve in 1882. He had been sent to a residential school, and, as one of the most promising students, had gone on to study at St. Boniface College in Winnipeg.[20]

Long Lance met the Pathmaker in the fall of 1922, when the air was sharp and chill, and the green poplar leaves were turning to gold. From the railway station at Sintaluta, where the grain elevators hovered like skyscrapers, he walked along the straight dirt road toward a substantial-looking farmhouse that he had been told was Kennedy's. It was conspicuous among the one-room log cabins, all nearly hidden by stacks of split wood piled up by the doors. The Indians' dogs barked as he entered the yard, then playfully romped about him as he shut the gate.

Kennedy looked remarkably like Long Lance himself. He was forty-seven, but looked as young as Long Lance, who was thirty-one that fall. The Pathmaker was as handsome, as powerful, and despite certain warrior-like features, his smile was kindly and his manner warm. He invited Long Lance inside, and told him he had just finished his harvest of three hundred acres of grain, using his own threshing machine. Kennedy also owned forty head of cattle.[21] As they talked, Kennedy explained the frustrations of living under the Indian Act and the strict supervision of the resident agent, which combined, at the beginning, to make life on the reserve "a veritable concentration camp."[22] Things had improved, he said, but much of the government paternalism remained. Kennedy agreed with Long Lance that Indians needed political organization. For his efforts to spread the idea, Long Lance reported to S. H. Middleton, Kennedy presented him with a gift of a beautifully decorated firebag.[23]

Long Lance's special gift as a journalist was his ability to draw people out, especially the older people, men and women who were eager to tell their stories of the "buffalo days." Through Kennedy, he met the oldest Plains Indian warrior left in western Canada: Chief Carry-the-Kettle. When they met, the aged chief wore the coat given to him by the Canadian government. How incongruous to see the ancient Assiniboine leader wearing what was essentially a mercantile marine officer's coat in the middle of the Canadian plains.

Chief Carry-the-Kettle was believed to be 107 years old. He had been on war parties when Sitting Bull and Crowfoot were in their infancies. Long Lance talked to him through an interpreter, and gained even greater respect for the wisdom and integrity of the elders, who were far from the savages depicted by Duncan Campbell Scott and Commissioner Graham.

Later, Long Lance wrote: "Though Chief Carry-the-Kettle had killed more than a hundred men on the war-path, there was something in his face that was truly spiritual —a remarkable gleam of human goodness that made him bigger in my eyes than any man I have seen. When he had to refer to his killings on the war-path, he did it with a whimsical air of apology which made it evident that it was distasteful to him. In spite of his destructive record, Chief Carry-the-Kettle was one of those men in whose fearless hands a person would gladly place his life, if it depended on a matter of fair judgment and the kindness of human nature."[24]

By the end of the fall, Long Lance was acquiring a more accurate grasp of Indian life, past and present. He felt genuinely at ease on the reserves, comfortable enough to relax and sit around telling jokes with the mission-educated Indians. He was especially interested in Indian dialects, being a lover of words and language. He noticed how elaborate the Indian languages were, how distinctive, in many cases as different from each other as English is different from Turkish.[25]

Even in swapping jokes with the young Indians and the elders, Long Lance never ceased to observe and learn. On the matter of Indian humor itself, he found that "there are few races that have a deeper vein of humor than the Indian. But his humor inclines to funny situations and actual happenings rather than toward manufactured jokes, which seldom 'get over' with him. If a person tries to act or be funny, then he is not funny in the eyes of an Indian. Instead, he is ridiculous, and will sometimes bring forth scornful laughter that freezes into stolid-faced contempt." Long Lance included an example of an effective Indian joke in an article in *Mentor* in March, 1924:

> George Brass, a Cree interpreter for Polley [Pelly] Agency, Saskatchewan, was interpreting a sermon for the Anglican missionary of that agency. The missionary was a cockney Englishman who took extreme liberties with his h's. In this particular sermon he quoted: "Do not be afraid, (h)it is I." George interpreted it thus: "Ahkah-waye-kesakeshew-pukama-oskeesikook" ("Don't be afraid, hit him in the eye"), accentuating the word "pukama" (hit) by banging his fist into the palm of his hand. I have repeated this occurrence to many Cree gatherings on the plains, and each time I have had to stop under the laughter before I could go on talking.[26]

Throughout December, 1922, Long Lance summarized his interviews with the Cree, Sioux, Ojibwa (Chippewa) and Assiniboine Indians in the *Leader*. If the series had a theme, Long Lance's comment in his second article provided it. He wrote that the Indian does not fear change, but worries that his son "be made into a white man, and that he might be lost to his home and people."[27]

11

A NEW IDENTITY

T HE TIME HAD COME. In the summer of 1922, Long Lance decided to alter his identity again. The public knew the "real Indian" as a mounted horseman in beadwork, moccasins, embroidered jacket and feather headdress. In the movies, on stage and in the rotogravure sections of the weekend newspapers, they had been conditioned to recognizing the Plains warrior as the genuine article. If he advertised himself as a Cherokee, he knew that his writings would have little impact. The Cherokee of Oklahoma, his current tribal designation, had already adjusted to the white man and wore business suits or workman's overalls. This did not sell. It made more sense to become a Plains Indian.

Before Long Lance left Vancouver, he wrote in his last article in the *Sun* of his "fellow-tribesmen, the Blood Indians of Alberta."[1] Taking out his clippings, he carefully removed all references to Cherokee and wrote Blackfoot or Blood in pencil over the blank spaces. Finally, in Regina, he had two photographs taken of himself in his "tribal regalia."[2] Not wanting to leave any possibility of doubt about his Plains origin, he appeared in buckskin pants and vest, wearing a tobacco pouch and a headdress. He even borrowed a wig with two long braids to cover his cropped hair.

To the old Indians, of course, these portraits must have looked ridiculous. In the 1920s the tribes' distinctive styles of dress had not yet blended. In the photographs, however, Long Lance wore a Blackfoot vest, a Blood tobacco pouch, Crow Indian pants — worn backwards — and a headdress used in the Chicken Dance.[3] To anyone not familiar with Indian dress, doubtless it looked authentic.

In early November, Long Lance justified his decision to S. H. Middleton. He explained that he had not lived with his own people since he was sixteen, and that he now knew more about the Indians of Western Canada and the Pacific Coast "than I do about my own progenitors." By presenting himself as a Blood he could, he added, give his writings "an additional touch of interest." He concluded: "Furthermore, I believe that as a Canadian Indian, which I have become in toto, I can do more for Indians who need something done for them."[4]

Middleton was perplexed, and he took nearly three months to reply to Long Lance. The decision upset the missionary, though he could understand how Long Lance would enhance his credibility if he wrote on the Indians of Western Canada as one of them, instead of as a Cherokee. Middleton rationalized that Long Lance, through his writing and personal contacts, could perceptively change the whites' negative impressions of Indians. After some apparent hesitation, the missionary accepted Long Lance's new literary identity. When he replied in early February, 1923, he ended his letter: "Write soon, the longer the letter — the better."[5]

Long Lance also told Commissioner Graham of his decision, but there was not the slightest problem in this quarter. Commissioner Graham already idealized Long Lance as the Indian athlete, the Indian war hero, and the successful Indian writer. He invited Long Lance to Regina's Armistice Ball. Years later, Long Lance recalled the "look of pride on his face as he took me from guest to guest, introducing me as Captain Long Lance."[6] The fact was, Commissioner Graham was delighted that Long Lance chose to present himself as a Western Canadian Indian, in a sense, one of his own.

When he arrived in Winnipeg early in 1923, Long Lance

followed his usual routine. After selling himself to the editors of the *Tribune*, the newspaper agreed to buy a series of stories on the Manitoba Indians. That winter he crossed the province by train from the Sioux Reserve at Oak River in the southwestern corner to the Peguis Saulteaux (Ojibwa) Reserve immediately north of Winnipeg. By dogsled he visited the Crees on the southwestern shore of Lake Winnipeg.

The *Tribune* liked his work and asked him to become a regular contributor. One of the two shots that he had brought from Regina graced his first article, and the *Tribune* captioned it: "Arrayed in the full regalia of his tribe, Chief Buffalo Child Long Lance...presents a picturesque and striking appearance."[7] Luckily for him, few Indians then lived in Winnipeg, and there were fewer students of Indian culture. His bizarre, pan-Indian costume escaped comment or criticism.

During his first winter in Winnipeg, a more cosmopolitan city than Regina, rumors of Long Lance and his accomplishments raced through the city, and he did not discourage them. In May, 1923, the *Tribune* described him as "the youngest chief west of the Great Lakes and one by blood inheritance." Garnett Clay Porter, another journalist working in Winnipeg at the time, understood that Long Lance held two university degrees. Long Lance managed to convince Professor W.T. Allison of the Department of English at the University of Manitoba, and the *Tribune*'s literary editor, that he had won the Italian War Cross as well as the Croix de Guerre.[8]

Inevitably, Long Lance received numerous invitations to speak, and he accepted nearly all requests. He was at ease at the podium. His favorite topic was "The Red Man, Past and Present," and it was always well-received by curious white newcomers to Western Canada, who rarely saw Indians in the cities. Through experience, Long Lance had mastered the basics of public speaking—voice modulation, gestures, humor, maintaining eye contact with the audience. He spoke to gatherings of authors, to church clubs and to local service clubs.[9]

Winnipeg served as his home base for the next four win-
ters. While the Panama Canal had hurt the city by allowing
Vancouver to take over the western markets it had once
supplied, Winnipeg still remained the most important city in
Western Canada in the 1920s. Like Chicago, its American
counterpart—Winnipeg was known back then as "the
Chicago of the North"—the city had great railway marshal-
ling yards, repair shops, roundhouses and grain-handling
facilities. Downtown Winnipeg was the financial heart of
Western Canada, home to the head offices of the chartered
banks and the trust and insurance companies. From 1901 to
1911, a million immigrants passed through Winnipeg's gates,
many staying. The population rose from forty-two thousand
in 1901 to one hundred and forty thousand by 1911 and to one
hundred and eighty thousand by 1921.[10]

Of all the Canadian cities in which he had lived, Long
Lance found Winnipeg to be the most European. In the
streets, he saw Mennonite and Hutterite farmers in their old
world dress. He mingled with men and women with broad
Russian, Greek and Slavic faces. In spite of their ever-
increasing numbers, a strict quota system ensured that all
but a small number of Jews and Slavs, regardless of their
academic standing, were kept out of the Manitoba Medical
College.[11] Discrimination against Jews and foreigners in the
job market was nearly universal. The ethnic division
between North and South Winnipeg had increased during
the thirty-seven-day General Strike of 1919, when the strik-
ers of the northern working-class area were pitted against
the middle and upper classes of South Winnipeg.

As an Indian, and as a successful journalist, Long Lance
escaped much of this abuse and strife, although on his first
visit to the Fort Garry Hotel, a doorman refused him entry.
When his friends at the *Tribune* privately complained, the
hotel management promptly apologized to him.[12]

Reporter Allan Bill, then in his mid-twenties, stayed in
the same rooming house as Long Lance, which was close to
the *Tribune* at Smith Street and Graham Avenue. Bill got to
know him well, or as well as Long Lance would allow. He
regarded Long Lance as "a good-natured soul... built like a

wedge" but a man "who never harmed anyone."[13] Always, Long Lance was out for good times, and rarely could he resist a dare. Once a fellow reporter challenged him to duplicate one of the feats of the Human Spider, and Long Lance responded immediately by standing on his head on the parapet of what was then considered a skyscraper in Winnipeg.[14]

After work, Long Lance and Charles L'Ami, one of the *Tribune*'s editorial writers, walked to the local YMCA and boxed. After this, for he still had energy to burn, Long Lance ran the indoor track and vaulted on the parallel bars. He was invited to all the newspaper parties and never played the wallflower. When the "black bottom" rage hit Western Canada, Long Lance was one of the first Winnipeggers to try it.[15] Sometimes at these parties, egged on by colleagues, Long Lance assumed the role of the backwoods Indian, as much to shock and impress his friends as to remind them of his personal history. One New Year's Eve, the *Tribune*'s editor, Wilfred (Biff) MacTavish, invited the staff to a gathering at his home on Oak Street. Long Lance was there, too, and after some coaxing he announced that he would do a war dance, right there in the dining room. L'Ami imitated the sound of tom-toms on the keyboard as best he could and out came Long Lance, "the chief," wearing a headband and two towels as a breechcloth. He began slowly, and, with sweat gleaming on his powerful torso, his feet made intricate patterns on the polished floor. He danced faster, and faster, and for a moment his frenzy convinced even the most skeptical onlookers that he had indeed reverted to some wild, atavistic state of mind. He had "gone Indian" was how some remembered it years later. The dance became so frenetic that Long Lance had to be forcibly stopped.[16]

Sometimes, too, for the same reasons, he let out his war whoop. Professor Allison's son, Carlyle, then a student at the University of Manitoba, once invited Long Lance to join a group of his friends at a university dance at the Royal Alexandra Hotel. That night, he made himself the hit of the evening. All the young, pretty coeds clamored for his attention. Enjoying the spotlight, Long Lance asked Carlyle as they were walking to a restaurant after the dance, "Did you ever hear an Indian war whoop?" Carlyle replied that he never had, and so Long Lance, at the corner of Portage and Main, let go with his best effort, one that split the night and turned heads for blocks in all directions. Carlyle remembered it as sounding "like several fire sirens and air-raid warnings lumped into one...blood curdling and exciting...."[17]

For all his exuberance and flamboyance, Long Lance acquired a reputation as a warm, generous friend. Vernon Knowles, the managing editor, told of the evening when his daughter was very sick, and Long Lance "left the office after a terrific day's work, and spent a large part of the evening sitting by her bedside regaling her with Indian stories."[18] He often took the time to tell Indian stories to his friends' children even when they were not sick.[19] Such incidents hint at an inner longing for family, for the roots he wanted but felt he could not have.

Long Lance liked the *Tribune*. After three years of newspaper work, he had developed a smooth and popular style, and that winter he started selling some of his Indian stories to other magazines. *MacLean's* summarized his articles from the Regina *Leader* in a two-part series that appeared on February 15 and March 1 of 1923. The Toronto *Star Weekly* bought his *Tribune* article on the refugee Sioux Indians in Manitoba who had come north in 1862. (When the American government failed to observe the terms of its treaty with the Sioux, they rebelled in Minnesota, killing five hundred white settlers.) Two American newspapers, the St. Paul *Pioneer Press* and the Chicago *Herald*, bought the same story.[20]

In the summer of 1923, Long Lance, encouraged by his success, returned to the field. He traveled to the Duck Lake area of central Saskatchewan, the site of the Rebellion of 1885. There he researched two stories, one on the rebellion, the other on the last stand of Almighty Voice, a young Cree who in 1897, with two other Indians, managed to hold off an attacking posse of one hundred men for three days.

Father Henri Delmas, the local Roman Catholic priest, arranged for accommodation at the Duck Lake boarding school. Long Lance and Father Delmas got along well, and Long Lance described the priest as "an all-round good fellow with a fine sense of humor, and hospitable to a fault." In a postscript to a three-page letter to S. H. Middleton, written while he was staying at the school with Father Delmas, Long Lance explained: "If this letter seems somewhat jerky, put it down to the fact that I have had to turn around and talk or laugh with somebody at the end of every sentence."[21]

After his research in Saskatchewan, Long Lance took a detour through his old haunts in Alberta, where he looked up his friends Howard Kelly and Hugh Dann. For a lark, the three of them decided to go down to neighboring Shelby, Montana, for the world heavyweight boxing championship. As a promotional stunt, the tiny town, then in the midst of an oil boom, decided to host the championship on July 4. Some twenty-five thousand boxing fans descended on Shelby, which had a population of only five thousand. There was not a hotel room to be had, so Long Lance and his friends spent the first night in a big tent and the second sleeping on unironed clothes in a laundry.[22] It was worth it, for Long Lance watched from the grandstand as an old acquaintance, Jack Dempsey, defeated the challenger Tommy Gibbons in fifteen rounds.

After returning from Shelby, there was more excitement. In 1923, the Calgary Exhibition added bronc riding, calf roping and bull riding to its events, and it became known as the Calgary Exhibition and Stampede. For a frontier touch, Blackfoot, Stoney and Sarcee Indians were given passes and encouraged to set up an Indian tepee village on the Stampede grounds.

When the Exhibition and Stampede Board heard Long Lance was in town, the members sought him out and asked him to help with a publicity stunt. Unlike the Indian elders, who spoke little English, Long Lance spoke it fluently and articulately, and knew how to hold the attention of a large white audience. This time, instead of dropping a fake bomb in a door at City Hall, Long Lance agreed to organize a kidnapping of the mayor.

At 10:15 on the morning of July 12, Long Lance, Running Rabbit, seven chiefs and a healthy assortment of Blackfoot, Stoney and Sarcee warriors, all painted and feathered and mounted on war ponies, charged down Seventh Avenue to City Hall. They hastily dismounted and, led by Long Lance, who knew the way, crowded into the mayor's office. Swiftly Long Lance ordered the mayor to vacate his official chair, then installed Running Rabbit, who spoke not a word of English, as mayor. Photographers scrambled to record the "kidnapping," then the war party took the mayor, dressed in chaps, blue silk shirt, pink handkerchief and huge Stetson hat,[23] to the steps of City Hall. There they tied Mayor Webster to a horse and rode him to the center of the city at Eighth Avenue and First Street West. In the hot July sun, the Indian mayor officially adopted the captive as a Blackfoot, naming him Chief Crowfoot, and then returned charge of the city to the white chief, who was now one of them.

The stunt made a great splash in Eastern Canada. According to the *Herald*, several eastern Canadian reporters covering the Stampede "declared the ceremony the most striking and picturesque they had ever seen."[24] Long Lance never forgot it. As a memento, he had a photograph taken of himself at the tepee village in his white buckskins, moccasins and war bonnet, mounted on an Indian pinto. The Stampede Board rewarded him with an official medal and made him a publicity agent and Indian committeeman for the 1924 Stampede.[25]

In late July, 1923, Long Lance left Calgary to visit the Stoney Reserve, thirty miles west of Calgary. Short of money, he wrote some articles quickly and sold them to pay his bills. With an interpreter, he went directly to the old Indians and sat with them at a camp fire, collecting their stories of this isolated group of Assiniboines, separated more than a century earlier from their parent group in southern Saskatchewan. When he approached his old employer, the *Herald* swallowed its pride and bought what unquestionably was a fascinating and compelling piece of journalism.[26]

Two years earlier, in 1921, Long Lance first heard of the Blackfoot Sun Dance from the Indian agent, George

Gooderham. Back in the days of the buffalo hunt, the tribe always gathered after the long winter to give thanks to the Creator. Through the medium of the Sun Dance, they sent their prayers to the Great Spirit. They prayed for the animals, for the grasses on which they fed and for all the peoples who lived under the mercy of the sun, without whose life-giving rays nothing could endure. Half a century after the buffalo, the Sun Dance remained a great spiritual celebration, and it was something Long Lance had always wanted to write about.

He returned to Gleichen, Alberta, on August 3, 1923, and headed for the Sun Dance flats on the north bank of the Bow River. By wagon and buckboard, some seven hundred Blackfoot Indians converged on the site carrying tepee poles and canvas covers. Their colorful green, red, blue and yellow tepees with boldly painted designs rose in a large circle. Gates to the east and west marked the sun's path across the sky.

At the encampment, there was a large lodge that had the same significance to the Blackfoot as any cathedral has to Christians. During the Sun Dance ceremony, the Blackfoot used the leafy branches of the poplar tree to build this sun dance, or medicine, lodge. It stood in the center of the camp, and from a distance looked like a grassy hillock.

George Gooderham arranged for Long Lance to stay with Joe Calf Child for the week before the Sun Dance and for the four days of the actual ceremony. Long Lance found his tepee accommodation surprisingly comfortable. Joe's wife had constructed embroidered back rests made of willow rods, and from the tepee poles hung a variety of attractive objects: bags, belts, pipes, shawls, rattles and headdresses. At night he fell asleep to the sound of drums throbbing outside, and in the morning he awakened to the smell of burning sweet grass and his host singing his medicine song. [27]

Until this visit, Long Lance had never stayed long on a reserve, perhaps a few days at most. Also, he had never been entirely on his own. He had worked through intermediaries: Indian agents, missionaries, or residential school graduates such as Andy Paull and Dan Kennedy. This time he was alone, and he did not find it easy. The Blackfoot received him politely, but it was obvious they did not regard him as one of their own. His easy friendliness and his enthusiasm to write about the sacred ceremonies made the Blackfoot suspicious, and they kept their distance.

Long Lance also knew just enough about the Indian way of life to get into trouble. He knew nothing about tepee etiquette, and inevitably he made mistakes. It unsettled the old people when he walked between his host and the fire. He did not know where to sit, unaware that male guests always sit on the host's immediate left. And when he was introduced, Long Lance always gave his own name, which the old Indians never did.[28] To the Blackfoot, he talked and behaved like a white man.

The elders actually objected to Long Lance's presence. Although they had agreed to allow him to visit the camp and to stay with Joe Calf Child, they had insisted to Gooderham that the stranger stay away from the inner circle, containing the Sun Dance lodge and the tepee of the Sun Dance Woman.[29] They did not want their sacred rites to be publicized, especially by someone they considered—for good reason—an outsider unfamiliar with their language and the religious significance of the event.

Long Lance talked as much as he could with Joe Calf Child, his host. He peppered him with all sorts of questions on the Sun Dance. After a few days he also made another friend, an attractive young woman, Mary Only Owl. Shunned as he was by the Blackfoot, he appreciated her very enjoyable company. She was extremely friendly, but that was her profession, as the lonely Long Lance soon discovered.[30] His already shaky image plummeted still further by being seen constantly with this woman, whose easy charms made her one of the tribe's fallen women.

Long Lance had difficulty in arranging suitable photographs to illustrate his article. He could not photograph the Sun Dance Woman, Mary Wolf Leg,[31] the virtuous maiden who had organized the ceremony and who stayed fasting in a tepee. The Sun Dance Woman was as sacrosanct as the

Virgin Mary in Christendom. Long Lance neatly side-
stepped all obstacles by photographing another Blackfoot
woman, Mary Only Owl! He boldly captioned it in his first
article: "Cat's Woman, the Blackfoot Virgin, who Bought
and Put on the Sun Dance this year."[32]

Whatever his tribulations in covering the story, his
glimpse of the ritual provided enthralling copy for more than
one future article. In a piece published in *Good Housekeeping* in 1927, he offered a convincing eye-witness account of
"our Blackfoot Sun Dance." In his usual opportunistic way,
and with the best instincts of the magazine freelancer, Long
Lance devoted nearly the entire *Good Housekeeping* article
to the role of Indian women in the ceremony. Again he used
the photograph of Mary Only Owl, introducing her this time
as "Miss Ghost Skin, the Blackfoot girl who 'put on' the 1926
Sun Dance."[33]

His rebuff at the Sun Dance hurt, but Long Lance did not
dwell on it. He knew he could trust Gooderham, and he knew
that few outside would ever hear that he had been rejected
by those he called his "own people." As he often had before in
such circumstances, he took the offensive, and about this
time he began to promote himself as a Blackfoot or Blood
chief. When John Murray Gibbon, the CPR's general publicity agent, approached him that fall to write up several
Blackfoot tales for use on the CPR menu cards, he eagerly
accepted.

During the winter of 1923-24 Long Lance prepared brief
stories about "The Indian Scout," "Blackfoot Travois and
Cayuse," and "Indian Medicine Practices."[34] In the summer
of 1924, the handsomely printed cards appeared in the CPR's
luxury dining cars, placed on the white linen tablecloths
between the monogrammed china and the cut flowers that
were part of first-class rail travel in the 1920s. At the bottom
of each card was a short note explaining that extra cards
could be obtained in envelopes ready for mailing, on application to the dining car steward. Soon they were being sent out
across the continent, nicely publicizing both the railroad and
Chief Buffalo Child Long Lance.

After the Blackfoot Sun Dance, Long Lance wrote his

articles on the Rebellion of 1885 and Almighty Voice. In his haste to convert his notes to stories, and make money to pay his bills, Long Lance sacrificed accuracy. When his article on the Rebellion of 1885 appeared in the Saskatoon *Daily Star*, a local historical society strongly complained that he had taken severe liberties with the facts. In a letter to the newspaper in early November, two executives of the Prince Albert Historical Society said that while the story was "quite entertaining," it contained "many errors regarding the participants and actual happenings."[35]

Long Lance often erred in small ways, for he was ignorant of much of Canadian history and more interested in the color of an event. He was one of those journalists who fancied himself more a writer than a reporter, one of those who never let the facts ruin a good story. In his article on the Stoneys for the *Calgary Herald*, he said that the French *coureurs de bois* Radisson and DesGroseilliers reached the foothills of Alberta around 1800. Even if the claim were true (most reputable authorities believe that they never traveled further west than what is now Minnesota), the dates are totally inaccurate. By 1800, Radisson and DesGroseilliers had been dead for nearly a century![36] Long Lance also frequently confused Indians of the same or similar name. In his *MacLean's* article, for instance, he referred to the great Blackfoot warrior "Running Rabbit, who took a prominent role in a raid on the Assiniboine in 1863." Long Lance wrote that Running Rabbit "was still living, well and hardy, the last time I heard of him." The original Running Rabbit had died in 1918, three years before Long Lance visited the Blackfoot Reserve, and the well and hardy Running Rabbit that Long Lance mentioned was the great warrior's son.[37]

The public knew little about Indians, and even those who should have been vigilant did not always spot the errors. John Hawkes, the librarian of the Saskatchewan Legislative Library, wrote in 1924 in *Saskatchewan and Its People:* "The Chief is a highly educated man who... has had considerable press experience, and his bright literary contributions to the lore and history of the tribes are not only interesting and well written but are valuable because of their authenticity."[38]

To his credit, Long Lance never hesitated to travel great distances and to at least attempt to achieve a rapport with the characters of his stories. He was never content to pick up material from secondary sources. In late May, 1923, for example, he went out of his way to visit Almighty Voice's parents, Sounding Sky and Spotted Calf, who still lived only four miles from the bluff where their son had fought to his death.

Long Lance was blessed, or cursed, with the novelist's imagination. He knew how to inflate a story to make it read well, and to enhance its sales potential. He embellished upon the known details when he sat down to write his version of the last stand of Almighty Voice, going so far as to invent dialogue and to include scenes that had no factual basis.[39] It was, nevertheless, a good story of a young Cree who killed a Mountie and who then evaded capture for two years. He sold it to the Winnipeg *Tribune*, the Montreal *Family Herald* and *MacLean's*.[40]

When Almighty Voice was found, it was, Long Lance said, because he wanted to be found.[41] Joined by his cousin Going-Up-to-Sky and his brother-in-law Topean, he had decided to die in a last, defiant stand. They chose a thicket in a half-mile clump of bush growing on rolling, open prairie. According to Long Lance's version, which is still cited today as an accurate account,[42] the large force of Mounties and volunteers charged twice. Topean was killed, but Almighty Voice and Going-Up-to-Sky killed two Mounties and the postmaster of Duck Lake. The police called for reinforcements, and more Mounties and volunteers arrived from Duck Lake, Prince Albert and Regina. That night, Almighty Voice shouted from the bluff to his attackers: "We have had a good fight today. I have worked hard and I am hungry. You have plenty of food; send me some, and tomorrow we'll finish the fight." All during the night, his mother chanted to him from a nearby hill, urging him "to die the brave that he had shown himself to be." Throughout the night, Almighty Voice yelled back in the darkness: "I am almost starving. I am eating the bark off the trees. I have dug into the ground as far as my arm will reach, but can get no water. But have no fear—I'll hold out to the end."[43]

By the next morning, field guns were positioned, a nine-pounder and a seven-pounder, and at six o'clock the first shells were sent thundering into the thicket. For three days, Almighty Voice had not eaten, drunk or slept. The barrage continued for hours. When it stopped, Almighty Voice shouted: "You have done well, but you will have to do better."[44]

That night, Almighty Voice's mother changed her chant to a lament: a death song for her son. As Long Lance described it: "At six o'clock the next morning, the big guns began belching forth their devastating storm of lead and iron in deadly earnestness. It was obvious that no living things could long endure their steady beat. At noon the pelting ceased." Almighty Voice was dead. The bluff where he and his two companions died, Long Lance continued, "marks the spot where the North American Indian made his last stand against the white man."[45]

After the summer of 1923, Long Lance headed back to Winnipeg, and the *Tribune* sent him to New York to cover the Dempsey-Firpo fight. On the evening of September 14, a crowd of eighty thousand—more than the entire population of Calgary—gathered at the Polo Grounds, the home stadium of the New York Giants of the National League.

Long Lance welcomed the assignment, for he was by now wearying of the Indian stories. He followed the fight blow by blow. Firpo, the Wild Bull of the Pampas, stormed into Dempsey, knocking him clear out of the ring. Fortunately, reporters at ringside pushed Dempsey back through the ropes at the count of nine, and the champ rallied and went on to knock out Firpo. It was one of the classic boxing fights of all time, and Long Lance was there. He wrote back to the *Tribune*: "There may have been a fight more savage, spectacular and brutal than the slugfest here Friday night between Jack Dempsey and Louis Angel Firpo, but it must have been back in the dark ages when men wore leopard skins around their loins and wielded tree stumps instead of eight-ounce gloves."[46]

The *Tribune* loved his report and later sent him on to

other fights. In May, 1924, he went to Michigan City,
Indiana, to cover a bout between Georges Carpentier and
Tommy Gibbons. In September, 1924, the *Montreal Star*,
Edmonton Journal, *Calgary Herald*, *Saskatoon Star*,
Regina Leader and *Winnipeg Tribune* all carried his story
from Jersey City on the fight between Firpo and Harry
Willis, the "Black Panther." A fellow journalist described
Long Lance's fight stories as "virile, red-blooded,
graphic. . . ."[47]

It had been seven years since Long Lance had visited
New York, and he was happy to be back in the big city. He
stayed at the Commodore Hotel on Forty-Second Street and
Lexington Avenue, right next to Grand Central Station. The
Commodore was the largest of the Grand Central hotels,
twenty-eight storeys high, with more than two thousand
rooms, but it was dwarfed by other skyscrapers in central
Manhattan.[48] After eleven days at the Sun Dance flats in
Alberta, the buildings seemed even bigger, more immense,
than he remembered them. They completely blocked the
sun.

Long Lance stayed an extra three weeks in New York,
and from there he wrote again to S. H. Middleton to report
that he was getting around and meeting people worth knowing. "Have been out to dinners, theaters, ball games, and
have had several good motor trips and games of golf," he
wrote in a letter dated October 8. He did not mention it, but
he was also running out of money.

Introducing himself as "a full-blooded Indian, a chief of
the Blood tribe of Alberta,"[49] he arranged to write a story of
the Indians of the Canadian Plains for *The Mentor*, a small
American educational magazine. On his way back to Winnipeg, he stopped in Toronto and called on Herb Cranston,
the editor of the *Star Weekly*, which had bought his article
on the Manitoba Sioux that spring. Cranston was anxious to
meet and discuss work with Long Lance. He wanted light
human interest stories and Long Lance's Indian pieces were
exactly what he wanted for the *Star Weekly*. As he was fond
of saying, "We seek to entertain rather than to instruct."[50]
Using this formula, Cranston had managed to raise the

circulation of the *Star Weekly* to more than one hundred and fifty thousand, making it the largest periodical in the country. [51] He bought Long Lance's article on the Sun Dance and asked for more.

Long Lance returned to Winnipeg in November and became a full-time reporter again. On weekends, he assisted with boxing programs in the city, helping to judge the City Amateur Boxing Championship in mid-February. He dated many women, and paid much attention to a particularly striking piano teacher. [52] When summer arrived, like a migrating bird, he returned to Alberta, and in late June he set off for the Macleod Jubilee, the Calgary Stampede and his new summer job as a CPR public relations representative at the Banff Springs Hotel.

Macleod, founded as a North West Mounted Police post in the fall of 1874, was the oldest white settlement in southern Alberta, older by a year than Calgary. To help the town celebrate its fiftieth anniversary, twenty-five hundred Blackfoot, Bloods, and Peigans and fifteen thousand tourists had joined the two thousand citizens for the Jubilee. Long Lance moved easily from the white town site to the Indian village, keeping fellow reporters abreast of the pow-wows and contests among the Indians. [53]

He tried to improve his image with the Blackfoot, for the rebuff at the Sun Dance still smarted. This time, he looked for ways to forge stronger ties with the Blackfoot tribe that had adopted him.

At the Indian village, he approached old Eagle Speaker, the veteran of several Blood war parties against the Cree. He had corresponded with his son, Mike, whom he had met on his first trip to the reserve in August, 1921. Mike had recently become the first Blood to enter agricultural college, and S. H. Middleton suggested that Long Lance write to encourage the young Indian in his studies. Long Lance approached Eagle Speaker and asked if he and his son could adopt each other. To his joy, the old man said yes.

The ancient ritual took place in Eagle Speaker's tepee in the Indian encampment. Three Blood elders, Spear Chief, Morning Bird and Mike Oka, joined Eagle Speaker. Spear

Chief led the ceremony. He took a piece of rawhide, tied Mike's and Long Lance's hands together as they knelt, then painted their faces with the sacred red paint. After raising them up, he asked them to walk four times around the fire. When this was done, Spear Chief untied the rawhide, and the two were blood brothers. They would remain close for life.[54]

Despite becoming a blood brother, Long Lance never won full acceptance from the Bloods. As part of his adoption ceremony at St. Paul's in February, 1922, Old Mountain Horse had pushed him away, reminding the new Buffalo Child of his place among his fellow tribesmen, but now some of the Bloods were shocked to see photographs of Long Lance in "tribal dress" splashed across newspapers and in magazines. It appeared that he was consciously using his adoption by the Bloods for personal publicity. On July 30, a month after the celebrations at Macleod, Middleton wrote Long Lance to say that some of the leading Bloods felt he was "using" his "Blood Indian name and tribal connections to commercial advantage."

Long Lance knew that by flaunting his false credentials he was upsetting, even antagonizing, the Bloods, and he knew he had reached a turning point in his life. Five years later he would tell a reporter that his dream was to "find a young Indian girl, and settle down on the reserve."[55] In 1924, he might even have done this. Using Middleton's good offices, he could have visited the Bloods and apologized to those he had offended. The missionary would have been delighted to introduce him to suitable female graduates of St. Paul's, and he could have married. But this he rejected; he wanted more.

He was beginning to feel let down by the Indians, whom he thought he had helped by promoting a better understanding of them among his white readers, and by organizing them politically. He could not understand why the Blackfoot did not appreciate his efforts, and something in his spirit seemed to sag.[56] He became a little more hardened, a little more cynical. His political activism came to an end.

After the Calgary Stampede, in which he headed the Indian contingent,[57] Long Lance took up his new job at Banff. His responsibilities included writing publicity, entertaining VIP's and accompanying horse-riding groups of guests staying at the CPR's luxury hotels at Banff and Lake Louise.[58] When he received his next invitation to lecture as an Indian chief, he accepted without hesitation.

The invitation came from John Carlisle, vice-president of the Ohio Historical Association,[59] and Long Lance saw in it an opening that might lead to more lectures in the United States. In early October, Long Lance set off for Columbus, Ohio, to speak at the fourth annual Ohio History Day.

In Columbus, officials of the historical society reserved the Governor's Suite at the expensive Chittenden Hotel for him, and everywhere he went he was treated as a distinguished visitor. He spoke at length of "his people" to the local Chamber of Commerce, the State Archeological and Historical Society and the Exchange Club. Over radio station WEAD, a woman sang "The Song of Love" in honor of Long Lance. Excitedly, from his well-appointed suite in the Chittenden Hotel, Long Lance wrote Middleton to say the people of Columbus "looked after me as though I were really 'somebody.'"[60]

The highlight of his visit was his address on Ohio History Day to an audience of six thousand. He spoke at Logan Park, about twenty-five miles south of Columbus in the Pickaway Plains. At this same site, exactly 150 years earlier, Chief Logan gave one of the most famous speeches in North American Indian history. After white frontiersmen had massacred his entire family, Logan took up arms against the white man. Under a tall elm tree he defended his stand, saying: "There runs not a drop of my blood in the veins of any living creature. This called on me for revenge. Who is there to mourn for Logan? Not one."[61]

The small elm of 1774 had grown to an immense girth of 25 feet and a height of over 150 feet.[62] When Long Lance spoke, though, not a single reservation remained in all of Ohio. The Indians had been expelled a century earlier, driven west of the Mississippi, or murdered like Chief Logan's family. Long Lance spoke beneath the same elm and his words hit their mark, reminding his white audience of the injustices of years past.

He spoke for half an hour on the North American Indian, past and present, and his eloquence stirred them. When he reached the end, the crowd surged forward so enthusiastically that the timber under the platform snapped just minutes after Long Lance and the others had climbed down. For another half hour, Long Lance shook hands with hundreds of well-wishers until the organizers whisked him away.[63]

The reaction to his speech convinced Long Lance that as a Blackfoot chief he could go a long, long way.

12

BANFF TO NEW YORK

IT WAS WHEN he was covering the Dempsey-Firpo fight in New York in September, 1923, that Long Lance got a taste of that gratuitous publicity that can suddenly bring an unknown to center stage. He was at the Polo Grounds, covering the fight for newspapers in Western Canada, and although ringside was studded with celebrities, Long Lance managed to attract notice.

A journalist covering the fight dropped into his story a reference to this conspicuous young Indian who happened to catch his eye as blows were exchanged in the ring. He wrote:

> Among the newspaper men at the ringside of the Dempsey-Firpo fight in New York sat a young chap of athletic build. The casual observer might have thought this fellow had acquired a healthy tan at one of New York's popular beaches. Looking him over more carefully, the observer would have noticed that this individual's skin was copper-colored, that his hair was jet black, that his cheek bones were prominent and that he had an unflinching eye. Inquiry would have brought out the fact that it was Chief Buffalo Child Long Lance, a full-blooded Indian chief representing a syndicate of newspapers in the Canadian Northwest.[1]

Long Lance pasted the reference in his scrapbook, already bulging with other clippings and photographs.

119

Long Lance excelled in sportswriting, especially in covering boxing, and it did not have to be a world championship
fight staged in New York City. He immersed himself in the
amateur sports of Winnipeg when he worked for the
Tribune. As at several other points in his life, he could have
chosen to make it his career, and he might have been one of
the very best, filing vivid copy on boxing, for example,
"where crushing blows are swishing through the air like
nine-pounders, where bulky frames are tottering like giant
buildings in an earthquake."[2]

He wanted more than this, however, though in the fall of
1924 he probably was not certain where he was going or
where he wanted to go. He accepted nearly all invitations to
speak, if he thought he could win publicity from them. In
November, 1924, he addressed, as a Blackfoot, the Canadian Club in Montreal, then the Women's Canadian Clubs in
Toronto and Hamilton. His press clippings grew, including a
feature article in the Toronto *Star Weekly* that carried a
full-page caption: REDSKIN EXTRAORDINARY IS THIS
INDIAN CHIEF.[3] He might have found being a "professional
Indian" repugnant, and in his letters there is evidence to
support this,[4] but it did not stop him from exploiting the
role.

During the winter, Long Lance worked as a free agent for
the *Tribune*, another indication of how highly he was
regarded. He could be assigned, or assign himself, to just
about any location in Canada, and usually be assured that his
stories would be bought. He covered the ski championships
at Mount Revelstoke in British Columbia,[5] then returned
eastward to Banff to welcome New Zealand's "All Blacks"
rugger team. The New Zealanders, having completed a
twenty-eight-game exhibition tour of Britain, were returning home. The team of thirty included several full-blooded
Maoris and others of mixed Maori and white blood. Most
noticeable to Long Lance was the utter lack of discrimination among them. They were a fun-loving crew, who went up
and down the toboggan slide at Banff at all hours of the
night. Often during their two-day stay at Banff, they performed Maori dances to a drum and native chants. The All

Blacks took to Long Lance as easily as he took to them, and before they left Alberta the New Zealanders made "Chief Buffalo Child" an honorary member of their team.[6]

By the 1920s, the Banff Springs Hotel had become a showplace and something of a Canadian legend. The gigantic hotel-castle lay anchored to the base of Sulphur Mountain on a pine-covered bank above the swift-flowing Bow River. Here, every summer, came the rich and powerful with their huge steamer trunks and servants. They came for the peaks and valleys and the stunning, green-blue lakes of one of the last great wilderness regions of North America.

Long Lance's job, as the CPR Assistant Press Representative at Banff, was to make sure influential guests had a pleasant stay. With his wide range of conversational topics and his warm and friendly manner, he performed his duties with ease. After a visit to Banff in the summer of 1924, the English journalist Eldred Walker included a sketch of Long Lance in his book *Canadian Trails Re-Visited*. What Walker remembered vividly was a chance meeting with Long Lance on the hotel's veranda. The immaculately attired Long Lance approached the portly, elderly Englishman, introduced himself and asked what he thought of the Rockies. Over drinks, the two men had a lengthy conversation, discussing art, literature, journalism, agriculture and science. Walker was impressed to find someone in such an unlikely place to whom no topic seemed foreign. He could compare the delights of Banff with those of New York and London; the Englishman was impressed. Suddenly, as Walker describes in his book, this dark-skinned stranger stopped talking, paused and bluntly asked: "You are looking hard at me. Can you tell to what nationality I belong?" Long Lance waited, and seeing that the Englishman was baffled, told him: "I am a full-blooded Blood Indian. I am Chief Buffalo Child Long Lance of the Blood Tribe."

"Had the heavens opened," Walker concluded in his book, "I could not have had a greater surprise."[7]

Long Lance enjoyed his work at the hotel, for it allowed him to play his favorite role of "noble red man," freely rubbing shoulders with the wealthy and socially prominent of the continent. In these, the hotel's golden days, many of the visitors arrived with letters of credit worth $50,000, all earmarked for a stay of two or three months in Banff. It was a make-believe world of which an old Banff banker observed: "The men would fish and play golf, and the women would change their clothes."[8] Long Lance cut an imposing figure on any dance floor, and at the Banff Springs Hotel he was a much-sought-after partner.[9]

The summer of 1924 ended quickly enough, and at the end of August he was on his way east again, this time, at the request of the hotel management, to accompany a visiting party of British scientists heading to Toronto. Long Lance was the ideal host. During the two-day journey across the prairies and down through northern Ontario, Long Lance spent much of his time with Sir Richard Paget, a famous English voice specialist. Long Lance told him what he knew first-hand of various Indian songs, and Paget was fascinated. In a fine bass voice, Long Lance chanted the songs as the train rattled on through the country. According to Long Lance's later comment to a reporter from the Toronto Star, Sir Richard caught on quickly: "Many of the Indian songs I talked to him about and illustrated for him were most difficult. They were in a very minor key with all sorts of peculiar Indian inflections graded down from ordinary sounds to a grunt. It is next to impossible for anyone except an Indian to pick them up. It was astonishing. . . . before he left the train at Toronto he was singing them as accurately as a native Indian."[10]

Long Lance pushed his Indian identity whenever and wherever he could, and he became bold and even reckless about it. To help a Star Weekly writer with the feature story on "The Redskin Extraordinary," Long Lance loaned him two clippings books and actually gave him a photograph of an old Plains Indian in a war bonnet and said it was his father. In due course, the photograph appeared with the article, captioned: "Old Chief Long Lance, father of Chief Buffalo Child."[11]

When summer arrived, he returned to Calgary and to Banff. The Stampede Board had invited him months earlier.

The official guests in 1925 were Long Lance's Supreme Commander in World War I, Field Marshal Earl Haig, now nearly seventy, and the Countess Haig. Haig was touring Canada to speak to ex-servicemen's associations. He was a somber Scot, with a full mustache, bluish-gray eyes and a handsome face. He walked with the rangy, swinging stride common to men who ride a great deal.[12] At the request of the Stampede Board, the Sarcee Chief, Joe Big Plume, was to adopt Haig into his tribe, with Long Lance acting as the interpreter.

On that fine July day, the weather was perfect. After the field marshal had led the Stampede parade through the heart of the city, mounted cowboys and cowgirls, Indians and chuckwagons rumbled to a stop at the corner of First Street West and Seventh Avenue. Thousands watched as Chief Big Plume, in buckskin and full headdress, conducted the ceremony. As instructed, Haig knelt on an Indian blanket, and Long Lance began translating the Sarcee chief's words into English:

> Field Marshal Earl Haig, I am going to make you a chief of the Sarcee Indians. The Sarcees had a great warrior killed one hundred years ago. He was the greatest warrior that the Sarcees ever had, and you are Great Britain's greatest warrior. . . . The name that the Sarcees are giving you is Big Chief Akahtse, which means Chief Bull's Head.[13]

Not knowing any Sarcee, Long Lance's interpretation was loose and free. Improvising, he said that the original Bull's Head died a hundred years earlier, in 1825, when actually the old Sarcee warrior had died in 1911.[14] But the error was not detected. Unlike Chief Big Plume, Long Lance's narrative was smooth and polished, in the finest English he could muster. He knew what to deliver to the predominantly white audience, and it worked.

After an eagle-plume headdress was placed on Haig's head, Long Lance carefully adjusted it, as if he had been doing this sort of thing all his life. When the ceremony was over, Long Lance extended his hand, broke into a wide smile, and welcomed the newest Chief Bull's Head into the tribe. [15] The performance was such a success that the Stampede Board invited him back for the following summer.

After the Stampede, Long Lance returned to the Banff Springs Hotel, where his public relations job awaited him. Again in return for his room, meals and a modest salary, Long Lance eased into his role as the resident Indian at the hotel. This time during his stay at the Banff Springs, he appeared in a comic strip, "Cicero Sapp," published in the New York *Evening World* on August 18, 1925. In the comic strip, the visiting Mr. Cicero Sapp had been told by the manager of the Banff Springs Hotel that he would introduce him to a real, full-blooded Indian chief. Not wishing to meet him looking like a city slicker, the bourgeois Mr. Sapp dresses up in a ten-gallon hat, cowboy duds, a gun and a holster, then proceeds to the lobby to meet the chief. He is astonished when the hotel manager presents a handsome Indian wearing a tuxedo, looking as much like a real Indian chief as a Broadway dandy.

When his duties at Banff were over for another summer, Long Lance rejoined the lecture circuit. In the early 1920s, public lectures were a popular entertainment. Movies were new and popular, to be sure, but until 1927 they were still silent. Through his article in *The Mentor*, Long Lance had gained an audience in the United States, and after the Ohio History Day speech other requests came in. A suave, well-spoken Indian chief was a great novelty, and Long Lance took full advantage of it. In the fall of 1925, he went to New York, then lectured at a dinner of the British Empire Club in Providence, Rhode Island. [16] After that, he went back to New York and spoke at the Dutch Treat Club, whose membership consisted of the editors of many of the leading newspapers in the United States.

At the Dutch Treat Club, Long Lance was introduced by Ray Long, editor-in-chief at *Cosmopolitan*, then a general interest magazine, and vice-president of Randolph Hearst's magazine chain. Long Lance gave one of his best talks, prompting applause that rang out for five minutes. Long, a director of the club for ten years, said he had "never heard a

more interesting address before this club than that given by
Chief Buffalo Child Long Lance."[17] Afterwards, he invited
his guest to visit his home at Greenwich, Connecticut, [18] and
there he suggested that Long Lance use his lecture notes for
an article for *Cosmopolitan*.

Long was a man of expensive tastes. He was a short,
dapperly dressed man, with a sporty, upturned mustache,
and he was the proud owner of some forty suits — all
custom-tailored in London — and shirts and pajamas made in
Paris. At forty-seven, Long was reputedly the highest-
salaried editor in the world, earning $180,000 a year. He was
a prodigious worker, and a typical weekend's work involved
reading thirty-three short stories, two novels, four or five
magazines, several trade papers and all of the New York
Sunday newspapers, which he clipped, sending pertinent
items to his assistants. *Cosmopolitan* received some three
thousand manuscripts a month, of which it accepted
between twenty-five and thirty. [19] Ray Long wanted Long
Lance's article to be one of these, in a magazine which could
boast ten times the circulation of the Toronto *Star Weekly*.

Long Lance stayed a month in New York. He loved dropping names, and in his letters to Canon Middleton in
Alberta, he told of the famous writers he was meeting.
Twice he had met Sinclair Lewis, who had just published his
two devastating reviews of American middle-class life in his
novels *Main Street* and *Babbitt*. He also had talked with
Kathleen Norris, the popular romantic novelist, and Peter
B. Kyne, the writer of westerns, and he spent many
hours with Vilhjalmur Stefansson, the Arctic explorer and
lecturer.[20]

Between the parties and the hobnobbing, he managed to
line up work. The American Bureau of Commercial Economics invited him on a lecture tour of the American Midwest.
The bureau was a private non-profit organization sustained
entirely by memberships and voluntary contributions. In
cooperation with President Coolidge's national outdoor recreation program, the bureau sent lecturers and films
throughout the United States, urging Americans "to take a
greater interest and part in outdoor life." The bureau paid

all expenses, plus an honorarium, and secured passes for
Long Lance on nineteen American railways. The tour
started in Washington, where the organization's headquarters was located, and it continued on to Illinois, Michigan,
Wisconsin, Indiana, Iowa and Missouri. [21]

One of his first lectures was to the University Club in
Evanston, Illinois, just north of Chicago. For forty-five
minutes, as a Blackfoot chief, he told of his people's origins,
language, customs, sports and religion. He concluded his
talk with slides and a question period. Dr. James Washington Bell, an economics professor at Northwestern University, later remarked on how much he enjoyed Chief Buffalo
Child's answers, when his "ready wit and native point of
view quite captured the hearts of his listeners." In a thank-
you letter to the bureau, one Charles MacConnell wrote:
"His talk was crammed with interesting information — just
the sort of things we have asked over and over about the
Indians since we were children." [22]

In all six states, Long Lance attracted large crowds. As in
Ohio, the Indians had been killed off or brutally exiled from
Illinois, Indiana, Iowa, Missouri and from lower Michigan
and most of Wisconsin. The treatment of the Indians in these
areas remained a sensitive issue with the white Americans.
As Long Lance traveled through Illinois to Alton, Cham-
paign, Chicago, Greenville, Moline, Normal, Peoria,
Springfield and Urbana, and to dozens of other centers in
other states, he knew he could expect waves of sympathy
from his audiences. The moral indignation over the Indians'
plight seemed to increase with the distance from the scene of
the crimes. He spoke to business groups, service clubs and
college students. At Eau Claire, Wisconsin, he addressed
fifteen hundred people at the Opera House. In Milwaukee,
he stood before two thousand at the auditorium in Juneau
Park. [23]

In another letter to Canon Middleton, this one on February 18, Long Lance described the details of his tour, and
concluded by saying that he would "probably go down into
Oklahoma for a few days before returning up west." He told
Middleton about all the railway passes he was using, and

how easy it was to make "jumps" from train to train. Long Lance left no record of private thoughts he had on these long train trips and in the hotels, where he saw more blacks than he ever encountered in Canada. He probably did entertain thoughts of dropping in on his home town in North Carolina; he had the railway passes, and a trip for old time's sake would hardly have cost him a penny. But ultimately, for whatever reasons, he resisted the temptation.

By 1926, Long Lance had been separated from his family for seventeen years, nearly half his life. He must have known the risks of returning home—the risk of being exposed, the risk of succumbing to the warmth of family and old friends, the risk of the ghetto. With this far-ranging lecture tour, and with his assignment for *Cosmopolitan*, he felt he was on his way up, at last, and the easy accessibility of Winston-Salem could not have come at a worse time. It had been so long since he had been accountable to those who knew who he was and where he came from that he had grown accustomed to a very different, totally unreal life. Sylvester Long lived in one realm, and Chief Buffalo Child Long Lance lived in another.

His lies were becoming more compulsive and more outrageous. In March, 1926, he was interviewed by the Minneapolis *Sunday Tribune*, and the story that appeared on March 7 said: "To the Plains Indians, Chief Long Lance is 'Big Boss'—all their tribes, in addition to the Blackfoot Indians of Alberta, are said to look upon him as a leader." In the winter of 1925-26, Long Lance pushed his "Indianization" even further. He resolved to erase his past completely, simply by trying to forget it himself. In June, 1926, Ray Long published the autobiographical article Long Lance had worked on over the winter. It was titled "My Trail Upward," and in it Long Lance said: "I took [the trail] because I, a Blackfoot Indian, wanted to live like a white man." He summarized the story that he had recently been telling in New York, Washington and throughout the Midwest. He wrote of his Blackfoot boyhood, his years on western cattle ranches, traveling with Buffalo Bill's Wild West Show, Carlisle, his service in the Canadian army in France and his career as a writer in Western Canada. Fact was carefully blended with fiction, and the whole story fit neatly within the bounds of credibility. It was great reading. *Mac-Lean's* printed an expanded version in Canada in May, 1926. *McClure's*, a widely circulated American magazine, carried the story in July, 1927.[24] Selling the story three times brought Long Lance badly needed income.

When the *Cosmopolitan* article appeared, Long Lance hastily wrote Canon Middleton, urging him to buy a copy, but warning that the editor had made many uncalled-for changes. He claimed it was the editor's idea that he had attended "a mission school in southern Alberta," instead of "at Wind River, Wyo., where it should have been."[25] Middleton again was puzzled, for Long Lance earlier had told him that he had attended a mission school in Oklahoma, but he kept silent about his doubts.

It hurt Long Lance that even with his best white friend he could not be honest. Six months later, he wrote Middleton again, this time to tell him "it is good for a globe-wanderer like me to have one good confidante like you; one whom I can be myself to, always, and speak what is in my mind. . . ."[26] In fact, even with Middleton, Long Lance could only tell of the ripples on the surface of the pond, not the turbulent waters below, and never the muddy bottom that gave the pond its color.[27]

"My Trail Upward" begins:

Missionaries on a Blackfoot Indian Reservation in southern Alberta taught me my ABC's — but an old-fashioned bartender out in Laramie, Wyoming, first thrilled me with the idea that I might become educated and really make something out of my life.

This man was a Pennsylvania Dutchman and so he happened to know about Carlisle Indian School. He asked me one day when I was in the old Central Bar with a crowd of cowboys why I did not go there and become educated. He explained that it was free for Indians.

"But I can't even speak good English," I told him.

"Well," he said, "you can educate yourself for entrance to Carlisle by reading. Read, read all the time—anything and everything you come across."

I think that bit of advice changed the trend of my whole life. I was at that time sixteen years old and a full-fledged cow-hand. I could break and ride bucking horses. I could barely sign my own name and spell out words; but I could ride almost anything that stood on four feet. I was proud to be a cowpuncher; that was doing pretty well at that for an ignorant, half savage young Indian buck.

A few days before I met this old bartender—I'm ashamed that I've forgotten his name—I had been fired from a ranch fifteen miles west of Laramie. At that time my temper was as wild and unbridled as a wolf's, and this was the cause of the trouble.

This all happened in 1907, and I'd come down from the reservation to follow the round-ups. I had made this step on my own initiative, because I was curious to know about this Pale Face who had conquered my people and compelled us to live on comparatively small reservations. Up to this time I had never done anything but follow the Indians' line of least resistance—hunt and fool around with horses. I always went on the trail alone and I thought a lot. Finally one day I made a resolution; I was going out to meet the white man on his own grounds, study him and find out just what sort of fellow he was. . . .

He describes in rich detail a series of adventures as he went about studying the Pale Faces. When he arrived at Carlisle, he writes, "my brain was as tough as raw buffalo meat. . . ." It was when he was traveling with Colonel Cody and the Wild West Show that, he says, he got his first good opportunity to study these white people at close hand.

One afternoon the chiefs and some of the older Indians were taken out to a wealthy American's home and served with refreshments; and some of us youngsters were taken along. This chap had a lot of friends in to meet us, and he introduced

us as "real Americans. . . ." [These people] were different from
any I had ever met. They had the dignity that the Indian likes,
and they did not *yapiota* — talk too much. An Indian distrusts
anyone who talks a lot. These people so impressed me with
their bearing and their environment that I decided on the spot,
"I am going to be like that."

Finally, the *Cosmopolitan* article ends:

Two or three times a year I go back to my Indian reservation,
where I spent my boyhood and where my people still live. I
was proud when they elected me a Chief. I had won my spurs
fighting side by side with the white men — and my tribe had
recognized this.

I'm proud to be as much like a white man as I am — but I'm
proud, too, of every drop of Indian blood that runs through my
veins.

I'm proud of my Indian heritage — and I'm proud, too, of the
land and people of my adoption.

I have reached no dizzy heights of material success, but I
have succeeded in pulling myself up by my boot straps from a
primitive and backward life into this great new world of white
civilization.

Anyone with determination and will can do as much.

Shortly after the *Cosmopolitan* and *MacLean's* articles
appeared at the end of May, 1926, Long Lance returned to
Calgary for the opening of the Stampede. Mounted on an
Indian pony, he wore white buckskin and a full eagle-plume
headdress in his usual place at the head of the Indian section. [28] After the Stampede, he took the train to Banff for his
last summer in the Rockies. Probably because he was
embarrassed and ashamed of his distortions in the magazine
articles, he did not visit Canon Middleton on the Blood
Reserve. The next Middleton heard of Long Lance was after
a messy — and nearly fatal — incident involving a married
woman.

Throughout the years Long Lance enjoyed the company
of many women, but he never allowed himself to get too

close to any of them, and he never maintained lengthy relationships. He knew that the rules of racial mixing were against him, but it did not stop him from enjoying innumerable one-night stands. Affairs with married women were preferable, for they were for the passing moment, and involved very little personal disclosure.

In Banff, Long Lance met Florence Sheridan, a vivacious young woman married to a man twenty years her senior. She and her husband had come up from Chicago for the summer, renting the old Dawson house on Buffalo Street. The wealthy Chicago lawyer's first wife had died in 1917, and on September 10, 1924, at the age of fifty-six, he married the former Florence K. Donovan of Aberdeen, Washington. [29] After thirty-one years of heading a busy and important law firm in Chicago, John Jay Sheridan was exhausted and weak. He came to Banff for rest. To ensure that their vacation would be comfortable, the Sheridans brought along their black butler, Athay MacFarlane.

Long Lance met Florence on a trail ride. [30] Soon they became constant companions, and were together on the night of September 9, the eve of the Sheridans' second wedding anniversary. That night, feeling "indisposed," John Jay went to bed early, and Florence and Long Lance were left alone. They made a fire in the living room to break the cold of a chilly autumn night. The time passed quickly. About eleven, Florence left the living room to ask Athay, the butler, to prepare drinks. Unfortunately, he was inebriated, and loudly refused. Hearing the noise from the kitchen, Long Lance rushed to the lady's assistance.

The butler, drunk and resentful of Long Lance's affair with his boss's wife, pulled out a razor and angrily struck Long Lance on his front right thigh, making an eight-inch gash. Long Lance chased him out of the kitchen, but, hurt and bleeding, could not catch him. He limped to the living room, there to be comforted by Florence. After a few moments, there was a crash in the kitchen, then the butler rushed into the room, thrashing the air with his razor, determined to finish Long Lance once and for all. Long Lance siezed a heavy iron poker from the hearth and smashed it over the butler's head, knocking him senseless. Neighbors heard screams from the house, hurried in, and found blood splattered on the furniture, a body unconscious on the floor, a badly wounded Indian, and a hysterical woman. The next day, Florence's husband told the Banff newspaper that he had not heard a sound. [31]

For two days, Athay MacFarlane's life hung in the balance; he survived, and Long Lance escaped a murder charge. But he lost his job. John Murray Gibbon, fearful of publicity surrounding CPR employees who became involved in scandalous affairs, dismissed him without delay. Through it all, public opinion sided with Long Lance. The Fort Macleod *Gazette* commented that Long Lance lost his job "by taking a lady's part against a 'nigger.'" The Banff *Crag and Canyon* joked: "Anyone in future employing negro servants should keep them supplied with safety razors."[32] The *Calgary Herald* on September 10 said that "only the thickness of the negro's skull saved him from instant death as the poker was almost double with the force of the blow."

At the hearing held a month later in the Banff police court, Athay MacFarlane testified that Long Lance had caused "grievous bodily harm," but as MacFarlane could not recall the details — because of drink and the knock on the head — the charge was dismissed. The court also dismissed a charge by Long Lance against the butler.[33]

When Long Lance ran into Fred Kennedy, one of his Calgary newspaper friends, he explained how he had been attacked and slashed and how he had nearly lost his manhood. Kennedy could not resist. If Long Lance had lost his manhood, he later wrote, it would have been "a fate worse than death so far as the gregarious Indian was concerned."[34]

Long Lance was entirely on his own again, but he was not worried. He already had a substantial assignment, a story that he had been working on for four years. In early October, he left for New York to see Ray Long at *Cosmopolitan*. (Never a man to miss an opportunity, he stopped off in Chicago to see Florence one more time.[35])

When he arrived in New York, he took a small apartment at The Clarkson, a huge Victorian building on the Upper

West Side, near the northwestern corner of Central Park. It was only a block from Riverside Drive, and he enjoyed walking by the Hudson River in the crisp autumn air. In a letter to Canon Middleton on November 2, 1926, he said it is "hard to feel perfectly natural and at-home on such furtive friendships as I must maintain, from place to place." He called New York a "noisy and extremely smutty old city" and said he wished he were back with him in Alberta. "I go out on Riverside Drive, a block from here, and walk alone and breathe in the fresh breezes from the ocean, and imagine that I am back on the prairies. That is my only safety valve from this clamorous environment."

Ray Long was still enthusiastic about Long Lance's work, and encouraged him to write a story about General George Armstrong Custer. Indian life and experiences were becoming distant for Long Lance; it had been four years since he had had any real contact with Plains Indians. When asked to give a Blackfoot name to the baby daughter of a friend with whom he boxed at his athletic club, the only one he could think of was "Napi," the name of one of the most significant mythic figures in Blackfoot folklore. Napi was the Blackfoot's "trickster," a spirit who had helped to create man and who had made many of the rivers, mountains and grasslands. It was hardly appropriate for a baby girl; Napi meant "old man."[36]

During the winter, Long Lance worked on his story of the Battle of Little Big Horn for the June, 1927, issue of *Cosmopolitan*. Long Lance's first sketch of the story had appeared in the Winnipeg *Tribune* on February 24, 1923. It was a fantastic tale, stretched to the limits by Long Lance's imagination. Based on what he learned at Carlisle, and from interviews with old Sioux warriors in exile in Western Canada, Long Lance claimed that Custer had not been killed by Indians at the Battle of Little Big Horn in 1876, and had not died spectacularly, with pistols blazing in both hands, besieged by thousands of Sioux. According to Long Lance, there had been no last stand at all. At the end of the battle, the man generally acclaimed as one of America's bravest military heroes had committed suicide.

In "The Secret of the Sioux," Long Lance said he first heard the real story of Custer's death "whispered around the Indian campfires of the Montana prairies when I was a boy." More accurate is his second statement that "years later, in 1910, while I was attending Carlisle Indian School, I heard more from Wesley Two Moons, son of Chief Two Moons, who commanded the Cheyennes who were with Sitting Bull in the Custer Massacre." (Long Lance was safe here, for Wesley Two Moons had died of pneumonia in 1911, when Long Lance was in his third year at the school.[37])

Even if he had not heard the story directly from the young Cheyenne, other Indian students could have told him, or he might even have read it in the Carlisle *Arrow*. While Long Lance attended Carlisle, the rumor of Custer's suicide was widely circulated. On October 21, 1910, the school newspaper published an Indian version of the Battle of Little Big Horn. In the article, Moses Friday, an Arapaho Indian, stated that when the Indians located Custer's body they "discovered that he was not scalped or mutilated in any way." All they found was a bullet hole in his head. Friday suggested that Custer killed himself rather than be taken by the Sioux, for "Indians never scalped the bodies of persons who had taken their own lives."

When Long Lance visited the old Sioux near Moose Jaw, Saskatchewan, and at Oak Lake, Manitoba, in the winter of 1922-23, they confirmed the story. Even so, Long Lance was not satisfied with this. He wanted still more drama. In "The Secret of the Sioux," he added the bizarre twist that Sitting Bull wanted to save General Custer because he considered Custer to be his blood brother.

According to Long Lance's story, the Sioux medicine man had met Custer at West Point in 1859. After discussing Sioux land rights in Washington, D.C., Sitting Bull and his party were escorted to the United States Military Academy "and shown the young embryo officers who were later to come out onto the plains and help establish peace between the Indians and pioneers." Having taken a liking to the young cadet who had shown him and his party around the grounds, Sitting Bull called young Custer *Weh-*

hunka-wanzi or "blood brother." Seventeen years later, just before the Battle of Little Big Horn, Sitting Bull warned his followers to spare his *Weh-hunka-wanzi*. His warriors carried out his orders. At the end of the battle, Custer was standing alone, the only survivor of his command. Before the Indians could give the peace sign, Custer put his gun to his head and pulled the trigger.

The story is incredible. Long Lance is the only one of all Custer's biographers who says that Sitting Bull met Custer previously in 1859. Even accepting this unlikely event, how could Sitting Bull have ensured that his message was relayed to everyone before the battle? There would have been many Sioux and Cheyenne who did not know him by sight, let alone pick him out amidst the smoke and dust of battle.[38]

In an era of wonderful nonsense, "The Secret of the Sioux" attracted widespread attention. In the 1920s, Americans turned for an entire decade to many light-hearted diversions — a heavyweight boxing match, a craze for the Chinese game *mah-jong*, the Charleston. It was the Age of Ballyhoo. After the war, they wanted to be entertained, and the times were uncritical. Even the sober *New York Times* was smitten by Long Lance's yarn, commenting that, if true, "then the mystery surrounding the death of General George Custer in the Battle of Little Big Horn is a mystery no longer."[39]

The article distressed others. Long Lance later told his friend Howard Kelly in Calgary that Mrs. Custer, the general's eighty-four-year-old widow, threatened court action. In Norfolk, Nebraska, a reunion of renowned frontiersmen protested against the inaccuracies.[40] In the long run, however, the publicity worked in Long Lance's favor. It won him instant fame.

13

THE AUTOBIOGRAPHY

AMONG RAY LONG'S RESPONSIBILITIES in William Randolph Hearst's organization was the Cosmopolitan Book Corporation, the book publishing arm of *Cosmopolitan*. Founded in 1914, the Corporation had published several popular authors, and each year the firm released some forty-five titles.[1] After seeing Long Lance's articles, Long knew that Long Lance had a book in him, and he wanted it for the Cosmopolitan list.

In late March, 1927, they met in Long's large, luxurious office in New York. The editor's enormous desk and wide-backed chairs were carved from heavy oak, as was an ornate and richly panelled chest. Behind the desk rose shelves of books, and directly in front of him, on the opposite wall, hung a portrait of the conglomerate's monarch, the king of sensationalism, William Randolph Hearst.[2] The imposing painting showed a smiling Hearst, the owner of twenty-two American dailies, fifteen Sunday papers, seven magazines.[3]

The busy editor no doubt came straight to the point, telling Long Lance that there was a market for a boy's adventure book on Indians, and he was the man to write it. Long Lance contained his excitement with some difficulty, for this was the chance he had been waiting for. He accepted the proposal and asked Long the expected professional questions, as if he considered such offers every day. How long a book? The editor suggested seventy thousand words.

When? Long told him he wanted *The Story of an Indian Boy* by the end of the year. Editing, layout, printing and promotion would take eight months. He would schedule the book to appear in the fall of 1928.

Long Lance signed a contract at the end of March, agreeing to submit a manuscript of seventy thousand words by November 1, 1927. The terms were those of a standard literary contract: ten per cent on the list price of the book, an advance of $500 against royalties, half to be given on submission of a first draft and half on completion.[4] If the book sold, as planned, for $2.50,[5] Long Lance would make twenty-five cents on each copy. Just before the contract was completed, Long, with Long Lance's consent, made a critical editorial suggestion.

For his articles and books, Long preferred a personal, or confessional, style.[6] It helped keep circulation and book sales mounting by injecting an easily identifiable narrator. Instead of *The Story of an Indian Boy*, he suggested instead *Long Lance*.[7] It should be his own life story, along the lines of all that he had written and spoken of in earlier articles and on the lecture circuit. It should begin in the 1890s, when he was growing up.

Long Lance knew as a journalist that telling the story in the first person would considerably enhance it and give it more impact. He wanted to reach the largest possible audience, but he also realized that to write it as a Blackfoot would involve great risk. But who would expose him? Both his autobiographical article and his story of Custer had been heavily embellished with fiction, and no one had unmasked him, so what should stop him now?

Before plunging into the project, Long Lance decided to contact his family. Sometime in the spring of 1927, he became Sylvester Long again and met Abe, his oldest brother, in Philadelphia.[8] He had not seen him in eighteen years. Abe had aged; there were wrinkles at his eyes, flecks of gray in his sideburns, and he had a slight stoop to his shoulder. When Sylvester had left for Carlisle in 1909, Abe, then twenty-eight, had recently married. Now he was forty-six. His daughter, Vivian, of whom he had written so proudly, had died at the age of eleven in 1919. His wife, Aurelia, was in good health, however, and she and Abe were happy. To help with expenses, she had started a hair-straightening shop in the basement of their home in Winston-Salem.[9]

As Long Lance listened to Abe's news, ghosts of the past rushed back at him. For Abe, as for their parents, religion and the activities of the First Baptist Church were the universe. Abe was intelligent and hardworking, but his horizons were limited. He spent his days directing patrons up the fifty or so stairs to the colored gallery of the Auditorium Theater, and he thought that the world was being good to him.[10]

Everyone at home still lived on top of each other in the little house on Brookstown Avenue. Walter still operated his own detective agency in the black community. Joe, their father, worked into his mid-seventies as a janitor, and each Thanksgiving the students at West Winston School expressed their gratitude to "Uncle Joe" by presenting him with a live turkey.[11]

Long Lance showed Abe his scrapbooks. He explained that he had managed to obtain a complete secondary education. In the unsegregated Canadian army he had risen to become an officer. As a Plains Indian, his articles were published in the big magazines, and now he was being asked to write a book. The contrast between their lives could hardly have been greater. When he left Abe and returned to New York, Long Lance knew more clearly than ever that he could not go back to Winston-Salem.

In the summer of 1927, Long Lance returned again to Alberta to do his research in Calgary at the public library and consult some of the local Indians. To pay his expenses in crossing the continent, he first completed several sportswriting assignments. Earlier in the year, he had written an article for the Winnipeg *Tribune* on Gene Tunney, the ex-marine who in September, 1926, had outboxed a weary Jack Dempsey and won the world heavyweight crown. Before leaving New York, he covered the Sharkey-Maloney heavyweight fight at Yankee Stadium on Friday, May 20,[12] but that night the fight was of secondary importance.

That morning, *The Spirit of St. Louis* had lifted off a muddy runway at Roosevelt Field on Long Island bound for Le Bourget Airport near Paris. During one of the preliminary bouts, the fight announcer broke in to report that a ship three hundred miles off the Atlantic coast had sighted Charles Lindbergh's plane. He asked the crowd to pray for him. The response was immediate, and electrifying: as one, the thirty thousand hard-boiled fight fans stood, and bared and bowed their heads to pray for the aviator's safe passage over the ocean.

The next day, the first reports of Lindbergh's successful arrival in Paris reached the United States. In the next few weeks, there was a mass excitement and enthusiasm that upstaged even the Age of Ballyhoo itself. Millions identified with the pilot-hero, and Long Lance was one of them, for Lindbergh had won all the fame he wanted himself. The morning after the flight, the usually restrained *New York Times* devoted nearly the whole of its first five pages to the feat. Across the nation, newspapers consumed an extra twenty-five thousand tons of newsprint. The American press paid more attention to the voyage of a stunt flyer crossing the Atlantic alone (for that was the feat; Britain's Alcock and Brown already had flown from Newfoundland to Ireland in 1919) than to the Armistice in 1918 and to the abdication of the German Kaiser.[13] Lindbergh's heroics — his sudden rise to fame from obscurity, success against great odds, the story of how someone with determination and will could achieve just about anything, no matter who he was or where he came from — fascinated Long Lance, and must have encouraged him in his own struggle for fame and recognition.

Long Lance traveled to Calgary by train, paying his own way this time — the CPR had withdrawn his pass after the fracas at Banff the summer before. He brought with him his large trunk heavy with books, a wooden box containing his typewriter, and a suitcase. Finances, as always, were tight; fortunately, he managed to sell three major articles that summer. One was a reworked version of "My Trail Upward," which he sold to *McClure's* in July. He redid a Toronto *Star Weekly* article on the Sun Dance and sold it to

Good Housekeeping. The third article was a lively, well-written account on the Prince of Wales and other European aristocrats who had recently bought ranches in Alberta. It was titled "Princes Go West, But What of the Young Man Without Money?" It appeared in *McClure's* that November. The fees from the three articles covered his summer and fall expenses until his return to New York in December.

In Calgary, he took a room next to the Vaheys' home on 4th Avenue, where he last stayed in 1921 and 1922. It had been six years since he spent a full summer in Calgary, and much had changed. Many of his friends of the early 1920s had married and were starting families. Howard Kelly, still sports editor of the *Herald*, was studying for a law degree at the University of Alberta. Hugh Dann was well launched on a new career with the John Deere Plow Company, making frequent trips across North America.

Long Lance was left on his own for the first few weeks. He went for long walks, watched baseball games at Mewata Park and St. George's Island, and worked out often at the YMCA where he became good friends with Maurice Fidler. Fidler was a strong, husky man of twenty-one, and had been in Long Lance's boxing class at the YMCA in 1921 and 1922. During the summer of 1927, they met daily and boxed, wrestled and played handball. Fidler was perceptive and could see behind Long Lance's easy, happy manner. He found him a "warm-hearted, wistful, lonely man." He knew that he was sensitive and that the lingering discrimination took its toll. After a workout at the YMCA one day, Fidler and Long Lance walked over to Rosie Helmer's poolroom two blocks away, but Long Lance could not enter. Large signs on the poolroom walls declared NO INDIANS ALLOWED. As an Indian, Long Lance could not step into a tavern or buy liquor at the vendors.[14]

That summer, Long Lance drew closer to the local Indians, and tried to help Indian children in the area. Never one to carry a grudge, he long ago put his embarrassment at the Blackfoot Sun Dance behind him. Once a week, he visited the reserve at Gleichen, where he conducted boxing classes for the boys, always urging them to take pride in their race. Every so often he brought the boys to Calgary to let them practice in the gymnasium at the YMCA.[15]

In his book, Long Lance wanted to emphasize the proud history of the Plains Indian and to win tolerance and understanding for them. He worked on his manuscript all summer, writing most of it at the Vaheys' next door to his rooming house. He seemed always to be at the Vaheys' at mealtime, and the Vaheys' oldest daughter, Jean, devoted most of her summer to his project. She proofread and corrected his text, and kept a pot of strong coffee on the stove.[16] Long Lance still found the spirits friendly at the Vahey house.

Long Lance often told Fidler of the effort, self-discipline and concentration the book required. By his own admission, he was a slow writer. Once at the YMCA, he admitted to Fidler: "What I write is well-written, but it takes so long to get it out."

Fidler knew the area that Long Lance was describing in the book. His grandfather and two uncles had a ranch at Boundary Creek, four miles north of the Montana border and just southwest of the Blood Reserve. They had arrived in Alberta in 1883. When he spent the summer of 1917 at the ranch, Fidler had learned much about the history of the area. Once, after Long Lance asked him to review parts of the book, he asked Fidler what he thought of it. Fidler tried to be encouraging and supportive, but pointed out a discrepancy. His father had played minor league baseball and his grandfather had a fully operating ranch in the area that Long Lance described in his manuscript as Indian and buffalo country in the 1890s. Without explaining why, Long Lance simply told him that this fictional touch was necessary for the book. Fidler let it go at that, but it troubled him.[17]

Long Lance incorporated many of his Indian interviews of the early 1920s into the manuscript, along with several of his published stories, such as those about Chief Carry-the-Kettle and Almighty Voice. He also used information supplied by his "brother," Mike Eagle Speaker. And, when it served his purpose, he did not hesitate to invent.

In the early, stronger chapters of *Long Lance*, Long

Lance relied heavily on what he learned from Mike Eagle
Speaker. Since their first meeting at St. Paul's mission in
August of 1920, Long Lance had kept in touch with the
young Blood Indian. When Mike left the reserve to study at
Claresholm Agricultural College in 1922, Long Lance
encouraged him, sending him letters as he traveled across
Canada writing for the western dailies. In 1923, he spent a
weekend with Mike at the school, which was sixty miles
south of Calgary. They met again after their adoption as
brothers at Macleod in 1924. When Mike came up to Calgary
in 1926 to enter the rodeo events at the Stampede, he saw
Long Lance, and in the summer of 1927, Long Lance invited
him to Calgary.[18]

Mike respected Long Lance. He looked up to him as a
great warrior, an Indian hero in the Great War, and also as
someone like himself who left his tribe to acquire a white
man's education. Blood brotherhood in Plains Indian society
meant a perfect sharing, and when Long Lance asked about
the Bloods' customs, Mike eagerly told him all that he could.

Mike's great-grandmother had raised him after the death
of his mother and grandmother. She was born in the 1820s,
half a century before the buffalo disappeared. In 1914,
before Mike was sent to St. Paul's Mission School at the age
of ten, she had told him and his brothers all that she knew of
the Blood ceremonies and culture. Their father, Eagle
Speaker, who had trained under some of the best-known
medicine men in the Blackfoot Confederacy, also taught him
much. Mike was a curious student, a keen observer, and
during his childhood many of the old customs were still
practiced. Everyone had horses and the travois was still
used. Few adult Bloods in the years before World War I
could speak English, and few had joined the Christian
church.

Mike Eagle Speaker and Long Lance spent two weeks
together in the summer of 1927. They stayed in Calgary for a
week, in Banff for four days, then traveled to Golden, just
across the Alberta border into British Columbia, where
they lingered another four days. Long Lance questioned
Mike on the Blood tribal dress, the Blackfoot language and

tribal customs, and Mike soon realized that Long Lance really knew very little.

Long Lance's opening chapter began with an arresting scene: "The first thing in my life that I can remember is the exciting aftermath of an Indian fight in northern Montana. My mother was crying and running about with me in my moss bag-carrier on her back. I remember the scene as though it were yesterday, yet I was barely a year old. . . ." He remembered that his mother's hand was bleeding, and years later, he wrote, his aunt confirmed this "startling impression."

> One day, when I had grown into boyhood, I asked my aunt about it. I described the scene to her and told her the position in which she was standing in relation to the pony, where my mother was standing and how she handed me to her; I gave her a word-picture of the whole circumstance, as it was so indelibly inscribed on my memory. As I talked, I could see my aunt's features taking on a gradual look of wonderment. And when I was through, she looked at me in great surprise and exclaimed:
> "Can you remember that! You were only fourteen months old then. It was when your uncle, Iron Blanket, was killed in a fight with the Crows—and your mother had cut off one of her fingers in mourning for him, as the women used to do in those days."

After that, Long Lance writes that he relapsed "into the mystic sleep of infancy again" until he was four, from which age he could remember things distinctly. The colors he remembers from those early years were "a dull, deep bluish gray."

> Everything I saw was tinted with this mystic grayness. It represented danger, mystery, and distance. We were not yet entirely at peace with our ancient enemies, the Crows, the Assiniboines, the Sioux, and the Crees; and stories of a new peril which might spell our doom—the White Man—were being whispered about our camp fires. Danger lurked every-where, even in the animals from which we secured our food. [19]

Having drawn the reader in, Long Lance then makes
Mike Eagle Speaker's childhood his own, pushing it back into
the late nineteenth century and grafting onto it stories that
he had collected from the old Plains Indians. He did a skillful
job of it.

Early in the book, Long Lance explains how Indian
children were taught to ride horses soon after they learned
to walk. He relates how the fathers hardened their sons to
make them "brave and stoical, and good and courageous
fighters." Every morning, summer and winter, they were
taken down to the river for a plunge in an icy stream or a roll
in the snow. From their mothers, they learned the moral
teachings of the tribe. Lying was severely punished. "We
had a legend for everything that was good, and the more we
youngsters lived up to the legends which our mothers told
us, the more highly respected we were in the tribe."

All this was accurate, and the book manages a strong and
legitimate Indian flavor. Short references to aspects of
Plains Indian culture keep appearing, such as the Indians'
ancient courtesy of not interrupting anyone while he is
talking, and their respect for old people "so deeply bred into
us that to this day I have not the courage to dispute the word
of an old person."[20] Mike Eagle Speaker's finest reminiscences are scattered in the book like raisins in the dough, all
carefully selected by a craftsman who knew how to use
anecdotes.

When he went beyond Mike's reminiscences, it was
always to make a point. While among the Lillooet Indians in
British Columbia in June, 1922, Long Lance heard of a
fascinating whipping custom. To toughen the children's
bodies, the men whipped them each morning with fir
branches. Anxious to emphasize the hardiness of Blackfoot
youth, Long Lance simply added this practice as another
aspect of Blackfoot culture, even though it had never
occurred among the Bloods.[21] Nor did they burn dry fir
needles on the backs of their hands to see who could endure
the torture the longest.[22] Still, the essence of what he wrote
was true: the Blackfoot insisted on a harsh, rigorous up-

bringing to make warriors of their sons and to make them tough enough to withstand the elements.

Long Lance relayed numerous, colorful incidents from tribal life, some of which he heard from the elders, some he had read and some he made up. He described the Indians' domestic life, the Sun Dance, the awesome powers of the medicine men, and the band's desperate search for the vanishing buffalo. A book reviewer commented: "Inevitably one is reminded of Hiawatha and Fenimore Cooper's adventure tales... startling accounts of dances, rites, famous medicine men of the past, battles, pony raids, great hunting expeditions in the Rockies—all told with verve and remembered with clarity." [23]

Long Lance also borrowed from his own childhood. Throughout the manuscript of *Long Lance*, his mother, not his father, is the dominant figure. In North Carolina, it was his mother who had attended church every Sunday and who insisted on a strict religious atmosphere in the home. There is an element of truth in the statement that his Blackfoot mother "trained us to live right." [24]

After wild adventures in the Rockies, where his band hunted mountain sheep and goats and captured a large herd of wild horses, they returned to the plains only to find that their fellow tribesmen had signed treaties with the governments of the United States and Canada, and "were living on reservations and getting along well." Under Crowfoot, their tribal leader, members of the last roving Blackfoot band decided it was time to lay down their arms, take up their reserves, and send their children to the missionaries' schools "that they might learn to work with their hands and become as white men." [25]

Our day as free rovers of the open plains had ended. A few years later we boys were in mission schools, learning our ABC's and how to hoe with our hands. How this shamed us: to have to work like women, when we had thought that we were going to be warriors and hunters like our forefathers. This manual labor so humiliated us that whenever we looked up and saw any of our old warriors passing the school, we would lay down our hoes and stand still until they had passed.[26]

Long Lance's conclusion, however poignant and evocative, was historically inaccurate. Crowfoot was not living "on that bright day in 1897."[27] He had died in 1890. Nor could the Blackfoot band have been roaming freely over the prairies and into the Rockies in the mid-1890s, as they had made treaty in 1877 and were settled on their reserves in the early 1880s.

Long Lance completed the first draft by late November, then checked with Canon Middleton some of the spellings of Blackfoot words before heading back to New York. Three more weeks of work there, and the final draft was ready.[28] The day after he submitted the manuscript, it was being circulated around the office, page by page, avidly read by half a dozen people at once.[29] After final editing, the book was printed to be ready for August and the fall book trade. Cosmopolitan liked the book so much it decided on a first run of ten thousand copies instead of the usual three thousand.[30]

Long Lance dedicated the book to Canon Middleton and Commissioner Graham, the inclusion of the latter a sign of his growing cynicism. The inscription reads: "Dedicated to the two White Men who have guided and encouraged me most since I have taken a place in civilization." To be safer still, he included a thank you to Duncan Campbell Scott, the Deputy Superintendent of Indian Affairs in Ottawa, whom he termed "a friend of the Indian." He then signed it, two thousand miles from the site:

BUFFALO CHILD LONG LANCE
Blood Indian Reservation
Cardston, Alberta
July 1, 1928

When it was published in August, 1928, the international press praised the book extravagantly. The Philadelphia *Public Ledger* called it "a gorgeous saga of the Indian race."

From the south, the New Orleans *Times-Picayune* hailed it
as "by all odds the most important Americana offered this
year." In Britain, the *New Statesman* wrote: "This book
rings true; no outsider could explain so clearly how the
Indians felt. . . ." Ernest Thompson Seton, the distinguished naturalist and student of the North American
Indian, called the book "one of the best pictures ever offered
of the old-time Indian at his best."[31] Dr. Paul Radin, the
well-known anthropologist, went even further, giving it his
academic stamp of approval in a review in the New York
Herald Tribune.[32] A year earlier, Dr. Radin had published
The Story of the American Indian, an exhaustive study of
all the major native groups in the United States. Dr. Radin
received his doctorate in anthropology from Columbia University in 1911, and devoted his life to the study of what was
then called "primitive man." For years, he worked with the
Winnebago tribe, a small Siouan-speaking group in the Midwest, publishing ten good-sized monographs and several
articles about them.

In his review of *Long Lance*, Dr. Radin began by commenting on the tragedy that so few biographies and
autobiographies existed of the first Americans. One was
forced to learn about them, he wrote, from works written by
sophisticated Europeans and Americans "who, no matter
how detailed may be their knowledge, can never properly
understand the workings of a society so utterly alien to them
as is that of so-called primitive man." For this reason, he
welcomed the appearance of such an "authentic" autobiography. He praised the book as an "unusually faithful account
of his childhood and early manhood. . . . I cannot think of any
work that could act as a better corrective of the ridiculous
notions still prevailing about the Indians than this autobiography of Long Lance."

Dr. Radin, however, expressed one reservation. While
Buffalo Child had described the "external side of the Blackfoot culture" with "remarkable realism," the anthropologist
felt that he had done very little to illuminate the Indian
mind, since he "consistently refuses to reveal much about his

inner self." He forgave this, though, explaining that in fact it serves to establish the book's authenticity, for "no Indian talks much about himself."

Long Lance was a success and sold well across North America and Europe. The first run nearly sold out by the end of 1928, and Cosmopolitan ordered a second printing. In England, a publisher printed a special British edition, and in 1929 German and Dutch translations appeared.[33] Long Lance was about to become one of the most famous Indians of his day.

14

PARK AVENUE

IN JANUARY, 1928, in the Crystal Room of the Ritz Hotel in New York, Ray Long gave a luncheon to honor Emil Ludwig, whose popular biography *Napoleon* had been riding the best-seller lists for nearly a year. As Ray Long's latest prodigy, Long Lance was a special guest at the luncheon. Sipping a cocktail before the luncheon, Long Lance heard a drawling voice behind him. "Chief Long Lance, I've been wanting to meet you for a mighty long time." He turned to find that the voice belonged to Irvin S. Cobb, the writer and humorist, then at the height of his fame.

"Well," Long Lance replied, "you don't have to tell me who you are."

Long, ever the opportunist, rushed over and said to Long Lance: "Chief, why don't you make Irvin write a foreword for your book?"

Cobb puffed on his cigar. "I'd be delighted," he said.

The deal was made on the spot. [1]

Over the next few months, Long Lance and Cobb saw a good deal of each other. Cobb and his wife, Laura, invited Long Lance to their attractive white house at East Hampton, on the eastern tip of Long Island. It was a pretty two-storey home with green shutters, festooned in summer with rambler roses. [2]

Cobb and Long Lance were exact opposites. Cobb liked to

hunt and fish, but that was the extent of his sporting life. He was a bulky man with heavy jowls and a triple chin. He loved to eat and it showed, but he made light of it, once describing himself as "an ugly-faced old man, with beetled brows and a big 'bay' window."[3] Thanks to his amusing tales of Judge Priest, a wise old southern judge fond of mint juleps and helping innocents in trouble, Cobb had became the most widely read and highest paid short-story writer in America.[4] He had come a long way from his first job as a reporter on the Paducah *Daily News*.

Cobb never forgot his Kentucky roots, and Judge Priest always described the South in the most affectionate terms. His father had been a Confederate army veteran, and Irvin himself had proudly joined and become a colonel in the United Confederates organization, always championing the cause of the soldiers who marched in gray. Cobb loved to tell "darkie" stories. His friend Bob Davis, of the New York *Sun*, once wrote that from 1918 to 1928 he had listened four or five hundred times to Cobb's "one hundred Southern Ethiopian classics."[5] Cobb's first novel was about Judge Priest's servant, Jefferson Exodus Poindexter, or as Jeff called himself on a visit to Harlem, "Col. J. Exeter Poindexter, Esq. (the 'Col.' standing for 'colored')." Still, Cobb was fascinated by the North American Indian. Once, in Oklahoma, a magazine had reported that he "is said to have declared himself to have a small strain of aboriginal blood."[6]

Since his boyhood in Kentucky, Cobb had gathered Indian artifacts. He decorated his study with Navaho rugs, Plains Indian war bonnets and Flathead buffalo spears. One of his most prized possessions was a goodluck necklace worn by Chief Joseph of the Nez Percé, whose famous retreat from the U.S. Army in 1877 General W.T. Sherman called one of the finest pieces of military strategy he had ever known. Cobb loved Indian legends and traditions. For years, he studied their sign language and had mastered much of it. In 1925, a band of South Peigans in Montana (where they are known as "Blackfeet") formally adopted him and humor- ously named the roly-poly Kentuckian "Piitaohpikis," or "Eagle Ribs."[7]

Long Lance endured Cobb's darkie stories, and Cobb never suspected Long Lance was an impostor. Instead, in an enthusiastic foreword to Long Lance's book, Cobb praised the book and the author in the fullest terms, telling of how he emerged from the war "as a captain of infantry, his body covered with wounds and his breast glittering with medals bestowed for high conduct and gallantry." Again, it was Long Lance who provided Cobb with all the details.

The foreword continues:

> ... sinking his own engaging personality, his own individual
> achievements into the background, he depicts graphic phases
> of a life which has altogether vanished, of a race which rapidly
> is vanishing. I know of no man better fitted than Chief Long
> Lance to write a true book about the true American Indian,
> and I know of no book on the subject which better reveals the
> spirit of the Indian in the years that are gone and the spirit of
> times the like of which will never be seen again.
>
> I claim there is authentic history in these pages and verity
> and most of all a power to describe in English words the
> thoughts, the instincts, the events which originally were
> framed in a native language.
>
> And I claim the white man will owe him a debt for this work
> of his and that his people the Indians already owe him a debt
> for having performed it. [8]

Several days after meeting Cobb at the luncheon at the Ritz, Long Lance attended a glittering cocktail party at Cobb's Park Avenue apartment. Long Lance had invested in a finely tailored $180 tuxedo, one that showed his athletic body to advantage. [9] The men arrived in full evening dress and the women in stylish, long-waisted gowns with strings of pearls circling their necks. Long Lance reveled in the chitchat, telling the guests stories of the Navaho, the Sioux and the Cree in his soft, cultured voice. When he referred to "my people," his voice took on a sad, arresting tone. One bejeweled matron asked Long Lance if he could demonstrate the Indian sign language. Graciously, he consented.

For spring, Long Lance made rapid movements with his

hands, suggesting rain, then, with a quick, upward thrust of his hand, he indicated the regenerative force of the land in spring. With long, curving movements he imitated summer's gentle winds, and with more hand gestures he made the sun set in fall and snow flakes dance in winter. He soon attracted a considerable audience and told how the Indian languages were descriptive and figurative. [10] "The Indian calls a looking glass, 'He peeped into the water and saw himself.' That comes from the old days when they would bend over water and see themselves. . . . " [11]

He resurrected all the material he used on the lecture circuit, and the Indian stories were not only a welcome relief from the usual cocktail party small talk, but also exactly what the rich and powerful whites wanted to hear about the noble red man. He explained that Indians had no "curse" words, and that the worst thing one Indian could say to another was to call him a "bad dog." He told them that Indians had no words for "How do you do?" or "Goodbye." Instead, he explained, "When we enter another's home, we just grunt and sit down. We take it for granted. When we leave we just 'Huh.' That is all." [12] He told of how in the old days the elderly never died of disease and their teeth never fell out, but after eating the white man's bread they died of diseases and their teeth rotted. [13] And he told how Indians acquired their names. "An Indian always has more than one name," he said. "The first name is given when he is born. Some circumstance will be noted and that determines his name. When he gets to be about six years old his playmates will give him another name, 'Crazy Horse,' 'Lazy Dog' — something like that. That name will stick until he is eighteen, and then he has to do something to earn a real name. When they were still fighting, he had to go out on an exploit and do some brave act; then they would change his name perhaps to 'Sheet Lightning' or 'Uses-Both-Arms.' These names are like medals in the army, like decorations, and that is why an old Indian will never tell you his name. If you ask him his name, he will turn to some third person to answer, because he does not want to brag." [14]

Irvin Cobb was showing off Long Lance, who proved to be

the hit of the party. During the evening one of the ladies remarked to her companion: "Isn't it wonderful that a dark-skinned person can look so distinguished?"[15]

Dark-skinned persons were a rare sight at Park Avenue parties in 1928. By the late twenties, blacks constituted ten per cent of Manhattan's population, and Harlem was known as the "Negro Capital of the World." When the blacks moved in, the whites sold their homes and moved further out. Many New York hotels, restaurants and theaters refused blacks admission, and even some of the New York churches denied them membership.[16]

The North American Indians, whether dark-skinned or copper-skinned, were not in that category. There was something of the woods and range and mountains about them, something of America's early history. There was also a certain shame and guilt felt by these affluent, upper-class Americans about the plight of the Indian, whose land was stolen, whose numbers were receding to the vanishing point and who posed no threat to real estate values. What little was known about the Indian came from such romantic treatments as Longfellow's *Hiawatha* and the works of James Fenimore Cooper.

The audiences Long Lance spoke to at the cocktail parties and on the lecture circuit were aware of their own shallow roots. Men such as Irvin Cobb and Ray Long had come from small towns and second-, third-, perhaps fourth- and occasionally fifth-generation immigrant families. But what were one hundred or two hundred years compared to thousands —to "time immemorial"?

Long Lance knew what they wanted to hear and he delivered. He acted the modern noble savage, the twentieth-century Hiawatha. He talked plainly and directly, and in reply to any question he always looked the questioner straight in the eye.[17] To the women crowded around him, he seemed the embodiment of all that was free and natural, and vaguely dangerous.

Long Lance stopped worrying about being unmasked and basked in the adulation. He discussed with confidence many subjects, even chromatic aberrations. When asked about mixed marriages and the physical appearance of the children from such a relationship, he explained that white couples might have a black baby because of "a Negro-element a generation ago." But he quickly added that this never happens to those of distant Indian ancestry. "After the fourth generation of intermarriage between white and Indian, all Indian features disappear," he said. There are no "throwbacks."[18]

Cobb helped to launch Long Lance socially in New York. He made valuable contacts at the party and at Cobb's house on Long Island and more dinner invitations arrived for the Chief. Once, at another party at the Ritz Hotel, he met Natacha Rambova, the wife of the late Rudolph Valentino. Without hesitation, Long Lance asked her to dance, and Natacha, wearing a blood-red dress with a red turban around her head, accepted. They fox-trotted around the floor as the orchestra played "The Sheik of Araby," the song Rudolph Valentino inspired.[19] To onlookers, Long Lance looked like a sepia version of the Latin lover himself.[20]

There were many other women. That winter, Long Lance dated Mildred McCoy, the actress, and Vivian Hart, the light-opera singer.[21] So successful was he with women that Cobb nicknamed him "the Beau Brummell of Broadway."[22] He became close friends with Princess Alexandra, the ex-wife of Prince August-Wilhelm, the fourth son of the German Kaiser, whom she divorced after the war. In 1926, the red-headed princess had left Europe with her second husband, a retired German naval officer, to earn her living as a painter in New York. Princess Alexandra later drew an appealing sketch of Long Lance in his Broadway tribal costume: top hat and tails.[23]

Long Lance's name inevitably surfaced in the newspapers. O.O. McIntyre, who wrote a chatty and informal column called "New York Day by Day," spotted him first. He wrote on May 20, 1928: "A social lion of the season is an Indian—Buffalo Chief Long Lance, who has been invited everywhere." McIntyre described him as "straight as an arrow, with smoothly brushed black hair, broad shoulders and waspish waist. . . . " He called him an intellectual, who had "graduated from three universities." Across the United States, in more than three hundred newspapers, some seven million Americans read of "Buffalo Chief," who, in the words of the gossip columnist, had become "a social wow."[24]

In mid-January, 1928, Long Lance visited West Point. Through Frazier Hunt, a senior editor at *Cosmopolitan*, he had met Lieutenant Bonner Fellers, a West Point English instructor, and his wife, Dorothy. Lieutenant Fellers invited Long Lance to speak to his classes.[25]

Long Lance wrote to his friend Howard Kelly in Calgary to tell him about the visit to the military academy, and he included in his letter the somewhat stilted remarks of a young cadet named W.D. Moore, who obviously had fallen under Long Lance's spell. "We saw in him the man developed by proper training from a people we consider far inferior," Cadet Moore said. "He was built like an athlete; carried himself like a soldier. His lectures showed a brilliant mind for research. His clothes betrayed a fine taste, and his smooth, regular flow of language showed him a master of our language. The ease with which he took hold of his audience showed leadership. So, in this civilized savage we see an athlete, soldier, scholar and leader. He is wholly a man."

The remarks sound almost too flattering, too much of what Long Lance's own self-portrait might have been. Indeed, they were, for an examination of the records reveals that no cadet named W.D. Moore ever attended West Point.[26] Long Lance had, unnecessarily it seems, invented him. In the same letter to Kelly, Long Lance told of a practical joke he took part in on his visit to West Point. It involved "a very beautiful girl about twenty, married to an 'old major' about thirty-seven."

For some reason or other, none of the other officers nor their wives like this particular Major very much. And since the young wife had been looking at my picture in one of the officers' suites and asking his wife to introduce us when I came up, every damned officer and his wife on the Post had conspired to get her over to their big party for me, alone. Well, it was the funniest thing you ever saw. They framed the Major

with a lot of examination papers, and about four of their wives
went over to their [the major and his wife's] home and, only as
women can do, managed to get her over. Then my host, a
captain, said: "Now, Josephine will be there by the time we
arrive; she's crazy to meet you, and don't be afraid to give her a
thrill. That's what she's looking for; that damned husband of
hers is a dead old stick; so as soon as the party gets started,
get her out into the kitchen and rub her up a little; wait until
you see her—she's a beaut."

When we got back to his apartment in the officers' quarters,
sure enough, I got a glance of the queen sitting in the drawing
room. She was so damned good-looking that I went into the
bathroom with the Captain to primp up a bit. And, before I
knew it, here she was in the bathroom, saying, "I couldn't wait
for you to come in." Oh, boy, what a beauty she was—exactly
like Jean Gardiner—only her eyes were more beautiful than
any I ever saw. A throbbing knock-out! She is what they call
"an Army girl"; that is, she is the daughter of a General and
was born in the army and has lived all over the world. She is
quite a flash in Washington society, where she goes every two
weeks for a social whirl—and she neither drinks nor smokes.
What I enjoyed about the whole thing was that it was open and
above board and everybody was a party to our little flirtation.
I am glad that I have had the unpleasant experiences that I
have; for now I can play up to a little innocent frame-up like
this without any thoughts of allowing it to go too far. To the
evident joy of everyone present, we had many quiet little
moments in the kitchen, and it was all very nice. I think
everyone of the officers and their wives was much pleased with
the way I conducted myself; though we were all drinking, and
now the whole post, that is, our big circle, refers to her as my
"Sweetheart." As I said, Howard, thank goodness, I know
what it is all about now; this married proposition, and I would
never think of going any further than playing just a little
before all the gang. . . . [27]

Back in New York, Long Lance continued to impress the
interviewers, among them Gladys Baker, the New York
correspondent for the *News-Age-Herald* of Birmingham,

Alabama, which called itself "the South's Greatest Newspaper." After *Long Lance* was published in the fall of 1928, Baker met the author in a small French restaurant on Eighth Avenue. The former debutante from Jacksonville, Florida, left the interview captivated by the dark, handsome stranger. In her article, she described Long Lance as "distinguished looking," and added for her Alabama readers the supreme compliment: "Were it not for his straight black hair, which is cut close to his head, and his skin, which is not red but more the color of ivory-tone parchment, he might be taken for a Wall Street broker." [28]

Long Lance confided very little to his friends in his many letters, but he methodically listed all his social successes. In June, 1928, he wrote to Howard Kelly in Calgary to tell him about the fabulous house parties he attended on Long Island. "You know the kind we've often seen in the movies but never in practice," he wrote. "Well, I can tell you now that they exist." He rattled off the same superficial letter to Kelly, Canon Middleton and the Fellers, telling of an evening at Irvin Cobb's, a lunch with celebrities in downtown Manhattan, the dinner party where he met Princess Alexandra, a weekend trip to Washington, D.C. [29]

By the fall of 1929, Long Lance was a celebrity in good standing himself and others might now boast of being at a party that he attended. He gave out opinions on everything from genetics to presidential politics. When reporters asked him about the presidential campaign building up, Long Lance urged all the chiefs of all the tribes to support the Republican ticket of Herbert Hoover and Senator Curtis of Kansas. Curtis's grandmother, after all, was one-half Kaw Indian. (The federal franchise had been extended to all American Indians in 1924. [30])

Long Lance eagerly accepted speaking invitations, which paid him honorariums of $100 per lecture, a not inconsiderable sum at a time when the average annual income was less than $1500. [31] In early October, he returned to Columbus, Ohio, to speak to the Chamber of Commerce, and again at Logan Park on Ohio History Day. From there he went to Cleveland to speak at the Halle Brothers Book Fair. At the end of the month, he was in Utah, speaking in Salt Lake City to the Bonneville Club, composed of four hundred of the state's most influential businessmen. [32]

Before leaving Ohio, he stopped in Akron at the request of the B.F. Goodrich Company. The Goodrich people wanted Long Lance to design and then endorse an improved canvas running shoe. He liked the idea and brought with him a pair of old moccasins, suggesting that Goodrich make up an experimental pair of running shoes modeled on them. When the shoes were ready, Long Lance tested them. In the words of a Goodrich publicist: ". . . not only did every bit of canvas, every stitch of thread, every ounce of rubber mean something to him, but he was able to explain it so that white men could understand." [33]

By the late 1920s it is apparent that Long Lance, after years of pasting stories and pictures into his scrapbooks, was beginning to believe his own press clippings and to regard himself in the same heroic terms as others. His smile was not as easy, or as genuine, and he began to take himself too seriously. In a manuscript he prepared in 1928, he called himself "a spokesman for the Indians of America" for the first time. [34]

Long Lance's other Indian stories were written to entertain, but this one had anger and fire in it. At the time, most Americans assumed that the Indians in the West were doing well, making progress, but Long Lance wrote that they actually were doing very badly—starving, in fact. The Bureau of Indian Affairs held a billion dollars in an Indian trust fund, money the tribes made through land sales, but Long Lance said the fund was not being used "to feed the starving stomachs of our old people who bore the brunt of this terrible thing that civilization has done. . . ."

This was the generation, he wrote, that had seen the white pioneers "surge across the West, killing their game, raping their women, giving them diseases that they had never heard of, picking fights with them and trading bad liquor for their buffalo robes." And the government itself had interfered, and "by trickery, promises and presents. . . bribed the Indians into signing away their rights to their reservations." So much for the "noble savage." Long Lance's attack on the white-administered Bureau of Indian Affairs is clear and direct. Few Americans, he said, realized the enormous powers the Bureau exercised:

> ...that the Bureau of Indian Affairs still controls both their person and their property; that the Indian tribes have no say as to whether their funds shall be used to support the government Bureau or not; that they can be declared mentally incompetent by the Bureau without resort to civil court; that the heirs of an Indian, even his own brother, can not administer his estate except through the approval of the Bureau; that the Indian Bureau can destroy the will of an Indian without having to show cause to any court.

Long Lance called for a reorganization of the Indian Bureau and the laws governing the Indian.[35]

It was all true. Charles Burke, Commissioner of the Bureau of Indian Affairs, recognized the evils of the system himself. In 1924 he told a reporter, "We are not even yet being square with the Indians. We are stealing land from some of them, depriving some of them of the water without which they must starve, making drunkards and loafers of others."[36] Burke tried to stop the abuses, but his critics charged that he had failed to do enough. He was the bureaucrat most easily vilified, the one with the highest profile, but the Bureau had by this time grown to be a huge, headless monster, and any criticism of an individual was useless and probably unfair.[37]

The reformers' attacks increased when the Meriam Report came out. In February, 1928, Lewis Meriam and his associates of the Institute of Government Research published a detailed study of American Indian Policy called *The Problem of Indian Administration*. It provided the first comprehensive description of what had happened to the Indians since the Indian wars ended. In the West, investigators reported that living conditions were wretched. General death and infant mortality rates were shamefully high. Entire communities suffered from trachoma, an eye disease resulting in blindness. Tuberculosis crippled and maimed, when it did not kill outright. Reservation housing was substandard. Hunger was the common lot. The Meriam Report concluded that unless drastic measures were taken immediately, the Indian in the United States appeared to be on the verge of extinction.[38]

Long Lance's outspoken manuscript never was published, and the fault must lie with the Cosmopolitan Book Corporation. Unwittingly, the corporation set in motion an investigation of Long Lance's origins, when, as a gesture of courtesy, it sent a complimentary advance copy of *Long Lance* to Commissioner Burke. An accompanying letter, dated August 3, 1928, read:

Dear Mr. Burke:
Chief Long Lance recently submitted a manuscript for a book that has the makings of a standard work. We are publishing it under the title of "Long Lance."[39]

The emotional reaction of those who have read it is enthusiastically favorable. Irvin S. Cobb has dramatically expressed this feeling in a foreword to the book.

Under separate cover we are sending you an advance copy. It would interest us very much to know what you think of "Long Lance."[39]

It was a straightforward and simple request, which Commissioner Burke decided to try to satisfy, but first he wanted to learn more about the distinguished author who had attended the Bureau's school at Carlisle and West Point.

On August 29, he contacted Major General Wahl, Adjutant General at the War Department, concerning Long Lance's record at West Point. Back came the surprising reply, dated August 31, that "Mr. Long-Lance" had failed the competitive examination. Burke decided to probe deeper, suspecting that the fraud might be greater. He sent off more letters in September, all of them asking, in different ways: Who is Long Lance?

By late November, Commissioner Burke had the evidence before him. Cobb, in his foreword to *Long Lance*, said

that the author was a Chief of the "Northern Blackfeet." On
October 4, Commissioner Graham wrote from Canada that
"this designation is only conferred on him in an honorary
capacity." Long Lance claimed to be a Blackfoot in his book,
but on October 7 another letter from Canada arrived, this
one from Percy Little Dog, the interpreter for the Blood
Indian Council:

> I am pleased to inform you, that we never saw or heard a thing
> about "Buffalo Child Long Lance" until the winter of 1922,
> when he attended the annual re-union of "The Old Boys and
> Girls" Association of the St. Paul's School, Blood Reserve. He
> was our guest, and there was given the name of Buffalo Child,
> by one of the older members of the tribe. He is not a Blood
> Indian, and has no tribal rights on the Reserve. We have heard
> he was a Cherokee Indian, but do not know definitely who he is
> and where he came from.

Little Dog's letter carried considerable weight with
Burke, who had met the Blood spokesman in the fall of 1927.
The tall, forty-four-year-old Plains Indian had been part of a
party of thirty-five Blackfoot Indians who toured seventy
cities in the United States as guests of the Great Northern
Railroad. In full regalia they took part in the Centennial
Railway Exhibition in Baltimore, parading every day. In
New York, Percy Little Dog initiated Mayor Jimmy Walker
into the Blood tribe, giving him the name "Many Rider" and
painting his face with war paint. In Washington, D.C., he
met Commissioner Burke, and in perfect English he laid
before him the Canadian Blackfoot claim for their share of
the sixty-two-million-acre lease in Yellowstone, Montana,
which by the Treaty of 1855 belonged to the Blackfoot Confederacy. [40]
Canon Middleton also wrote to the Bureau of Indian
Affairs, and the letter, dated October 23, said that Long
Lance was "a full-blooded Cherokee Indian, he received his
first education at a Reservation Boarding School in
Oklahoma, from there he went to Carlisle, and then pro-
ceeded to St. John's Mil. Academy, Manlius, N.Y." Other

letters from Oscar Lipps, a former Superintendent at Carlisle, and James Henderson, one of his former teachers, confirmed that Long Lance, or "Sylvester Long," had attended the Indian school as a Cherokee.

By the end of November, Commissioner Burke finally had enough information to reply to the Cosmopolitan Book Corporation. He wrote simply:

Gentlemen:
Through your courtesy receipt is acknowledged of a publication of fiction entitled "Long Lance," for which please accept thanks.
    This book is very interesting and quite readable.

Sincerely yours,
Chas. H. Burke
Commissioner

He said no more, but by that one phrase, "a publication of fiction," indicated that the book that had been praised to the skies by critics and by the Cosmopolitan Book Corporation was not authentic. The corporation had encouraged Long Lance to write another book,[41] but it never appeared. Nor did Ray Long ever again publish any of Long Lance's articles in *Cosmopolitan*. It was probably Commissioner Burke's short but devastating reply that ended Long's interest in Long Lance.

When Long Lance returned to New York at the end of October, he found dead leaves on the sidewalks and the grass in Central Park turned from a lush green to a drab brown and yellow. He must have been aware of the investigation into his past, and feared the worst. There is evidence that Canon Middleton wrote to him, enclosing the letter from the Bureau,[42] and Commissioner Graham in Regina also may have corresponded with him on the matter of Burke's inquiries.

Long Lance decided to flee, and he had a ready excuse. A few days after he returned to New York, he was approached to co-star in a silent film being made in northern Canada. He bought some heavy woolen shirts, a parka, some work boots, and in a day he was gone.[43] Two days later he was five hundred miles north of New York on Lake Temiskaming on the border of northern Ontario and Quebec. Once there, Long Lance filed away his article on the Bureau of Indian Affairs and hoped that the results of the inquiry would not unmask and destroy him. He knew he could not risk antagonizing the Bureau now, and he knew that if he wanted to carry on the charade, he would have to concoct a new and convincing explanation of his origins.

15

"THE SILENT ENEMY"

I T WAS DOUGLAS BURDEN, a young naturalist and explorer, who selected Long Lance to star in his film, *The Silent Enemy*. He first thought of making the film in 1927, after seeing the Meriam C. Cooper – Ernest Schoedsack film *Chang*, a documentary that depicted a Thai family's struggle for survival in the jungles of southeast Asia. It was shot four hundred miles north of Bangkok and included hundreds of extraordinary pictures of leopards, man-eating tigers and, in the final scene, a herd of stampeding elephants.

For years Burden had objected to Hollywood's inaccurate and demeaning portrayal of the Indian as a wicked savage of the plains. He knew the reality was different and wanted to record it on film before both the Indian and the wilderness vanished. In 1908, when he was nine years old, he camped with his father in northern Canada and came to admire the Ojibwa (Chippewa) Indians' mastery of the woods.[1]

"With an Indian you tend to be silent — you speak softly, if at all," he said. "You become increasingly sensitive to your surroundings, and as a result you find yourself endlessly listening to what the forest has to say."[2] In *The Silent Enemy* he hoped to show the Indians and their traditions and customs before the coming of the white man, and he wanted to film the wildlife in northern Canada the way Cooper and Schoedsack had done in Thailand.

164

By 1927, when he was twenty-nine, Burden was an experienced world traveler. After graduating from Harvard in 1922, he left on a round-the-world tour, which included hunting on the Mongolian border, in the jungles of Annam and in the high Himalayas. Before that, in the summer of 1921, he had mined diamonds in Brazil, and had spent 1924 looking for a lost silver mine in Central America. In 1926, the American Museum of Natural History sent Burden to the isolated island of Komodo in the Dutch East Indies (now Indonesia), and there he obtained thirteen specimens of the largest lizards in the world, capturing two alive for the Bronx Zoo.

For the film's legal counsel, Burden enlisted William Chanler, a friend from Harvard. Chanler worked in a New York law firm, but the idea of making *The Silent Enemy* excited him, and he asked for and was given a leave of absence. Burden and Chanler then arranged the financing with friends and private investors, eventually bringing the script to Jesse Lasky of Paramount, who agreed to distribute the independently produced film when it was completed.[3]

Burden, with Lasky's backing, managed to get enough money to start work on the film, and he began by reading all he could on northern Canada and the Indians who lived off the land before the whites arrived. He read Francis Parkman's histories of early Canada, then examined each of the seventy-two volumes of the R.G. Thwaites edition of the *Jesuit Relations*, the records of the travels and explorations of the Jesuit missionaries in what was then New France. For more detail, he studied Samuel Hearne's graphic account, first published in 1795, of his travels across the desolate Barrenlands between Hudson Bay and the Arctic Ocean.[4]

Once he had formulated a rough outline of *The Silent Enemy*, Burden looked for a capable director. He approached H.P. Carver, who had been for five years general manager of Cosmopolitan Productions, owned by William Randolph Hearst. Carver, who had already directed a film on Indians, was an excellent choice. In Burden's words: "He was somebody you could get along with; he enjoyed being away out in the wilderness. He was very fond of these people, so he could get a lot out of them."[5]

During the summer of 1928, Burden and Carver traveled by train and canoe throughout northeastern Ontario and northwestern Quebec, scouting locations and seeking out photogenic and cooperative Ojibwa. The Indians gathered in small encampments to fish in summer, where they stayed together until fall. Then they dispersed, returning to their family hunting territories. Burden spent six weeks visiting the bands along the shores of Lake Abitibi on the border between Ontario and Quebec.

The Indians were experiencing bad times, and they were eager to work on the film. The building of the Canadian Pacific Railway, then two more transcontinental railways just before the war, brought ruthless white trappers into northern Ontario and Quebec. Fur was at a low point by the late 1920s, and the Ojibwa welcomed Burden's offer of employment. It would assure them of food and provisions and good wages all winter. Father Evain, a portly, white-bearded Roman Catholic priest, helped obtain Indian "extras" from his wide-ranging congregation. Most of the hundred Indians hired were Ojibwa from Lake Temagami, just west of Lake Temiskaming, but some came from Abitibi further to the north, Kippewa to the east, and Mattawa, on the Ottawa River to the south.

With the Indian actors signed up, Burden and Carver selected locations for shooting. For the fall scenes they chose Tem-Kip Camp (short for Temiskaming-Kippewa) at the mouth of the Kippewa River at the lower end of Lake Temiskaming, on the Quebec side. They chose Rabbit Chutes, halfway between Lake Temagami and Lake Temiskaming, for the Indian village and for winter scenes. The Chutes, unlike the area around Tem-Kip Camp, had never been cut over by loggers. A magnificent stand of red pine stood by the rapids where Rabbit Lake emptied into the Matabitchewan River. The high-wooded ridge, dramatically surrounded on one side by the rapids and on the other by Rabbit Lake, was ideal for the tepee village in the film. Everything was ready for late fall shooting when Long

Lance arrived on location at Tem-Kip Camp in early November. [6]

For several weeks the geese had been flying southward in their flying chevrons, a sure sign of the coming winter. The robins, white-throated sparrows and wood thrushes had long since gone. The nights were cold and the northern lights were beginning to play in the sky. The maples had dropped the last of their red and rust leaves, the birches and poplars shed their bright yellow foliage and now only the dark evergreen of spruce and pine remained. Everywhere in the woods there was the smell of dead leaves. [7]

It was in late October that Burden and Carver decided to ask Long Lance to play Baluk, the mighty Ojibwa hunter, "the epitome of manly development," as the script said. What convinced them to select Long Lance was his arresting portrait in the frontispiece of his book *Long Lance*. [8] Burden and Carver went over the script with Long Lance as soon as he arrived. It was getting late and the final fall shots at Tem-Kip had to be taken without delay. Throughout the film, they explained to Long Lance, hunger — "The Silent Enemy" — is dominant. They wanted to portray the Indians' search for the migrating caribou as a desperate struggle. Only when they are on the verge of starvation do they finally locate a herd, and the band narrowly escapes extinction. In addition to Baluk, there are four other principal characters: Chetoga, the wise old chief; Dagwan, the medicine man who is intensely jealous of Baluk; Neewa, the chief's daughter, who is the object of both Baluk's and Dagwan's affections; and Cheeka, Neewa's young brother. Baluk, needless to say, is the skilled hunter who finally finds the caribou. [9]

Over the next few days Long Lance got to know the other actors. Burden himself had selected the young Indian for the role of Cheeka. He met him and the boy's mother, who became an extra, at Lowbush, on Lake Abitibi. The thirteen-year-old Ojibwa, George McDougall, who had lived all his life in the bush, turned out to be a natural actor. Paul Benoit of Golden Lake, just west of Ottawa, played Dagwan, the villainous medicine man. Benoit was a skilled bushman and contributed much to the film, including a scene where he stalks a buck deer, calling it with a bone horn, then killing it with an arrow from his bow. For Neewa, the chief's daughter, Burden and Carver chose Molly Nelson, or Molly Spotted Elk, a beautiful Penobscot girl from Old Town, Maine. She was easier to find than the others—she danced every night in New York at Texas Guinan's Night Club, a well-known speakeasy. [10]

Long Lance's co-star, Chauncey Yellow Robe, was a man in his late fifties who was born in the last days of the buffalo hunt, and actually killed one as a young man. His mother's uncle was Sitting Bull himself. Carver happened to meet the Indian by chance in New York when he was viewing exhibits at the American Museum of Natural History.

Long Lance was impressed by Chauncey Yellow Robe, a genuine Indian, but he was also fearful. After all, he was a real Sioux chief, born in Montana in 1870, and he had lived the experiences Long Lance invented for himself in his book.[11] Again Long Lance worried that he might be exposed. But with Burden, the producer, he always presented himself as a Blackfoot chief. Long Lance knew Burden was a stickler for authenticity.

On location, first at Tem-Kip Camp, then at Rabbit Chutes, Long Lance immersed himself in the job at hand. He dressed in a breechcloth, headband and moccasins, and rescued Neewa, who had gone to snare partridges on a cliff, from a black she-bear. He also captured the bear's two cubs and presented them to young Cheeka as pets. Willy Chanler, the party's legal counsel and an expert archer, actually shot the arrow that killed the bear, but Long Lance did seize the cubs. It was no easy task, as the cubs each weighed a hundred pounds and fought back when Long Lance went after them. They slashed him severely, and he had scars to show for it, but he did not complain.[12]

At Rabbit Chutes the crew filmed the tepee village just before freeze-up and the first lasting snowfall. Some of the film's best scenes show George McDougall as Cheeka spearing fish from a birchbark canoe and shooting rapids. Long Lance did not look nearly as comfortable in a canoe, but after freeze-up, when winter shooting began, he performed extremely well on snowshoes, which he attributed to experience gained at the St. Vital Snowshoe Club when he was a reporter in Winnipeg.[13]

After several weeks in the bush, many of the technicians grew tense as the strain of being isolated and cold began to tell. They were becoming "bushed," to use the northern expression. In a letter to his friend Bonner Fellers on January 27, 1929, Long Lance described what was happening.

> Supper and coffee was always a bright event at five, but after the first week we ran out of dirty stories with which to fill in the time from then until the late retiring hour of nine — and, as I said, the time surely dragged, with nothing to read or occupy our minds. We had not expected a second dog-team that brought in an extra load of supplies and the news that we were to stay out an additional two weeks; and so we were surprised to get a batch of mail up there — among it your letter! It made a whole evening for us — I mean your jokes. I read them all out aloud. . . .
>
> The white fellows on this trip have to fight like hell to keep from "going bush," anyway. They are not used to being out of the world for so long, and their remedy is to herd together all of the time: the very worst thing that they could do. I keep within normal bounds by the Indian method of keeping to myself a lot, alone. And because I have a cheery smile when I do join all of them in the mess cabin, they all flock to my cabin evenings, thinking, I suppose, "Well, the old chief always has a smile; I'll go down and see how he gets that way."[14]

Burden himself had a terrible winter. In Nicaragua in 1924, he had contracted a mysterious illness that returned and struck him down again at Rabbit Chutes. For three weeks he lay on his bunk by the woodstove, surviving on cans of tomato juice. (Eighteen years later, a doctor finally diagnosed his illness as amoebic dysentery.[15])

Long Lance kept active after the day's shooting. On and off the set, Ilia Tolstoy, who acted as the assistant director of the film, became Long Lance's closest friend. He and the fun-loving Russian engaged in spirited Indian handwres-

tling contests, which Long Lance invariably won. Long
Lance also put on Indian dances in the cook tent, which had a
board floor. Stripped to the waist, with a full feather
headdress streaming behind him, he did his war dance,
while Ilia Tolstoy, grandson of the famous Russian novelist,
beat on the tom-tom.

Throughout the winter, which was long and cold, Long
Lance kept to a daily regimen of exercise. With Burden's
cousin, S.C. Burden, he sometimes broke holes in the ice and
took short dips in Rabbit Lake. On cloudy days, when they
did not film, he boxed nine rounds in the gym, three rounds
apiece with each of the Hennessy brothers, the camp's con-
tractors. And every day, regardless of whether or not they
filmed, he chopped firewood for at least an hour with the
lumberjacks.[16] After that, he felt a clean, muscular exhaus-
tion.

Doubtless he felt the tension, knowing of the Bureau of
Indian Affairs inquiry, and the presence on the set of a real
Indian warrior in old Chauncey Yellow Robe. Once, in
Temagami, his anxiety exploded in anger at a young Ojibwa
girl, Agnes Belaney. She had simply remarked to him that
she had never seen an Indian with such dark skin. Long
Lance saw Agnes whenever the cast traveled in by dogsled
to Temagami, where she worked as cook and dishwasher at
the village's only restaurant. After serving him several
times, the seventeen-year-old Ojibwa's curiosity finally got
the better of her. She asked him where he came from, to
which tribe he belonged, and then said, "You must be a
different kind of Indian." Long Lance's smile withered, and,
bitterly, he told her he was a full-blood, and all the Indians
around Temagami were a bunch of halfbreeds.[17] In Agnes's
case, it happened to be true; her mother was Ojibwa and her
father an Englishman. In a most extraordinary coincidence,
her father was none other than Archie Belaney, the
English-born writer who "went Indian" and later wrote
under the name of Grey Owl in the 1930s. Archie lived in the
Temagami area from 1906 to 1911, and again in 1925, just
three years before Long Lance and the rest of the cast and
crew arrived to make The Silent Enemy. As Grey Owl,

Archie read *Long Lance* in 1931 and hailed the author as a "splendid savage."[18] The two never met.

Once again during that winter in northern Canada, Long Lance faced the central dilemma of his life. At Rabbit Chutes he again agonized over whether he should resign himself to the status of a colored and return home, or drop the charade and strike out as an honest actor, writer, reporter or lecturer. It was on Christmas Eve, 1928, that he decided on a course of action. He would continue his masquerade, but first he would alter a few things.

In his tent-cabin, after warming his fingers by the stove, he sat at his portable typewriter and wrote a letter to Canon Middleton in Alberta. He started by telling his missionary-friend about the movie, about how it would be "an all-Indian motion picture...to record the life of the Indians and wild animals of the north country previous to the coming of the White Man." Then he got to the heart of the matter.

> Now, here is the thing I want to talk to you about: I have several dangerous scenes to do in this picture — Well, to be exact, I have done all of them but one, but that one will by far be the most dangerous of them all; and for that reason they are leaving it to the very last shot of the picture in case anything should happen to me. When I was down in Wyoming, I learned that my foster-parents, the only parents I have had since I was a child — Cherokee Indians who took me out of a Wild West Show when I was run over by a horse and had my hip knocked out of place, and kept me for several years — I learned that these foster-parents had died since I lost touch with them during the war.

He made his point in elliptical fashion, by rearranging the pertinent details of his roots and upbringing under the guise of telling Middleton of the movie and the fact that now he did not have an heir.

> I have given considerable thought to this subject, and have decided that if I should suddenly be taken, I would want to appoint you as the Trustee of my estate, such as it would be;

and would want the money I should leave, and the future
royalties from my book, to be devoted to the higher education
of the most promising young graduates of St. Paul's School,
said graduates to be designated solely by you. I think that
about covers the subject in its entirety, though, before I take
the risk that I have mentioned, I will draw up a formal will,
send it to my lawyer in New York and have him make it legal
and send you a copy. [19]

This explained, to Middleton at least, why he was listed as
a Cherokee at Carlisle, and not a Blackfoot. The fact that his
"foster-parents" were dead made it more convenient. Saying he had fallen off a horse and displaced his hip as a boy
shows how Long Lance's mind worked under pressure. He
was clever enough to rely on real experiences, embellished
with his imagination. When he was a boy in Winston, a horse
had tripped and fallen on him at the fair grounds. One of the
horse's knees indeed had hit and smashed his hip. [20]

He kept emphasizing his Indian background during the
filming of *The Silent Enemy*. The writing of his will in late
March gave him the opportunity to stress again his Blood
Indian origins. He returned to Tem-Kip Camp for the final
sequence of the film involving the bull moose, which had
been kept in a large natural enclosure. The script called for
Baluk to spear it with a spruce lance tipped with a flint. The
scene opened with timber wolves chasing the moose; then,
just as the wolves closed in for the kill, Long Lance was to
enter, drive the wolves off and plunge his spear into the
moose. Burden waited off-camera with a rifle in case Long
Lance was in danger. Long Lance took no chances, and the
day before the scene he asked Burden, Ilia Tolstoy and
Charlie Bonn, the film laboratory technician, to witness his
will. The scene went well, however, and Long Lance managed to spear the moose. [21]

Long Lance's will, dated March 29, 1929, assigns all of his
personal belongings to "my brother, Michael Eagle
Speaker, Blood Indian Reserve, Cardston, Alberta," and all
his "Estate and currency" to the St. Paul's Blood Indian
School to be used "to send promising Blood youth through

higher schools on being graduated." He named Canon
Middleton as his sole executor and trustee. [22] By drawing up
his will, Long Lance had made provision to repay the tribe,
and the Indians who had adopted him. It also served, equally
important, to impress upon Burden and others in the film
crew that he was a bona fide Plains Indian.

By April, the filming was nearing completion. Its high
point came immediately after Chief Chetoga's death. Just
before he dies, Chief Chetoga appoints Baluk to succeed
him, which greatly displeases the evil Dagwan. Baluk then
leads the tribe to the Barrenlands in search of the caribou.
Dagwan begins plotting against his rival. Weeks later,
Baluk proves unable to find the herd, and the survival of the
tribe is threatened. Dagwan convinces his tribesmen that
Baluk has failed and is to blame and that he must die as his
punishment. Baluk chooses to perish as a warrior, by fire.

The scene is Long Lance's finest. Naked from the waist
up, at forty degrees below zero, a grim and silent Baluk
climbs the funeral pyre. Tension rises as the flames crackle
and pop, and Baluk sings his death chant. The producer and
director were astonished at the intensity of Long Lance's
portrayal. As the flames lick at his ankles, he beats the
tom-tom, slowly at first, then faster, and faster, until — as
one observer later wrote — "it seemed as though forty devils
were contriving to make one mad." [23] Long Lance changes
the rhythm, slower again, then faster, then a steady,
monotonous tom-tom-tom-tom-tom-tom-tom, and with this
an eerie, chilling chant — his death song.

In the film, the death scene concludes happily. Just as the
fire begins to catch Baluk, an Indian brave glimpses the thin
smoke rising from the scouts' distant signal fires, and the cry
comes: "Caribou!" The herd is sighted. Baluk is taken down
from the pyre, burned but alive, and like the great elephant
charge in *Chang*, the film ends with a magnificent shot of
thousands of caribou stampeding. The tribe survives. Baluk
and Neewa win each other, and the sinister Dagwan is
banished as an outcast, left to die a slow death, wandering
alone on the empty barrens.

Burden and Carver were immensely pleased with Long

Lance's work. He always arrived on time for a shooting,
never complained, took risks willingly and, unlike many of
the technicians, never asked for a leave of absence from
Rabbit Chutes. All through the making of *The Silent
Enemy*, he had been friendly and cooperative, but one member of the cast remained unimpressed. Chauncey Yellow
Robe was watching Long Lance with growing suspicion.

Yellow Robe grew up on the plains in the 1870s and 1880s,
learning the customs and traditions of his people. He was
one of the first Sioux to attend a white man's school. When he
was fifteen, General Pratt took young Yellow Robe to Carlisle, where he graduated with honors. After Carlisle, he
worked for twenty-five years as the boys' advisor, or disciplinarian, at the Federal Indian Residential School at Rapid
City, South Dakota.

Though in the pay of the federal government, Yellow
Robe remained a staunch Indian patriot. He was at Carlisle
in 1890, the year of Wounded Knee, when the Seventh
Cavalry attacked a Sioux camp that was flying a white flag of
truce. Three hundred men, women and children were massacred. When Buffalo Bill proposed to make a heroic
reenactment of the Battle of Wounded Knee on film, Yellow
Robe protested against it. It was not a glorious battle, he
said, adding that "women and children and old men of my
people, my relatives, were massacred with machine guns by
soldiers of this Christian nation. . . ."[24]

Before he agreed to be Chief Chetoga in *The Silent
Enemy*, Yellow Robe insisted that the picture be as accurate
as possible. He would not participate if it misrepresented his
people in any way. Burden and Carver assured him everything would be done to make it authentic, but Yellow Robe
still harbored misgivings throughout the shooting of the
film. More and more he suspected that Long Lance was not
the full-blooded Indian he steadfastly claimed to be. He first
sensed a masquerade in the mess hall, where the principal
Indian actors and film crew ate three times a day. Yellow
Robe watched and listened in silence. He noticed Long
Lance's punctuality, itself a small point, but it surprised him.
Indians rarely are punctual in this way, preferring to eat

when they are hungry and sleep when they are tired. Long Lance always arrived on time, like a white man. He was disturbed by Long Lance's boisterousness, his "cheery smile," his big-hearted, uproarious laughter and his easy small talk with strangers — all peculiar character traits for an Indian to possess. He lacked the natural reserve of the Plains Indian. And for one who took pride in knowing Indian sign language, Long Lance often made grievous mistakes.[25] His dancing, too, though pleasing to the whites, was not the dancing of the Plains tribes.[26] If Yellow Robe had read *Long Lance*, he would have known it could not possibly have been Long Lance's life story. The man playing Baluk could never have seen a buffalo hunt, for the herds were exterminated long before he was born.

The filming of *The Silent Enemy* finished in late April. When the ice broke up, the crew moved by canoe to the railway at Temagami and from there to points south. Yellow Robe headed west and Long Lance returned to New York. He felt some relief when he heard that Burke of the Bureau of Indian Affairs, suffering ill health and hounded by his critics, had resigned in early March.[27] In the reorganization of the Bureau, he hoped that the investigation into his origins would be forgotten, but Yellow Robe had other ideas. After spending the summer in South Dakota, Yellow Robe returned to New York to lecture on the American Indian.[28] He also had more work to do on *The Silent Enemy*, recording the prologue for the silent movie. (Such sound work was necessary as the "talkies" became popular.) When in New York, he made discreet inquiries about Long Lance.

Burden and Carver, meanwhile, cut and edited a quarter of a million feet of film down to eight thousand.[29] The final version would be an hour and twenty minutes, including Yellow Robe's prologue. To the completed film they added a musical score, now necessary, for the arrival of the talkies led many theaters to dismiss their orchestras. Titles for the screen were prepared and inserted. Yellow Robe wrote the prologue himself, and with great dignity and simplicity he began: "This is the story of my people. In the beginning the Great Spirit gave us the land. The forests were ours and the

prairies; the wild game was ours to hunt. We were happy
when the game was plenty; in years of famine we suffered.
We loved our country and our homes. Now the white man
has come; his civilization has destroyed my people. Soon, we
would have been forgotten. But now this same civilization
has preserved our traditions before it was too late; now you
will know us as we really are. . . ."[30]

For foreign distribution, the prologue and the titles were
dubbed by Paramount into German, French, Spanish,
Polish, Italian, Portuguese, Swedish and Dutch.[31] The evening of May 19, 1930, was opening night at the Criterion on
Times Square. First-nighters included George Sherwood,
director of the American Museum of Natural History;
Thomas Hitchcock, the United States' top-ranked polo
player; Kermit Roosevelt, the former president's son; Walter Damrosch, a leading composer and former conductor of
the New York Symphony; and William K. Vanderbilt, a
director of the New York Central Railroad. Long Lance
invited General Verbeck of St. John's Military Academy and
Commissioner Graham, but the two men could not attend.
He also invited Princess Alexandra and a new acquaintance,
Anne Morgan, the sister of J.P. Morgan, the illustrious
financier.[32]

The critics loved the film. Robert Sherwood of the New
York *Post* ranked it with *Chang*. *Time* wrote that "no
schoolbook, museum or government bureau will ever pre-
serve the vestigial red man as this picture does." The *New
Republic*'s critic declared it "the only significant film to be
produced in this country for a long time." The *Wall Street
Journal* called it a "striking picture."[33]

Of the five Indian actors in *The Silent Enemy*, Long
Lance by far won the most accolades. Irene Thirer in the
New York *Daily News* congratulated the entire Indian cast,
but added, "Chief Long Lance, who portrays Baluk,
deserves mention over the rest." In the New York *American*, Regina Crewe wrote, "The hero role is taken by Chief
Long Lance, a superb figure, agile as a catamount and
utterly fearless." *Variety* said: "Chief Long Lance is an ideal
picture Indian, because he is a full-blooded one . . . an author

of note in Indian lore, and now an actor in fact."[34] Grantland
Rice, the most revered sports journalist of the day, wrote in
the New York *Sun* on May 22, 1930: "Chief Long Lance, a
former Carlisle star, puts on a battle with a bull moose in
'The Silent Enemy' that rivals the first round of the
Dempsey-Firpo fight. Chief Long Lance nails the moose
with his pre-Columbus lance and then the moose nails him.
The chief takes the first fall, but the moose stays down for
the count. There is enough action through a minute here to
last three or four modern fights."

To further guarantee the film's credibility, Burden and
Chanler decided on a special screening of the film for Madison Grant, one of America's leading naturalists. The influential New York lawyer had spent years traveling throughout
North America to discover new animal species. In Alaska,
he had discovered a unique form of caribou that later was
named after him: *rangifer granti*. With Theodore Roosevelt
and others, Grant also played a leading role in the founding
of the New York Zoological Society in 1895, and since 1925,
Grant had been the society's president.[35]

Fortunately, Grant liked the film—so much that he chat-
tered enthusiastically all through the showing. After the
scene in which the timber wolves attacked the bull moose, he
leaned over to Burden and whispered: "They're really hus-
kies with lead attached to their tails to make them look like
wolves." When the caribou herd appeared on the screen,
Grant exclaimed with his usual self-assurance: "It's nice to
see you've really got caribou there!" Burden and Chanler
smiled. Grant was wrong on both counts. The wolves were
real and the "wild caribou" mainly were reindeer, a domes-
ticated version of the caribou.[36]

Grant was wrong on a third count, too. For years he had
researched race theory, and in his book *The Passing of the
Great Race* (1916), he alerted Americans to the danger of its
superior races, the Nordics, being submerged by inferior
immigrants. In his final work, *The Conquest of a Continent*
(later published by Charles Scribner's in 1933), he repeated
the theme, emphasizing the peril of racial miscegenation. As
the Negro was "inferior to the Nordic in intelligence," Grant

stressed that "states which have no laws preventing the intermarriage of white and black should adopt them." The Nordics also must be vigilant to unmask the "pass-for-white" mulattoes.[37] Grant failed to spot an impostor in *The Silent Enemy*. In a letter to Burden after the screening, Grant wrote: "I am thoroughly familiar with the country from the upper Ottawa River to the Hudson Bay region, and I can testify that your pictures are accurate in every detail."[38]

Despite all the work done by Burden and Chanler, and despite Grant's imprimatur and the fine reviews, *The Silent Enemy* failed at the box office when it was released in August. Perhaps it was too authentic, too "educational." One commentator cynically observed: "To say that this admirable production is 'educational' is to condemn it to be shown in empty theaters. There is no more demand for education among movie fans than there is among college students."[39] It also suffered because it was a silent movie, just as the talkies were sweeping the market. Finally, Paramount backed out of its promise to promote the independently produced picture, and it was doomed.[40]

The Silent Enemy was among the last authentic silent movies ever to play on Broadway, and though it failed commercially, fifty years later the respected film historian Kevin Brownlow called it a "priceless treasure."[41]

16

THE TRAIL NARROWS

EFORE RETURNING TO NEW YORK after the filming of *The Silent Enemy*, Long Lance stopped off in
Toronto for an interview for the *Star Weekly*. There
he talked to Wilfrid Eggleston, a young writer who
had grown up in Alberta, about the film project and the
north. He could still dazzle a young writer, and he impressed
Eggleston, who later wrote: "Chief Long Lance is an ano-
maly. A Blood Indian born on the border country around
Coutts, Alberta, and raised in the tribe, he is yet one of the
best stylists in Canada today."

Long Lance also enlarged on the adventures of the movie
project, fabricating tales of spectacular side trips to the
Northwest Territories and to Alaska. "Hard times up there
this winter among the Indians and Eskimos," he told
Eggleston. "Trapping was very poor. Game is getting
scarce, country's getting trapped out." He told of going to
Windy Lake, "the geographical center of the Territories,"
which he said was "thirty-six days by dog team" from The
Pas, Manitoba. He could deceive as easily as breathing in
and out by now. He mentioned that he had traveled 4,800
miles by airplane with a Captain Lenson of the United
States Air Force, flying north and west of Nome, Alaska.
All of these details — thirty-six days by dogsled, 4,800 miles
by airplane — were included in the *Star Weekly* story.[1] It was
Long Lance's forte that he could make anyone's experience

his own, for he never made either of these trips, though he knew others who had. His friend Ilia Tolstoy had tried to locate a caribou herd in the Barrenlands, and when he returned, unsuccessful, two cameramen flew to Alaska and managed to find and film a reindeer herd. Long Lance himself spent the entire winter at Rabbit Chutes.[2]

Canon Middleton invited him to visit Alberta, but Long Lance, edgy about the Bureau's inquiry and Yellow Robe's suspicions, declined. As a result, Middleton's well-intentioned attempts to act as a matchmaker came to nothing. Earlier, he had written from the Blood Reserve: "I suppose while staying in the wilds you have many times thought of taking unto yourself a partner for life. If you fail in your endeavours, please remember that we have a delightful Blood girl here, who I am sure would make you a charming life partner."[3]

Long Lance chose another season in New York instead.

Before he went up north for the film, Long Lance had agreed to appear in advertisements endorsing the B.F. Goodrich Company's line of running shoes. As he browsed through the newsstands in New York, he saw his picture in full regalia in such magazines as *American Boy, Boy's Life, Youth's Companion* and *Popular Mechanics*. The story in one of the advertisements read:

One winter we came near starvation. Our braves hunted over the plains for the frozen heads of buffalo they had killed early in the fall. They chopped the skin from the tops of the heads, and our mothers cooked it for food. We were saved by finding a herd of mountain sheep which had been driven down into the foothills by the big snow. We slew the entire herd and ate them on the spot. On many occasions like this, our lives depended on the endurance of our legs and feet in hunting game for food.

In our primitive life, nothing was more important than our feet. I wonder if the white race would not be sturdier if they took better care of their feet in childhood — by wearing shoes that allow free exercise of the foot and leg muscles.

As for myself, I always wear rubber-soled canvas shoes in

the stiffest climbing and the longest hiking, whenever the weather permits. They are more like moccasins in strength-building than any other modern shoe. [4]

That summer he also heard his name in Goodrich radio commercials prepared by the J. Walter Thompson Advertising Agency. Long Lance met frequently with the Goodrich people at the Thompson offices in New York, working on publicity for the "Chief Long Lance Shoe." Specimens of the shoes were manufactured in late summer of 1929 when orders for fall delivery were taken. [5] The Goodrich people asked Long Lance to write *How to Talk in Indian Sign Language*, a thirty-four-page booklet designed to publicize the new shoe. It was released in 1930. In the booklet, Long Lance is shown in a breechcloth and headband, his powerful torso bared to the waist, demonstrating the sign language of the Indians in eighty-three photographs. Goodrich also managed to persuade Jim Thorpe to write a glowing testimonial to Long Lance and his new shoe. It did not take much persuasion, as Thorpe by this time was in desperate need of money.

By 1930, at age forty-one, Thorpe was finished as an athlete. He played his last football game for the Chicago Cardinals in 1929 and retired from the game. Like many professional athletes, he had no savings to fall back on. He had divorced his first wife, Iva Miller, whom he met as a student at Carlisle, had remarried and now had a wife and two children to support.[6] Under the title "The Greatest All-round Athlete in Modern History Adds a Word," Thorpe said:

Like most Indians, I have always been a great user of canvas rubber-soled shoes. When my old schoolmate, Chief Long Lance, and I were running with and against one another on the track team of the Carlisle Indian school, I remember how we used to kick about the rubber-soled shoes we had to wear in our athletics. We spent most of an evening once discussing the kind of shoe we would like to see someone turn out.

Little did I think then that Long Lance himself would some day design this shoe. I have just tried out my first pair of the new Chief Long Lance Shoe and find that they remove the last objection we had to this type of footwear.

Long Lance and I trained together for the 1912 Olympics, and when the games were over at Stockholm, I told Long Lance that it was the stiff competition that he had given me in the mile run which had enabled me to win the World's All-Around Athletic Championship that year. He was always an intense trainer, using up dozens of pairs of rubber-soled shoes, and I don't know anyone better fitted than he to know what we want in a shoe of this sort.

I'll go the limit in saying that in all my years of athletics, I find the Chief Long Lance Shoe the smoothest, the best natural foot and leg-muscle builder of any shoe of any kind I have ever seen. It is the shoe that I have been looking for all these years. . . .

Long Lance spent the summer and fall of 1929 in New York, preoccupied with Goodrich's promotion campaign. The skyscape of the city changed dramatically that October, as wreckers knocked down the old Waldorf-Astoria to make way for the skyscraper to end all skyscrapers—the Empire State Building. [7]

The task of writing a booklet on the Indian sign language caused Long Lance not the slightest qualm, even though, as old Yellow Robe realized in an instant, he knew precious little about it. Fortunately, he had other resources, such as William Tomkins' *Universal American Indian Sign Language*, which appeared in 1926. Earlier illustrated works such as Ernest Thompson Seton's *Sign Talk* were readily available, [8] and Long Lance whipped out the booklet in short order, leaving himself plenty of time for New York's social life.

That summer, the Fellers, his West Point friends, were on leave in New York awaiting Bonner's posting to the Philippines in the fall. On several trips to West Point in 1928, to give special lectures, to referee track meets and to research an article on the military academy, [9] Long Lance stayed at their apartment. He was always a popular house guest. When asked if he wanted breakfast in the morning, he laughed and told his hosts that he "never felt right until he had his protein." The Fellers were happy to take the chief along to West Point parties, where he chatted and danced and told old Indian tales, and managed to lower everyone's inhibitions. At one of these parties Long Lance thumped on a tin wastepaper basket so loudly that people heard the noise three floors away.

One afternoon in New York, driving out with the Fellers to visit friends in Connecticut, Long Lance sat in the rumble seat of the small Pontiac, with Bonner and Dorothy sitting up front. On one of the rough roads, Dorothy turned to say something to Long Lance and to her horror saw that he was gone. The rumble seat was down. Just when the Bonners feared the worst, they heard whoops of laughter and watched Long Lance pop up again, perched in the rumble seat. "I thought I'd just disappear," he told them, as the threesome bounced on to Connecticut.

Dorothy Fellers noticed that no matter how agreeable Long Lance was in white society, and no matter how he seemed to be comfortable and at ease in new situations, there were times when he plainly was awkward. Once he made a well-meaning but completely misunderstood remark to a close friend of Dorothy's. The friend's scathing retort, Dorothy noted, obviously hurt and angered him. But he did not reply, and "just quietly disappeared perhaps to hide his hurt or control his short-fused temper. Or maybe both."[10]

That summer he rented a single room at the Explorers Club on Cathedral Parkway, just north of Central Park. The room in the attractive eight-storey building cost $15 a week, and he probably heard of it through Douglas Burden, who was a member. The Explorers Club was founded in 1904, and in twenty-five years it had become one of the most distinguished clubs in the world, organized with the objective of "uniting explorers in the bonds of good fellowship and promoting the work of exploration by every means in its power." Its members included the late Admiral Peary, Roald Amundsen, discoverer of the North West Passage,

President Theodore Roosevelt, Ernest Thompson Seton and the Arctic explorers Vilhjalmur Stefansson and Fritjof Nansen.[11]

It was at the club that Long Lance met Dr. Clyde Fisher, one of its directors and a man keenly interested in Indians. Fisher earned a doctorate in botany at Johns Hopkins University in 1913 for his thesis on cell division in the developing seeds of various species of *Pepero-mia*, tropical members of the pepper family. He had little interest in becoming a narrow specialist in the field, however, and read widely on zoology, geology and astronomy. He was familiar with flowers, insects and birds, and could name the stars in their constellations and discuss the theory of relativity. After he joined the Department of Education at the Museum of Natural History in 1913, he went on expeditions to Bermuda, Europe and the American West. On a 1927 trip to the Standing Rock Reservation in North Dakota to photograph and study Indian ceremonial dancing, the Sioux inducted him into their tribe. [12]

Long Lance's other friend at the Explorers Club was Seumas (James in English and pronounced Shamus), Chief of Clann Fhearghuis of Stra-chur and Clann Ailpein, who included among his Scottish ancestors Ferghus the Great, mightiest of the Ferguson clan's kings, and Duncan, murdered in Shakespeare's play by Macbeth. He was the club's most colorful member, known as "the wandering Scot." Seumas always appeared bekilted at the Explorers Club. He wore a dirk in his belt, a *sgian dugh*, or black knife, and the traditional Gaelic *sporan*, or leather purse. He was fifty years old in 1929, and the tall, handsome Scot claimed to have fought in armies around the world, serving in his late teens in Armenia and the Balkans with "the Bashi-bazouks (Irregular Horse) recruited mainly from the Hak Kari country of Kurdistan." He returned briefly to the Western Highlands, then set off for West Africa, and, when he was twenty-four, crossed the Sahara. During the Russo-Japanese War, he said he commanded seven squadrons of "Kuban Cossacks." He concluded his military career by serving seven years in South Africa with the "British Legion of Frontiersmen, Military Scouts." [13]

Not everyone at the Explorers Club believed the friendly Scot's exploits. Indeed, as his obituary in the *Explorers Journal* says, "there were often controversial discussions about the Chief among some of the members."[14] Perhaps because of this, he and Long Lance gravitated to each other and developed a warm rapport.

In late September, 1929, Seamus, Dr. Fisher and E.W. Deming, the artist, proposed that Long Lance be accepted for membership in the Explorers Club. To strengthen the application, the seventy-year-old Deming, who had lived in the American West in the 1880s and 1890s, studying and sketching Indians, wrote a strong letter of support. He had always believed that "the Blackfeet Indians are racially magnificent," and his paintings of the western Indians were highly regarded. Clark Wissler, the anthropologist, told Deming in 1921: "...you, above all, have been able to get inside the Indian life and to see the world as the Indians see it." In his letter, Deming's praise was unqualified. "Long Lance," he wrote, "although he is well educated and has lived the life of the white man for many years, belongs to the old time Indian and has written one of the best books on the old time Indian life."[15]

On October 11, the membership committee voted into the club "Buffalo Child Long Lance...a full-blooded Chief of the Blackfeet Indian tribe, who has long been well known and respected in Canada and the western states, not only as an explorer, but also as a writer and lecturer on Indian experience and affairs." It was a great honor. At the same meeting the Explorers Club elected Charles Lindbergh as an honorary member.[16]

Long Lance was the only non-white member living at the Explorers Club, though on the streets north of the building was Harlem, with a quarter of a million blacks. To the east was Spanish Harlem, with some one hundred thousand Latin Americans, blacks and West Indians.[17] Long Lance even had a cousin, Felix Graves, in Harlem, but he never invited him to the Explorers Club.

Long Lance put all his energy into the masquerade at the Explorers Club. He went out of his way to meet and talk at length with members such as Frederick Webb Hodge, Club

President George G. Heye, and Dr. Clark Wissler, all well-known students of the North American Indian. He became friendly with Hodge, who had edited the authoritative, two-volume *Handbook of American Indians* in 1910. Long Lance and Hodge liked to read in the club library. Hodge was sixty-five, but as a younger man he had done anthropological field work among Indians in Arizona and New Mexico. Heye, the club president, spent a lifetime collecting Indian artifacts and had founded the Museum of the American Indian in New York in 1916. He was interested in Long Lance's knowledge of Indian sign language. Long Lance read Wissler's *The American Indian: An Introduction to the Anthropology of the New World* (Second Edition, 1922) and Wissler read Long Lance's *Long Lance*. [18]

When Clyde Fisher asked Wissler what he thought of the book, the anthropologist was at a loss as to what to say and somewhat embarrassed. Twenty years earlier, he had done field work among the Sioux and then more systematically among the Peigan tribe of the Blackfoot Confederacy. Without question, he knew that Long Lance's autobiography was fiction. From his own field trips at the turn of the century, he knew that the Blackfoot were not chasing the last buffalo or organizing war parties in the 1880s. By that time, the Confederacy lay shattered, its member-tribes in Canada and the United States ill-fed, stricken by disease and confined to their reserves and reservations. Knowing all this, Wissler kept his silence. When Dr. Fisher pressed him for an opinion of *Long Lance*, Wissler replied as best he could. "If you begin it," he told him, "I think you will finish it." [19]

Wissler's reaction can be explained by his humanistic outlook on life, [20] and perhaps by a grudging respect for Long Lance and what he had accomplished. In an age when the Indians were viciously treated, as much by the slanderous stereotype pushed by Hollywood as by the ruthless bullying by whites on the plains, Long Lance succeeded at least in capturing something of the essence of the Indians' heroic and noble history. If it was fiction disguised as fact, then it was fiction done well, and in its own peculiar way, done accurately. Unlike his own dry monographs on the Blackfoot "Material Culture," "Ceremonial Bundles" and "Societies and Dance Associations," *Long Lance* reached a much wider public with an impact that caused many to abandon their erroneous notions about the Plains Indians.

Also, Wissler could not prove on his own that Long Lance was an impostor. Even if he could identify unmistakable Caucasian and Negroid physical traits in the man, it really established very little. Perhaps he was not full-blooded; by the 1920s, few North American Indians were. In Canada and the United States, the ancestry of many who were officially classed as Indian was, in fact, mixed. Jim Thorpe, the Sac and Fox Indian, was by his own calculation only "five-eighths Indian," and his first wife, Iva Miller, classed as a Cherokee, was at least half-white. On the South Peigan or Blackfeet Reservation in Montana, three-quarters of the population under thirty were of mixed racial origin by 1930, and it was a relatively isolated reservation. Most of the racial mix had been with whites, but there had been some with blacks, too. Even among the Bloods of Alberta, there were band members descended from Henry Mills, a black frontiersman from Montana, whom the Blackfoot called "Six-apekwan" (black white man). [21]

Culturally, too, it was becoming difficult even for anthropologists to determine racial ancestry. Neither the American nor the Canadian governments were interested in protecting the Indians' culture and religion. The Duncan Campbell Scotts and Charles Burkes partially succeeded in their attempts to eliminate the "primitive" customs and remake the Indians into brown white men. In Canada, for sixty years after 1869, Indian women lost their Indian status when they married a non-Indian, while white women marrying Indians gained it. [22] Long Lance easily could have been born of such a racial mix. Or perhaps he had simply done so well at the reservation mission school and at Carlisle that he had lost much of his native culture, which was the ostensible purpose of Indian education in those days.

Another advantage Long Lance enjoyed was his skillful use of Mike Eagle Speaker's childhood memories in his autobiography. Wissler would recognize many of the experiences in the early pages of the book as authentic, though Long Lance's description of Blackfoot history was not. His claim that he traveled in a travois as a child, took icy dips in winter and learned the tribal legends from his mother, all rang true.

Long Lance took pains to cover his tracks well, and as long as the results of Charles Burke's inquiry remained in the files at the Bureau of Indian Affairs in Washington, he was safe.

The fall of 1929 brought catastrophe to most Americans. The 1920s had been a decade of prosperity, when the United States moved from outdoor privies, ice boxes and horse-drawn buggies to electric refrigerators, cars, vacuum cleaners and telephones. Spending reached spectacular heights. The stock market broke in early September, recovered quickly, slid again in late September, recovered momentarily in early October, then suffered an alarming decline. Prices fell so rapidly on October 24 that panic seized the market. Overnight, men's hopes and fortunes vanished. As stocks plummeted, bankruptcies followed, and within two months of the crash, three million people were out of work. Factories closed, stores shut down, construction stopped, breadlines formed on the streets. November was the month of panic and December the month of melancholy adjustment. [23]

The Depression did not hurt Long Lance's lectures at first, for he offered his audiences something fresh and uplifting: "Be wise and persevere." In late November, he spoke at the American Museum of Natural History on "An Indian's Story of His People." He repeated the talk at the Explorers Club, where he was praised in the club's newsletter for his "brilliant and humorous account of the characteristics of the life and philosophy of his people of the northwestern plains." [24]

Economic hard times dampened but did not drown the social life in New York that winter, and Long Lance was more popular than ever as a much-sought-after guest. Fannie Hurst, to whom Ray Long paid $70,000 for the seri-

alization rights to her novel *Back Street*, invited Long Lance
to her New Year's Eve party.[25] At Princess Alexandra's
apartment, he met her cousins, Princess Nina of Russia and
Princess Xenia of Greece, both nieces of the late czar.[26] His
friend W.R. Edrington, the banker, included him in his
theater parties.[27] Several times, Long Lance lunched with
Carl Van Vechten, the New York music and drama critic
turned novelist. Van Vechten, renowned as one of the best
hosts in New York, loved it when Long Lance performed a
war dance for his guests, and the Chief was only too happy to
oblige.[28] He always found time, too, for the starlets and
Broadway showgirls, dating such standouts as Vivian Hart
and Mildred McCoy.

Even Walter Winchell caught him at play that winter, and
once wrote in his "On Broadway" column in the *Daily Mirror*: "Chief Long Lance, the Indian lecturer, and the first
Mrs. Guy Bolton are uh-huh...."[29] Seumas, the Scottish
chieftain, who occupied the room next to Long Lance's at the
Explorers Club, kept track of his friend's exploits the way a
box-scorer in baseball keeps track of hits, runs and errors.
He had a sprightly sense of humor, and when Long Lance's
women called, as they did day and night, his standard reply
was: "No, this is not Long Lance...I am Chief Longer
Lance."[30]

Long Lance's career as Indian-lecturer-showman began
to crest in the last two weeks of January, 1930. He spoke on
the Indian sign language to five hundred guests at the
Explorers Club annual dinner at the Hotel Astor on January
18. The next day, in the Sunday edition of the *Herald
Tribune*, Beverly Smith's article "One Hundred Per Cent
American" appeared. Before going into detail on the man
who was "Buffalo Child Long Lance, full blooded American
Indian, Chief of the Blood band of the Northern Blackfeet,
athlete, soldier, author, explorer and scholar," she began:

> You may find him some day at the American Museum of
> Natural History, delivering a learned lecture on Indian
> archeology before the trustees and directors; or at West Point,
> judging a track meet; or at the Explorers Club, writing a

report for the United States Bureau of Commercial Economics. He is, to use a much abused phrase correctly, a 100 per cent
American.

Again it was Long Lance himself who provided the
research material, and again he lapsed into a world of fan-
tasy. He told the writer that he "played tackle on the great
teams of 1910, 1911 and 1912 of which Jim Thorpe was the
bright star." He said he attended the Olympic Games at
Stockholm in 1912, when Thorpe triumphed over the world's
best. Instead of reporting that he had been wounded twice
in France, he raised the number to eight, adding that he had
been "decorated by three governments for gallantry in
action." His lies now were reckless, and could have been
exposed in an afternoon of checking, but they appeared, as
they usually did, just as he told them. All that winter he felt
something closing in on him and it was as if he wanted one
final fling at acceptance and acclaim; or, perhaps subcon-
sciously, he wanted to be caught.

On the evening of January 28, Katherine Hale (the pen
name of Mrs. John Garvin), the former book critic of the
Toronto *Mail and Empire* and in her own right a well-known
writer and poet, met Long Lance at the annual dinner of the
Poetry Society of America. The Depression had entered its
third month, and it was not a good time for American writers
whose books, new and old, sold as remainders in the book
shops and drug stores of New York. [31] Still, the dinner was a
gala affair. Four hundred guests attended the banquet at
the Biltmore Hotel, opposite Grand Central Station. Hale
spotted Long Lance in the lobby and later wrote: "His
clear-cut aquiline features, dark complexion and magnificent carriage set him entirely apart from everyone else in
the brilliant crowd. He moved among people, everywhere
recognized and smiled upon...." [32]

In the ballroom that evening, Long Lance was in his glory.
During the after-dinner poetry readings, he got up to demonstrate his evocative, if not perfectly accurate, Indian sign
language. Then, under the huge crystal chandeliers, in a
room decorated with hand-carved wood, velvet drapes and

acres of rare Venetian marble, he recited in a soft voice the words of his own death chant. [33]

> Oh, look down upon Long Lance,
> Thou knowest Long Lance,
> The Sun, the Moon, the Day, the Night;
> Tell me if it is real,
> This life I have lived,
> This death I am dying.
> Ah, the clouds are leaving my door,
> The Outward Trail is no longer dark,
> I see — I understand:
> There is no life, there is no death;
> I shall walk on a trail of stars. [34]

The evening was a tremendous success, a personal triumph in every respect. But the trail was narrowing. Chauncey Yellow Robe had recently contacted the Bureau of Indian Affairs in Washington, and shortly thereafter he informed William Chanler that Long Lance was not a Blackfoot. [35] A week after the banquet of the Poetry Society of America, Chanler, acting as legal counsel for *The Silent Enemy*, summoned Long Lance to his office.

17

"HELLO, SYLVESTER"

L ONG LANCE had not seen Will Chanler for months; then, on February 5, 1930,[1] a phone call summoned him to Chanler's office—as soon as possible. He walked east along Cathedral Parkway from the Explorers Club to the subway, deposited his five-cent fare and walked down to the Broadway level. The front page of the *Times* carried a story on former President Taft's ill health, another on New York Governor Franklin D. Roosevelt acting to end the dressmakers' strike, and a human-interest item on Charles Lindbergh, who had just celebrated his twenty-eighth birthday in Los Angeles.[2] Long Lance hopped off in the Wall Street district and walked toward the Mutual Life Building, while sheets of cold wind swirled through the office tower canyons. At 32 Liberty Street, he stepped inside and took the elevator to Chanler's office.

"Hello, Sylvester," Chanler greeted him.

Long Lance must have guessed that Chanler knew the truth, but he had lived with the masquerade and the fear since 1909 and his entrance to Carlisle—for twenty-one of his thirty-nine years. Instinctively he was on his guard. He glanced around the well-furnished law office, the walls lined with red, leather-bound legal volumes, and replied, calmly: "Sylvester? Who's Sylvester?"

Chanler zeroed in.

"You're Sylvester, Sylvester Long. You come from North Carolina, and you're not a Blood Indian."

Chanler was furious. Both he and Burden knew that the seemingly authentic, full-blooded Indian chief they had cast in the role of Baluk was a fraud. The day before, Charles Rhoads, Burke's successor at the Bureau of Indian Affairs, had confirmed Yellow Robe's story. Long Lance was a Croatan, not a western Indian, and he was Sylvester Long, not Chief Buffalo Child Long Lance.

Long Lance stood firm. "I've never heard of the Croatan tribe," he said, looking Chanler straight in the eyes.

"We know what the facts are," Chanler shot back, "and there's no use arguing about them."

Long Lance denied the charges; then, appearing to crack, he confessed to Chanler that he had in fact lied. The true story, he told him, was that he was not a Blood—but a Blackfoot! He patiently explained that he had kept his ancestry a secret because his father was a renegade Blackfoot around Laramie, Wyoming. He was "a wild character and not held in very good repute," and all along Long Lance sought to hide the relationship behind a claim that he was a Blood. He was ashamed of his father, he explained; he did not want to be known as an outlaw's son.

Pressed for more details, Long Lance told him he was born in Montana and had no memory of his mother. His earliest recollections were of the days he worked as a child on white ranches in Wyoming. At the age of nine or ten he ran away with the Wild West shows. When he was with Robinson's Circus in North Carolina, a horse fell on him and smashed his hip, dislocating it.[3] It was a convincing rebuttal, and years later Chanler remembered how sincerely Long Lance had defended himself, always with the steady gaze leveled on his inquisitor's eyes. Chanler related more of the story in a later letter to Commissioner Rhoads:

He was taken from the circus in a buggy by a doctor and nursed by a Cherokee family; he thinks their name was Long; he lived with them for about two years, although he says he ran away from them to join a circus at some time. He does not remember whether he went to school there but knows that he could read and write a little when he was sent to Carlisle from the Cherokee Reservation. He thinks he was given the name of "Sylvester Long" at Carlisle, although he may have been given that name by the Cherokees. . . . [4]

Long Lance urged Chanler to check out his story, to write to Canon Middleton and to James Henderson, one of his teachers at Carlisle. He then opened his scrapbook and showed it to Chanler in an attempt to prove he was a Blackfoot, but here he miscalculated. Chanler noticed that "whenever the name of his tribe in the earlier clippings referring to his West Point days appeared, the printed word was erased and 'Blackfoot' was written in pencil." [5] In his second letter to Commissioner Rhoads, Chanler suggested that Long Lance "call upon your office and endeavour to straighten out the records." He also thanked Rhoads for sending information on the Croatan Indians. [6]

Chanler knew the Plains Indians well enough. An uncle who had fought in the Indian wars in Arizona and New Mexico once sent him a full eagle headdress and buckskin suit, and he had worn it often as a boy. When he was about ten, he read George Catlin's two volumes on his travels among the western Indians in the 1830s, Francis Parkman's *Oregon Trail* and all of Fenimore Cooper's books on the Eastern Woodlands Indians. Just five years earlier, around 1925, he traveled west to visit the Blackfeet, or South Peigan, Reservation at Browning, Montana, in the company of James Willard Schultz, the white author who had married a Peigan woman and written many books on their old ways and customs. [7] Still, Chanler did not know of the Croatans, the tribe to which Commissioner Rhoads said Long Lance belonged.

Commissioner Rhoads had sent along an excerpt from the *Handbook of American Indians*, which was edited by Fred Hodge, one of Long Lance's friends at the Explorers Club. The entry on Croatans explained that the name was recently given to a group of people in North Carolina, previously classed as "free negroes," but who claimed to be Indians.

The term, according to the *Handbook*, "serves as a convenient label for a people who combine in themselves the blood of the wasted native tribes, the early colonists or forest rovers, the runaway slaves or other negroes, and probably also of stray seamen of the Latin races from coasting vessels in the West Indian or Brazilian trade."[8]

Chanler then wrote to James Henderson, the Carlisle teacher. Long Lance had been out of touch with him for nearly twenty years—perhaps he even assumed he was dead—and he made a grave mistake suggesting that Chanler check him out as a reference. Henderson was retired as superintendent and agent for the Eastern Band of Cherokees, a post to which he had been appointed after leaving Carlisle in 1912, and he lived in Canton, North Carolina.

Henderson wrote to Chanler on February 24 and repeated most of what he reported to the Bureau of Indian Affairs in October, 1928. He said he had once known "Sylvester Long who now calls himself Long Lance" but added that "he was never recognized at Carlisle by the Cherokees as a Cherokee Indian" and "it was alleged that he was more of negro blood than Indian." Henderson also said that, shortly after his appointment as the Eastern Cherokee Superintendent, he was asked to investigate the Cherokee background of Sylvester Long when President Wilson had nominated him to West Point. He looked into the matter, but "could find no one in the reservation who knew anything at all in regard to his life history." Later, Henderson continued, he learned about Sylvester's father from a chance meeting with a journalist from Winston-Salem. The reporter had read Long Lance's articles, and told Henderson that his father worked as a janitor at the Winston-Salem high school and "often spoke of having a son at Carlisle and that he was going to West Point."

Totally bewildered, Chanler scrawled across the bottom of Henderson's letter: "Mr. Henderson was Disciplinarian at Carlisle in Long Lance's time, and Long Lance himself referred me to him to prove he really was a Blackfoot from Wyoming!"

Shortly thereafter, Chanler heard from Charlie Bonn, who worked as a lab technician for *The Silent Enemy*. Bonn's boss at Eastman Kodak was Jules Brulatour, who formerly owned a theater in Winston-Salem, one of the theaters where Abe Long had worked.[9] All indications were that Long Lance, far from being a Plains Indian chief, was, by southern racial standards, a Negro. In early March, Canon Middleton's letter arrived.

Middleton enclosed copies of the previous Bureau of Indian Affairs inquiry and his reply to it, stating that the alleged Blackfoot really was a Cherokee from Oklahoma. He said that the story Long Lance told of his origins is "almost identical with the version he had given me at different times, but this he always communicated confidentially, and I have always treated it as such." Middleton proved to be a loyal friend. "Knowing Indian life as I do, I know him to be of true blue," he wrote. "He has wandered over no easy road, and so far as I know, has come through unscathed and unsullied. All honour to his Indian blood, his training, his character, and his respect for those who respect him." He concluded by saying, "Shall be pleased to hear, at your pleasure, the result of your investigations."[10] And so he would.

Canon Middleton's letter convinced Chanler that a full investigation was needed. He contacted Ilia Tolstoy, then visiting at Aiken, South Carolina, close to the Georgia border, requesting him to go to Winston-Salem and ask about Long Lance and Sylvester Long. He wanted the whole affair cleared up, and quickly; an extensive advertising campaign was being prepared for the movie, with Long Lance billed as a full-blooded Indian. Chanler wrote to Middleton in early March and said, "Certain Indians in New York and some others are spreading around a story that Long Lance is part negro."[11]

In February and March, the rumor that Long Lance had black and not Indian ancestry reached many of his friends. Irvin S. Cobb exploded in anger when he heard it. "To think that we had him here in the house," he raged. "We're so ashamed! We entertained a nigger...." Others simply dropped him from their circles. [12]

Those who stuck by him included crusty old Seumas, the chief of Clann Fhearghuis, his friend at the Explorers Club. Breaking his silence at last, Long Lance admitted his mixed ancestry to Seumas and the worldly wise Scot kept the secret safe. He told Long Lance how much the world's races had been mixed, and how, after Bonnie Prince Charles was defeated at Culloden, the Highlanders were dispersed all over the world and had mingled with many races. Many was the time, he counseled Long Lance, that part-Oriental, African and American Indian clansmen came to him "some clutching an old Bible or a piece of tartan, proud of their Scottish heritage."[13] Seumas, Middleton and Clyde Fisher of the American Museum of Natural History all stood by Long Lance. Curiously, so did old Chauncey Yellow Robe.

Long Lance probably confided in Yellow Robe soon after his interview with Chanler, who had revealed that it was Yellow Robe who saw through the masquerade. Long Lance must have confessed to Yellow Robe that he was a Cherokee, born and raised in a southern town that recognized only two races—white and colored. After he was adopted by the Bloods in Alberta, Long Lance decided to identify fully with the Bloods and the Blackfoot and to use Buffalo Child Long Lance as his pen name. Once the secret was revealed, the old Sioux finally understood. Yellow Robe must have respected the courage it took to challenge the color bar, for he apparently forgave and accepted Long Lance. When he fell gravely ill in March, 1930, he agreed that Long Lance should replace him on the publicity tour to Hollywood. Chanler and Burden had no choice but to send out their other headliner and hope for the best.

Yellow Robe's unexpected death from pneumonia in early April affected Long Lance deeply. He wrote to Yellow Robe's daughter, Rosebud, and in grief and despair said: "One thing I do know: he will never die in my memory. I think I thought almost as much of him as you his own children did." Later he offered to pay for the education of Rosebud's youngest sister, Evelyn.[14]

Long Lance undertook the promotion tour in late March. Because Burden and Chanler sent him, and because the trip

was important for the movie, he may have thought it meant
that the investigation had ended, or had come to nothing.
Whatever it meant, he loved Hollywood. Through his connections at Paramount, he met and was photographed with
Clara Bow, the "It Girl" of the late 1920s, who commanded a
salary of $5000 a week.[15]

Thanks to a letter of introduction from Fannie Hurst,
Long Lance also met Douglas Fairbanks at his studio home
on the United Artists lot. The talkies had hurt his career,
but Fairbanks, the silent star, was at the height of his fame
and the King of Hollywood. He had a proper queen, too, in
Mary Pickford, the most popular female movie star in the
country. In a letter to Canon Middleton, Long Lance said
that Fairbanks and Pickford "are greater in person than
they are even on the screen—very real people." In Hollywood, he also met Charlie Chaplin, Irving Berlin and the
comedian Harold Lloyd.[16]

He worked hard to publicize *The Silent Enemy* in Hollywood, where there were other Indian actors, but few as
articulate as Long Lance, the smooth and faultlessly
dressed, self-styled Blackfoot. The Los Angeles *Times*
described him as "a very clever young Indian of the new
school, a Carlisle graduate who fought in the World War and
has written things for good magazines." At a pow-wow held
in his honor by Hollywood Indians from fourteen tribes,
Long Lance danced the prairie chicken dance with a young
Cherokee named Iron Eyes Cody.[17]

On March 22, Long Lance was introduced to Anita
Baldwin, one of the richest women in the United States. She
was in her mid-fifties, five feet five inches tall, with hazel
eyes and a fine Grecian nose. A graceful woman of regal
stature, the Los Angeles *Times* had dubbed her "the lady of
the peacocks."[18] She was not the first woman to fall under
Long Lance's spell, and when he left California to return to
New York, the twice-divorced woman could not get him out
of her mind.

Unknown to Long Lance, Ilia Tolstoy set out for
Winston-Salem on his investigative mission for Chanler.
Tolstoy had lived a rich and varied life. He was born in 1903

at Toptikovo in Tula Province, south of Moscow, and on both sides of his family he boasted famous ancestors: Leo Tolstoy, the Russian novelist, was his paternal grandfather, and General Diterichs, a distinguished Czarist officer, was his maternal grandfather. He attended schools at Odessa and the Moscow School of Agriculture, then served in the Imperial Cavalry under General Kuropatkin near Tashkent in the deserts of Central Asia. A superb rider, he once traveled on horseback from Samarkand, across the mountains of Afghanistan to Peshawar in northwestern India (now Pakistan). Commissioned in Her Majesty's Leib Guard, he fought against the Bolsheviks in the civil war, and after the defeat of the White Guard armies he fled to the United States.[19]

Tolstoy arrived in Winston-Salem in early April, the most beautiful month of the year. The sky was clear, the temperatures were balmy; red, white, purple and orange azaleas were blooming everywhere. The first leaves were sprouting on the oak trees. [20]

Since Long Lance's departure, the population of Winston-Salem had quadrupled from nearly twenty thousand in 1909 to eighty thousand in 1930, due mainly to the good fortunes of the R.J. Reynolds Tobacco Company, the most profitable tobacco operation in the country. It employed twelve thousand local residents. The spire of the twenty-three-storey Reynolds skyscraper dominated the city, and spread before it for blocks were Reynolds factories and the gaudy signs proclaiming: CAMELS LEAD THE WORLD. In 1913, when Winston and Salem officially amalgamated, R.J. Reynolds introduced the cigarette that became the best-selling brand in the 1920s. In 1930, the Reynolds Company sold 38 million Camels, and North Carolina's second-largest city became known as "Camel City." The smell of tobacco was everywhere. [21]

On his first morning in Winston-Salem, Tolstoy called on the Longs at their home on Brookstown Avenue. He got the address from the West End School where Joe had worked into his mid-seventies, until bad health kept him from the job. Brookstown Avenue was a short, dirt road in the middle of white West Winston. Tolstoy noted that the one-storey frame house on a slight hill was "very poor, but good in comparison with the colored houses around." The Longs kept their hedge and front lawn well trimmed and on the lot stood many good-sized trees: oak, walnut, and a chinaberry tree. [22] His knock at the door was answered by a thin, elderly man, about five feet, eight inches, with a moustache, straight gray hair and rather dark skin.

Tolstoy's Russian accent startled Joe and Sallie Long, but when he introduced himself as a friend of their son — he used the name Sylvester — they relaxed and welcomed him. Ilia understood Joe quite well, but Sallie's accent was much thicker, with a rollicking Deep South cadence, and he could not catch everything she said. Still, Sallie was anxious to hear all she could about her son, and she fired one question after another at their visitor. When Ilia reciprocated and began to probe into Sylvester's background and origins, Joe and Sallie became suspicious. They told him abruptly that they were Cherokee and suggested that he talk to their son, Abe, who worked at the Carolina Theater. The interview was over.

Ilia found Abe at the theater, where he managed the colored section. Prominently displayed by the side entrance to the gallery, he saw the ticket prices listed at ten and fifteen cents. [23] Ilia liked Abe at once, whom he described as "quite decent and intelligent," but Abe pretended at first that he did not know who Sylvester Long was. Joe and Sallie had identified Sylvester Long as their son, so Ilia was puzzled. He persisted, and finally Abe admitted "that he had a brother by the name of Sylvester, who has not been home for twenty years." He said no more.

Ilia then went to see R.H. Latham, the superintendent of schools, [24] who spoke of Joe Long as an "exceptionally good man" who had never missed a day of work. He said he knew Joe was an Indian, and, yes, he would gladly have a chat with him and find out what he could.

Joe told Latham that he was born in Yadkin County and that his father was a prominent white man by the name of John Vestal and his mother an Indian. [25] After a forty-year search for his mother, he told Latham, he finally found her in a small town in Alabama. It was then that she told him she was a Cherokee. Latham also learned that Sallie Long's father was white and her mother a Cherokee. (From about 1913 to 1953, the Indians known at the turn of the century as Croatans called themselves Cherokee. Today they call themselves Lumbees, from the Lumber River in Robeson County.[26])

Latham referred Ilia to William Blair, president of the Peoples Bank, a man Joe said he had known since his arrival in the city forty-five years earlier. The white community held the seventy-year-old Colonel Blair in high regard. He had graduated from Harvard and from Trinity (now Duke University) in neighboring Durham, and he had traveled widely and read far beyond the narrow confines of banking. The Winston-Salem *Journal* once said that William Blair would have been the English philosopher Francis Bacon's ideal of an educated man. "He can name the bones in the human body, enumerate all the moons of Saturn, interest the children with animal stories, and discuss philosophy. . . ."[27]

Colonel Blair, of course, was thrilled to meet the grandson of the giant of Russian literature, and he cleared his desk immediately. Leo Tolstoy's vast novels and intricate plots, with their strong, bold characters, epitomized in his mind the complexity of Russia. The American South was complex, too, as any native-born Yankee trying to grasp the subtleties of the racial system soon realized. Colonel Blair summarized for Ilia the basic southern rule: anyone with any known Negro ancestor was colored, even if he or she had blue eyes, blond hair and the fairest of skin. He probably used the example of Russia's greatest nineteenth-century poet, Alexander Pushkin, whose great-grandfather, Hannibal, one of Peter the Great's generals, was black. In the South, an American with the same pedigree as Pushkin would be regarded as colored, simply because one of his eight great-grandparents had black blood.[28] It seemed ludicrous, but Colonel Blair had more surprises for Ilia when he told him all that he knew of the Longs.

He explained that Joe Long came to Winston in the late 1880s, when the town had a population of less than eight thousand. Because of his hooked nose, tanned complexion and straight black hair, he was accepted as an Indian and treated accordingly. He even managed to get a job as a store clerk where all the other clerks were white. "Long was employed because it was understood he was an Indian," Colonel Blair told Ilia. It was also known in the community that Sallie Long had "only white and Indian blood with no mixture of any other." Because Joe and Sallie were "Indians," Colonel Blair recalled that they were advised to act as such. "I remember perfectly well that the white people, and perhaps I was among the number, advised Joe not to associate in any way with the colored people, as it was understood that he was an Indian."[29]

Looking back on it all, the elderly banker realized the difficult and unenviable position in which Joe and Sallie found themselves when they arrived in Winston. If they had moved to the southern section of the state, where mixed bloods were more numerous, they might have been legally registered as Indians. There were thousands of Croatans in Robeson County. No one knew for sure where they came from, but it was believed that they were descendants of survivors of Sir Walter Raleigh's missing colony. Colonel Blair outlined to Ilia the abortive attempt to found an English settlement on the North Carolina coast in the late 1580s. The white survivors intermingled with the neighboring Croatan Indians and later migrated to Robeson County. In Robeson, there were three racial classifications: white, colored and Indian—not just white and colored, as in Winston. The Croatans in Robeson had their own schools and churches.

Joe and Sallie Long first tried to gain acceptance as whites of Indian background, and early on in Winston they nearly succeeded. There was already a local family in Winston, the Poindexters,[30] who were known to be of distant Indian ancestry. At the turn of the century, individuals of white and some Indian ancestry—like Will Rogers, the famous humorist—were treated as whites. The Virginian-born second wife of former President Woodrow Wilson never tried to hide the fact that she was a descendant of Pocahontas.[31]

When Joe and Sallie presented themselves at the local white church, they were admitted, but not for long. Someone from Iredell County probably reported that "back home" they were classified as "colored." When the white congregation made it known that they were not welcome, Joe and Sallie left and attended the colored churches.[32] The issue was settled, the racial barrier had crashed down, and the Longs forevermore were "colored." Joe's dark skin had already convinced many in Winston that he had black and Indian blood. When the Long children reached school age, they attended the black school because, as Colonel Blair explained, "the races here have separate schools." White children avoided the Long children.[33]

Colonel Blair's testimony proved so illuminating that Ilia asked him to repeat the most salient points in a sworn affidavit. He complied, and in the document dated April 9, 1930, Colonel Blair said that "it has always been my understanding that Joe Long's wife had only white and Indian blood with no mixture of any other. . . . I have known Joe quite well through all these years and I never heard anyone in this city or state express even a doubt but that his was Indian blood."

After his lengthy talks with Colonel Blair and Latham, Ilia returned to see the Longs, and this time they received him with open arms. In his report to Chanler, Ilia wrote: "I thought they would never stop talking and telling me about their lives and showing me pictures." Sallie and Joe by this time knew Ilia was a loyal friend of their son and was on their side.

Ilia interpreted the evidence favorably, and on April 10 he wrote to Chanler to say that the family was "delightfully pleasant" and that he had an enjoyable visit. Joe and Sallie undoubtedly told him that two weeks earlier they had celebrated their fifty-first wedding anniversary.[34]

Ilia interpreted the evidence favorably, and on April 10 he telegraphed Chanler in New York: "HAVE FULL INFORMATION AND AFFIDAVIT OF HIM BEING INDIAN AND WHITE." When the telegram arrived, followed by Ilia's full account of his investigation, Chanler felt enormous relief. Long Lance may have lied about his past, he may have come from North Carolina and not the western plains, but at least he was Indian. He told Ilia that being an Indian "is all we care about; what tribe he belongs to is entirely secondary." In a note to Colonel Blair and Latham, Chanler thanked them for their help and said he would talk to Long Lance and "see that he stops calling himself a Blackfoot."[35] As far as Chanler was concerned, the case was closed.

Ilia Tolstoy and Long Lance had a grand reunion when they met in New York in late May. At first, Long Lance was surprised to hear of his friend's visit to his home town, but he was delighted to know that everyone in his family was doing well.

Just as important was the news that Ilia's report to Chanler had been favorable. He took one of his portraits as Baluk in *The Silent Enemy* and inscribed it: "For Ilia Tolstoy whom I am honored to call the best Pale-face Friend I have anywhere in the world —*Netawa Hanka-wanzi* Long Lance —May 30 '30." "Hanka-wanzi" was the highest compliment Long Lance could bestow; it meant that he had taken Ilia Tolstoy as his blood-brother.[36]

18

THE LADY OF THE PEACOCKS

RUMORS THAT he was part-black cost him some society friends, but Long Lance nevertheless enjoyed a busy social life in the summer and early fall of 1930. He stepped out often in his formal evening coat, tails, silk hat and patent leather shoes. He kept in trim, too, working out daily at an athletic club on the roof of a New York skyscraper. [1]

The reviews of his performance in *The Silent Enemy* continued to appear, maintaining his status as a celebrity. In September, *Liberty* magazine suggested that a clever producer should schedule James Fenimore Cooper's *Last of the Mohicans* and "assign Chief Long Lance — who did such good work in *The Silent Enemy* — to the role of Uncas." *Screenland*, a movie magazine, said that Long Lance, if cast in a talking picture, would "give Gary Cooper, Richard Dix and the rest of our great outdoor heroes of the screen an awful run for their cinema money." [2]

Long Lance was as playful as ever with reporters, always good for a colorful story and a lively interview. He earnestly told one journalist that every day he ate rare meat and raw eggs, and drank two quarts of milk every night after his work-out. [3] When the *New York Times* interviewed him, he spoke about the drought that threatened many parts of the country that fall. Seeding clouds was not the answer, Long

Lance said. He suggested instead that concentrated thought could bring on the rain to save the fall harvest. "I have no doubt that the mind of man can be brought to such a state that it can control the forces of nature," he told the *Times*. [4]

The nation still lay in the grip of the Great Depression, and Long Lance knew he was doing much better than most. Every day on the streets of New York he passed beggars and panhandlers, and returning home at night he walked by homeless people sleeping in doorways and on park benches. In the poorer districts there were long breadlines.

He tried to do what he could to help, for he was essentially a generous man. In early July, a former Carlisle student showed up on the steps of the Explorers Club looking for him. His name was Dan Arapaho, an Oglala Sioux from Pine Ridge Reserve in South Dakota, and he was in desperate straits, with no money and clad in a soiled blue shirt and an old pair of trousers. Long Lance checked his closet and gave the man a suit, shirts, ties, socks, even some of his underwear. He also gave him money to tide him over until he found work, which he later did, driving a truck. [5]

One woman he saw frequently that summer was Te Ata, or Mary Thompson, a Chickasaw Indian from eastern Oklahoma. She was a striking beauty with long, black braids who had graduated from the Oklahoma College for Women and studied theater at the Carnegie Institute of Technology in Pittsburgh. After coming to New York, she appeared in several roles on Broadway.

Te Ata was not at all disturbed by rumors of Long Lance's background. She accepted without question his story that he was a Blackfoot who had been adopted by Cherokees before coming to Carlisle. She found Long Lance "gracious" and "very personable," and she simply liked being with him. She enjoyed his inquiring mind and found they had many common interests, among them a keen enthusiasm for new books and movies. [6]

However, the rumors were having an effect on Long Lance, and his friend Seumas knew it. Long Lance grew apprehensive and self-conscious at the Explorers Club, feeling he was always under scrutiny. In Calgary, he had never touched alcohol or smoked, but now he indulged heavily in both. He attended club meetings smelling of liquor. [7] Against the rules of the club, he kept alcohol in his room, in a bottle labeled "hair tonic." Seumas and Clyde Fisher stood by him, but the belief that he was a "half breed nigger" showed in others' hostile glances. [8] By the end of the summer he was ready to leave the Explorers Club.

An opportunity to move out gracefully came that fall when he was offered free flying lessons at Roosevelt Field on Long Island. With his savings, he paid for room and board at the Roosevelt Field Hotel. He began his training in early October, under an instructor named Lester (Husky) Flewellyn, and he first went aloft in a Consolidated Fleet biplane with a Kinner ninety-horsepower engine. [9]

After only five hours of flying time, Long Lance was eager for more excitement. He volunteered to demonstrate a new automatic Switlik Manufacturing Company parachute at the Air Races at Trenton, New Jersey, in mid-October—even though he had never parachuted before. On a cold and blustery Sunday afternoon he dropped through the cabin floor of the Switlik plane and, far below, thirty thousand spectators watched him float safely to the ground. [10]

Two weeks later, ready for more thrills, Long Lance went up and executed several unscheduled stunts. On his first solo flight he took his plane up to an altitude of about three thousand feet, then nosed it down with the engine in full throttle, pulled back on the stick and executed a perfect loop. He then went up again and did two more loops and some rolls and tailspins, outlandish tricks for a rookie flyer on a solo flight. On October 29, 1930, in the New York *Sun*, a story appeared detailing the feat and once again repeating the accomplishments of Long Lance's career, from a famous football player at Carlisle to West Point Cadet, to light-heavyweight boxing champion of the Canadian army. The item described Long Lance's aerobatics before an audience of instructors who looked on "aghast" while other students turned "a pinkish pale. . . ." The *Sun* continued:

Chief Long Lance says there is something about the air that agrees particularly well with the temperament of the Indian. The ranginess and freedom akin to that of this continent before the advent of the white man appeals to the redskin. The Indian aviator says he hopes to interest others of his race in the game of emulating the eagle. He is very confident of his ability to fly and is completing the course at the Long Island field rapidly. A week ago Saturday he made his first parachute jump, or rather he was dumped out by Parker Cramer, who flew Sir Hubert Wilkins over the pole. . . .

Chief Long Lance has always proved himself to be the master of the unexpected. Up until he was in his teens he could talk little English, could not read it at all and had never been inside a white man's house. He has since been an honor student at Carlisle, a West Point cadet, a winner of the Croix de Guerre. . . . [11]

Long Lance did not allow his social life to slip while staying at Roosevelt Field. He started dating a young woman flyer, Laura Ingalls, who came from a wealthy family and had been educated in Paris and Vienna. That same October when Long Lance parachuted and did his solo stunts, Laura Ingalls became the first woman to fly from Los Angeles to Roosevelt Field (in twenty-five hours and thirty-five minutes). [12]

Long Lance wrote to Mike Eagle Speaker in Alberta to tell him of his flying lessons and declared them "more fun than riding bucking horses." In mid-December, he sent a note to Dorothy Fellers' sister, Isabel, to announce that he had obtained his private pilot's license and was working on earning a commercial license. "I like it better than anything I have ever done," he told Isabel and her husband, who lived in Connecticut. "I seldom see New York anymore—thrown the old top hat into my locker at the Explorers Club, and forgot all about it." [13]

Climbing, diving, banking, making loops and rolls, Long Lance had never experienced such freedom. It rivaled anything he imagined of the freedom of the Plains Indians a century before. In the air he was not a "full-blooded Indian" or a "colored," but a man alone against the elements. There was nobody to report to, nobody to prove himself to, nobody to lie to. Among the clouds his only enemy was death, and he did not fear it. He escaped all the rumors and ugliness, literally rising above it all in the skies over New York. He would soon be brought down to reality.

On December 31, New Year's Eve, his brother Walter left Winston-Salem for New York. When he arrived in the city he discreetly inquired about Sylvester and learned of his flying lessons at Roosevelt Field. On January 5, the two brothers met, probably in Harlem, after a separation of twenty-two years. Walter told him that Joe and Sallie had been dangerously ill that fall. Their father, now seventy-seven, had been hospitalized for five days in late November. Abe and Walter could not afford the doctors' fees and hospital bills, and they needed help from Sylvester. [14] An awkward taxi ride through Manhattan followed, after which Sylvester blindly jumped out and ran up the steps at Penn Station.

After his meeting with Walter, he could not sleep. Next morning, he poured out his anguish in a letter to his brother.

I must have been in sort of a daze. I don't remember how I said goodbye. And it was only when I had gotten on the train and my brain had cooled a little that I remembered seeing you reaching for the taxi fare, and then realized that you, too, must have gotten out at Penn Station. I had been under the impression that you were going to take the taxi on to some other destination, and when I got out my mind was so fixed on not making a fool of myself saying goodbye to you, that my eyes actually saw things that did not register in my mind until I had gotten home.

I lay awake most of the night, wishing that I could phone you . . . kicking myself because I had not stayed at the apartment all night with you, and a thousand other things that came to my mind when it was too late. I would have given anything to have seen you again. I don't think that I have ever felt the emotions that my visit with you brought into being.

I have not yet fully untangled these emotions: my own

darling brother whom I used to romp and play with, coming to
me after twenty-two years, wondering if I were going to be
ashamed of him. . . . [15]

Long Lance felt pulled in opposite directions, frustrated and
guilty. His love for his family struggled against his uncom-
promising ambition and, though it did not surprise him, it
disturbed him that in the end his ambition won out. Once his
flying lessons were paid for, he sent checks home: $25 in
March, $30 in April, and, when he began working again,
$100 in June, $230 in August, $50 in December and $40 in
February. He wrote to Abe to thank him for being "so kind
and sympathetic with me." He asked him to tell his father
"that I love him as I have always done — more than anything
in the world now — him and our sweet mother." But he would
not come home. He wrote: "If there is anything in the
papers, Abe, you will be careful about names, won't you.
What a condition this is! Good night my dear brother — And
thanks a million times for what you and Walter are doing." [16]

Within two weeks of seeing Walter, Long Lance was at
center stage again, this time making a special appearance at
a showing of *The Silent Enemy* at a theater near Roosevelt
Field. At the end of the month he spoke to five hundred
people at the Hotel Pennsylvania in New York, and in the
audience were film stars Maurice Chevalier, Tallulah Bank-
head, Fredric March and Claudette Colbert. [17]

When a chance at a glamorous job in California surfaced,
he jumped at it. His new employer this time would be Anita
Baldwin, whom he had met earlier on his publicity tour in
Hollywood. Mrs. Baldwin was fascinated by Indian culture
and had written several songs about the tribes of New
Mexico and Arizona. She had traveled among the Hopi in
New Mexico to research their music and to collect artifacts.
From her first meeting with Long Lance, she was impressed
by the handsome Blackfoot chief, and when he left Hol-
lywood for New York, he promised he would send her a copy
of *Long Lance*. She kept in touch with him while he was in
New York, and early in the spring of 1931 she wrote to offer
him employment as her secretary and bodyguard on a trip to
Europe in the fall. [18]

Long Lance accepted. Once he received his commercial pilot's license in mid-May, 1931, he left for Chicago where he boarded the *Santa Fe Chief*, the express train to southern California. [19] A short-term job would allow him to send more money to his parents, and provide a temporary distraction from the agonizing decision of whether to return home.

On his way west, Long Lance looked up an old friend, Susie Curtis, at Elmira, New York. She had met him in Banff in 1926, the summer he had, in her words, a "fearful" affair with "a married woman of Chicago." Miss Curtis had corresponded with him ever since, and at her request Long Lance met her at the Elmira station. She traveled with him westward on the train for two hours, until they met the eastbound train on which she returned home. They never saw each other again. [20]

As the *Santa Fe Chief* chugged to the outskirts of metropolitan Los Angeles, it crossed the San Gabriel Valley. From the train window Long Lance caught his first glimpse of Anita Baldwin's immense ranch of more than three thousand acres. The Santa Fe Railway had been granted a right-of-way across the estate by her father, Elias Jackson, or "Lucky" Baldwin, in return for a station on the property. Included in the deed was a provision that all passenger trains must stop on signal at the Baldwins' Santa Anita station. When the train pulled in, Long Lance grabbed his bags and stepped down onto the wooden station platform. Mrs. Baldwin's chauffeur met him in one of her three Rolls-Royces and drove him to Anoakia, the Baldwin mansion.

Anita's father had worked for years to create a great fruit and livestock farm. He personally supervised the planting of avenues of eucalyptus and poplar trees and groves of fruit trees. After his death, Anita kept up the work, building her own home, Anoakia, on the northern edge of the estate so that she could work at it daily. The first two letters of the mansion's name are from Anita and the next three from the lofty oak trees scattered over the estate. It was discovered later that "Anoak" itself was an Indian word that meant "where no harm shall befall."

To enter the estate, the chauffeur first checked in at the guard house on Baldwin Avenue. A high, ten-foot concrete wall—nicknamed the "Great Wall of Anoakia"—surrounded the property, which was lit all night. A guard with a sidearm and dogs patrolled the grounds day and night. For more protection, barbed wire and six strands of low-voltage wires had been stretched along the top of the wall. If the circuit was broken, a revolving light on the roof of the mansion flicked on and a system of bells, gongs and sirens was activated.

Anoakia astounded Long Lance, having come from the breadlines and panhandlers of New York. The mansion and the grounds belonged to another world. After leaving the guard house, the Rolls-Royce passed a large stable, a garage and finally came to the house itself, built in Italian Renaissance style with a balustraded terrace, a grand stairway and a loggia with Roman columns. In 1928 the building was valued at $500,000. It stood on two levels facing Foothill Boulevard to the south and was shaped like a half-H, with terraces spreading about it. Built atop a knoll, the house looked over the San Gabriel Valley, and on a clear day one could see the ocean in the distance. [21]

The chauffeur carried Long Lance's baggage to the door. Edwin, Anita's Scottish butler, answered the bell, greeted Long Lance, then told one of the Indian maids to inform "Madame" that her guest had arrived. Long Lance's bags were taken to one of the guest suites, and he was invited inside.

The living room was on the main floor, equidistant from the dining room and the library. Through the opened doors he could look through all three rooms, a distance of more than a hundred feet. Rich oriental rugs covered the floors and custom-designed furniture filled the rooms. The oak leaf and acorn, the peacock and the California poppy—Anita's favorite symbols—appeared in the decor of all three. From where he sat, Long Lance could see the sculpted plaster oak leaves and acorns and the peacock theme in the Tiffany-designed luster glass chandeliers on the ceiling of the living room. The tiles in the fireplace were fired to a peacock hue.

When Anita arrived, she welcomed him and showed him around the house. Also on the main floor were bedrooms, the

"Cicero Sapp", a cartoon strip which appeared in the *New York Evening World*, August 18, 1925. (Joe Bradshaw)

A photograph of Long Lance taken by the White Studio in New York. (Glenbow-Alberta Institute, Canon Middleton Collection)

A drawing of Long Lance by Princess Alexandra Victoria of
Schleswig-Holstein-Glücksburg, completed in 1930. The illustration
appears in *Redman Echoes*, compiled by Roberta Forsberg. (Los
Angeles: Frank Wiggins Trade School, 1933)

Above: Long Lance, left, Ilia Tolstoy, center, and Bob Hennessy, on the wilderness set of *The Silent Enemy*. (Glenbow-Alberta Institute, Canon Middleton Collection)

Below: A still from *The Silent Enemy*. Chetoga (Chauncey Yellow Robe) greets Baluk (Long Lance). (Glenbow-Alberta Institute, Canon Middleton Collection)

Douglas Burden, from the program "How *The Silent Enemy* Was Made". (Douglas Burden)

William Chanler, from the same program. (Douglas Burden)

The Indian village of *The Silent Enemy*. (Glenbow-Alberta Institute, Canon Middleton Collection)

Above: Long Lance, Dr. Clyde Fisher, and Chauncey Yellow Robe, at the American Museum of Natural History, New York City, September 23, 1929. (United States Army Research Collection, Carlisle Barracks, Pennsylvania, and Glenbow-Alberta Institute, Canon Middleton Collection)

Right: Seumas, Chief of Clann Fhearghuis, in the library of the Explorers Club in New York, around 1930. (Lee Ash)

Left: Anita Baldwin, "the Lady of the Peacocks", around 1905. (Los Angeles Public Library)

Below: Long Lance as an aviator, Roosevelt Aviation School, Roosevelt Field, Long Island. (Roberta Forsberg)

Walter Long with his father, Joe Long, taken around the time of his visit with Long Lance in New York in 1931. (Newman Dalton)

Elizabeth "Bessie" Clapp, in a photo inscribed "Enni-Poka from Dakotawin". "Enni-Poka" is her spelling of Buffalo Child in Blackfoot; "Dakotawin" is the name Long Lance gave her. (Glenbow-Alberta Institute, Canon Middleton Collection)

kitchen and breakfast room, and a small North American Indian Hall decorated with scenes of the Indians of the northern plains. She had commissioned Maynard Dixon, a leading western artist, to complete the murals when the house was built in 1913. Upstairs were a number of additional suites, but because of the financial pinch, which even Anita felt, they were closed. There were gas and electric fixtures in all of the rooms and a fireplace in each bedroom. The basement contained a bowling alley wide enough for two lanes, a billiard room, a "jinks" or rumpus room, and a wine cellar with two huge barrels of wine (one of muscatel, one of port) and a rack with niches for as many as 549 bottles. On the north side of the house was a swimming pool seventy-five feet long and thirty feet wide. For a bathhouse Anita had built a miniature reproduction of the Athenian Parthenon, with six dressing rooms, all with private showers. There was a Greek-columned gymnasium that Long Lance was welcome to use. Throughout the grounds were aviaries with peacocks, birds of paradise and love birds. [22]

After a few days at Anoakia, Anita and Long Lance traveled to Tallac, her large, thirty-two-hundred-acre estate at the southwestern corner of Lake Tahoe on the California side of the California-Nevada border. To the southwest of Anita's home, surrounded by massive yellow pines and cedars, Long Lance saw the mountain the local Washoe Indians called "Great Mountain," or Mount Tallac. He fitted in well here, and at a party one day he demonstrated how the Indians let fly their arrows from the hip. He was an excellent shot with the bow and arrow and flung off bull's eye after bull's eye. [23]

At Tallac, Long Lance learned much about Anita Baldwin. Despite every apparent advantage, he discovered that she was a much distressed woman. At night when she could not sleep, she called Ralph Tweedle, one of her guards, and asked him to bring some Cokes to a little screened-in side porch at her lodge. There, in the dark, she talked about how worried she was about losing her property, about threats on her life and people trying to break in to see her, usually demanding financial help. It was assumed she was immensely wealthy and probably easy prey, but in fact she was house- and property-poor and could not even pay her taxes. [24]

Anita's life had not been happy. As a child, all she had enjoyed was money. Her father had risen from humble origins to become one of California's wealthiest men, but at the expense of any meaningful family life. Born on a farm in Ohio in 1828, Eli, or "Lucky," came west by wagon train at an early age. He made a small fortune from shrewd real estate speculation around San Francisco, then invested heavily in the Comstock Silver Mine in Nevada, making millions. He used his profits to buy up land around the small town of Los Angeles, eventually accumulating more than fifty thousand acres. During the great real estate boom at the turn of the century, he sold portions for prices ten times higher than he had paid and, with his coffers overflowing, he bought a huge estate at Lake Tahoe. On his death in 1909, his fortune was estimated at $10,000,000. [25]

Unfortunately, Lucky Baldwin did not have the same success with women. He had four wives and, in his biographer's words, "a well-defined but unsubstantiated rumor of a fifth, not to mention numerous sweethearts and a breach of promise and seduction suits."[26] It was said that he was so fearful of being poisoned by his second wife that he refused to eat anything she prepared until she had tasted it.[27] He had an affair with Jennie Dexter when he was in his late forties and she was sixteen, eight years younger than his daughter by his first marriage. Their child, Anita, was born in January, 1876, and three years later Lucky and Jennie were married.[28]

Anita's mother died when she was five years old, and three years later her father married again, this time a beautiful blonde named Lilly Bennett, who, at sixteen, was just eight years older than Anita. When she was older, Anita was haunted by her origins and undertook extensive genealogical research. She discovered that her mother was descended several generations back from a line of Flemish counts, who in turn traced their ancestry back to the Emperor Charlemagne.[29]

Anita's own experience with marriage proved to be as
disappointing as her father's. When she was fifteen, she
eloped with her first cousin. She gave birth to twins who
died in infancy and after seven years of marriage her husband deserted her. She then married Hull McClaughrey, the
son of a wealthy northern California family, but in 1913 this
union as well was terminated in the courts of law. Anita gave
him $300,000 as a settlement and won custody of their two
children, Dextra and Baldwin.[30] Anita told reporters in 1914
that she would never marry again. She once explained to the
San Francisco *Chronicle* that she preferred dogs to men.
"They are faithful and true. They are constant. In this
particular they differ most from men."[31] She changed her
name back to Baldwin.

When her second marriage ended, Anita immersed herself in community work, and during World War I she placed
her estate at the disposal of the government. The United
States Balloon School was established on her property.
Anita spent $10,000 a month on the U.S. Army soldiers until
the war ended. After the war she donated large sums for the
establishment of a hospital for crippled children in Los
Angeles. Anonymously, she gave $50,000 to an orthopedic
hospital in San Francisco. She contributed substantial
amounts to establish the Anita Baldwin Baby Clinic in the
city, and she was heavily involved in women's issues, upholding the right of women to vote. And she strongly supported
the North American Indian. "All my life," she later wrote, "I
have been interested in Indians and he [Long Lance] was
only one of many whom I have tried to help."[32]

By the summer of 1931 Anita was sad and lonely. Despite
all the care she had showered on them, her children's lives
were in complete disarray. Dextra had married and
divorced. Baldwin recently had left his wife and two children
to live in Paris with Suzanne Lenglen, the French tennis
star. And there were economic problems. As she wrote to
Baldwin on December 16, 1930: "Business is so very bad. . . .
There are countless suicides and so much red activity." By
spring, conditions had deteriorated further, and she had to
cut back Anoakia's staff to a chef, assistant chef, two Indian

house maids, three gardeners, two watchmen, a chauffeur and a handyman.[33]

Anita lived in fear at Anoakia, despite the elaborate security system. She was convinced each May 1 that Communists would storm her home. In late 1929 she announced that she intended to sell all her property in southern California, then estimated at a value of twenty to twenty-five million dollars, and live year-round at Lake Tahoe. "For years and years I have wanted to cut away from the worries and troubles which the management of this business provokes in order that I might have time to devote myself primarily to music and travel," she told a reporter. "There are many, many places that I still have not seen and that I would like to visit."[34] Unfortunately, the Depression made it impossible to find buyers, but she still insisted upon going to Europe to see her son, Baldwin, in the fall of 1931.

Anita found Long Lance a refreshing diversion. He was the perfect choice as bodyguard and secretary for the European trip. She wrote to Baldwin from Tallac on July 6 and told him all about her new Indian employee.

I am planning some work, musically, etc., with an educated Indian, who has gone thru Carlisle, Manlius and left West Point to join the Canadians in the World War and returned a Captain of Infantry. He has just completed his air course, being a commissioned pilot, etc. He had collaborated on a book and movie called *The Silent Enemy*, a story of the Indians in the North. He is a Blackfoot, born in Montana and must be about 35 years old. He is a gentleman and his ways are gentle, too, so I am glad to have him in the home while I assimilate all the knowledge he can impart of legend, customs, etc.

She trusted Long Lance and insisted on only one precaution, which was to warn Tweedle, the night guard, "to keep a special watch on the maids' quarters since Long Lance, as an Indian Chief, might assert his 'tribal rights' if he felt so inclined."[35]

Long Lance and Anita had long talks, and he spared no details about himself. When he drew up his American passport application at Tallac in early July, he asked her to witness it.[36] He began by stating he was born at Sweetgrass, Montana, and again he dropped years from his age, claiming that he was born on December 1, 1896. He added that his father, Pitah, died at Sweetgrass in 1900. On Anita's advice he marked the purpose of his journey as a "pleasure trip" to "France, Italy, Germany, Sweden, England, Austria, Spain, Switzerland, Belgium," with his mailing address as Tallac, El Dorado County, California.

If Anita had doubts about Long Lance's true identity, they were removed when an affidavit from Emma Newashe, dated July 1, arrived. In June, Long Lance wrote to his old friend from Carlisle, who had married shortly after graduation and lived in Luther, Oklahoma. He asked her to certify for the United States Passport Office that he was born in Montana, near Sweetgrass, and that she had known him since Carlisle.[37] Twenty-one years after Carlisle, Emma still believed his story of being a Blackfoot adopted by Cherokees. In her signed affidavit she testified that "to the best of my knowledge and belief he was born in Sweet Grass, Montana, on December 1, 1896."

In mid-July, Long Lance met with a State Department official in San Francisco. He brought his application, witnessed by Anita, and the affidavit from Emma Newashe, "an old family friend." Long Lance told the officer that he had asked his brother, Eagle Speaker, who lived on the Blood Reservation in Alberta, to make out an affidavit, but unfortunately he had not done so. The agent noted in his report: "Applicant claims that his brother is rather illiterate and would not perhaps understand how to attend to this matter." Long Lance said that Emma knew Eagle Speaker "intimately" but had forgotten to state this in her affidavit. Almost casually, he advised the State Department to check the records of the Carlisle Indian School to verify his tribal identity. He gambled that it would not go to the bother of checking with the Bureau of Indian Affairs. All went well. The Carlisle records were not checked. Satisfied that the applicant was "a full-blooded Indian of the Black Foot tribe," and "a very high type, intelligent person," the agent recommended that the passport be issued.

The night before Anita and Long Lance departed for

Europe, Elizabeth Analla, a Yankton Sioux from South
Dakota who was living in Los Angeles, visited Anoakia. She
knew the Indian maids who worked for Anita. While there
she spoke with Long Lance and learned of the Sioux he
admired most, Chauncey Yellow Robe, who had been "like a
father to him."[38] It is a revealing comment. Despite his
outward confidence, Long Lance always sought an authority figure—a Canon Middleton, a Chauncey Yellow Robe,
and, as the weeks passed, an Anita Baldwin.

Anita and Long Lance viewed the trip to Europe somewhat differently. For Long Lance (he wrote Emma
Newashe) it was a "vacation given me as a forerunner of
some work that I am going to do for the Indians upon my
return in November. . . . I am getting a four-place Lockheed
plane, as my travelling vehicle, and will devote all of my time
from then on to helping our people, with private backing."
The understanding was that as long as he behaved himself
he would be given his airplane, but, according to a later
statement by Anita, there was no such promise. He was
simply hired on "a salary as secretary-bodyguard, etc." to
accompany her, her daughter, Dextra, and Lowry McCaslin, the manager of her Los Angeles office, to Europe. On
August 26 they all sailed from New York to Le Havre on the
Ile de France.[39]

Lowry McCaslin was a recent graduate of the University
of Southern California, and just twenty-three years old. At
university he had been on an athletic scholarship and played
for the basketball and football teams. One of his best friends
was a young man with acting ambitions whose name was
John Wayne. On his frequent visits to Anita, McCaslin often
found Long Lance there, and the two men got along well.
They boxed at Anoakia's gymnasium. It was arranged that
McCaslin would leave the party in southern France, see
Europe on his own, then join Anita, Dextra and Long Lance
in Berlin a few weeks later.

During McCaslin's absence, Anita, Dextra, Long Lance
and a hired chauffeur drove from Cannes to Nice, Monte
Carlo, Monaco, Cap d'Antibes, Juan les Pins and Barcelona.
In the mornings Long Lance was introduced to the skimpy

continental breakfast of coffee and croissants. In the evenings came his reward: exquisitely cooked French meals and fine wines. At the villa Anita rented at Cannes, he installed a boxing ring and every day he ran along the beach. [40]

On the way to southern France, Anita visited Baldwin in Paris, where he ran a radio import shop near the Etoile. At his apartment Long Lance would have seen his collection of French impressionist works, particularly those of Henri de Toulouse-Lautrec, which Baldwin had been buying for some time. Long Lance told Anita that her son was "a fine chap." His remarks pleased her, as he knew they would, and she passed them on to Baldwin. [41]

In October, Anita and her entourage traveled through Italy, Austria, Germany, Belgium and Holland. They stayed at the best hotels: the Excelsior in Rome, the Hotel Bristol in Vienna, the Adlon in Berlin. All the while, Long Lance took notes. Years earlier he had read of ancient Rome in *Ben Hur*, [42] and many times Princess Alexandra had told him about Germany. Now he was seeing it all firsthand. He found Spain "unsettled politically," as indeed it was, just five years before the onset of its civil war. In Rome he made no comment on Mussolini's government, but wrote in a letter back to North America that the city was "far more interesting with its ruins than I had anticipated." He liked Vienna and Berlin most of all, for their "cleanliness, industry and stately beauty."

Of the five countries they visited, Germany and Austria seemed to be in the most serious economic straits. In Germany, there were more than seven million out of work. Long Lance wrote that "no one knows what will ultimately happen to them. Hundreds of gigantic factories are closed tight, throwing the villages which depended upon them into utter unemployment." [43] The year before, a new party, the National Socialists, had won a hundred seats in the *Reichstag* elections. If he had inquired, Long Lance would have learned that Princess Alexandra's ex-husband, Prince August Wilhelm, had recently declared that Adolf Hitler was God's gift to Germany. The ex-Kaiser's fourth son had just joined the Nazi Party. [44]

There are contradictory reports of Long Lance and his state of mind on the European trip. Clearly, something happened. He was not one to reveal much of his innermost thoughts, certainly he never did so in any of his letters, but from Anita's remarks it is apparent that not all was well. Publicly, she stated that he was "a man of estimable character and gentlemanly in all respects (his conduct being always of the highest type)." Yet, privately, she recorded different impressions. Six months after the trip, Anita reported that he had made several suicide attempts in Europe. In August, she said, "the first night out on the *Ile de France*, he was saved from jumping through a porthole. In Cannes and Berlin he was also saved."[45]

There is more evidence of his bizarre behavior. In Berlin in late October, Anita, McCaslin and Long Lance were invited to a formal dinner party of thirty to forty people at the Adlon Hotel, sponsored by German friends of Anita. Long Lance was late. When the dinner began, his chair was the only one unoccupied. A number of the Germans had read *Long Lance* (the German translation appeared in 1929) and were anxious to meet him. When finally he did arrive, he stumbled in, drunk.

The waiters had just carried in on a large tray a roast pig with an apple stuffed in its mouth. They placed it at the head of the table. At that moment, and to everyone's horror, Long Lance ran to the head of the table and grabbed the huge carving knife. He hovered menacingly over McCaslin, looked him in the eyes and shouted, "I'm going to cut your heart out." McCaslin turned white. When Long Lance finally calmed down, McCaslin took him to his room. The dinner party was ruined.[46]

Anita and her party returned in mid-November from Amsterdam. She later wrote that Long Lance "was left in New York in Nov. given up as too much of a responsibility."[47] He still belonged to the Explorers Club, and he stayed there in New York, momentarily lifted out of an inexplicable but deep depression. Through his old friend Seumas, he met Elisabeth Randolph Clapp, known to her friends as Bessie, a dancer who lived with her girlfriend in a Greenwich Village apartment.

Bessie was an unlikely candidate for the bohemian life, having come from a wealthy and influential family. She had attended the Dwight School in Englewood, New Jersey, the exclusive Ethel Walker School in Simsbury, Connecticut, the Holy Cross Convent in Washington, D.C., and, finally, the Collège Féminin in Paris. Her socially prominent grandmother, Mrs. Charles E. Clapp, was the niece of Henry Clay Frick, the famous industrialist. Her grandmother had high hopes for her vivacious granddaughter, as did her parents, but Bessie chose instead a life style of her own in New York and Greenwich Village. [48]

She was eighteen years old and believed that she was part Indian; as a result, she "always felt drawn to them as one might be drawn towards a magnet." [49] Long Lance became an irresistible attraction, and Bessie fell in love with him. She told him all about herself. Her parents had separated several years earlier; her father moved to Mississippi and her mother, with a new husband, to Kinderhook, New York. Bessie's uncle worked as a stockbroker in New York. [50] Her grandmother's uncle, Henry Clay Frick, was a coal and coke baron who had ruthlessly amassed a fortune at the turn of the century. On one of their walks, they passed Frick's home on Fifth Avenue at Seventy-first Street, and Bessie, laughing, told Long Lance how Frick built his five-million-dollar mansion to "make Carnegie's place look like a miner's shack." Inside the mansion were paintings by El Greco, Van Dyck, Vermeer, Rembrandt and Rubens. [51]

Long Lance warmed to her, telling her of his boyhood among the Blackfoot. They spoke a great deal about Indians, and about old Seumas and his eccentricities. He mentioned Anita and the airplane she had promised him. Bessie believed that "if a person really loves someone, no matter what nationality he is, she has a perfect right to marry him." [52] The pretty brunette wanted to marry Long Lance who, she said, "apparently had no worries or cares in the world." He gave her the Sioux name "Dakatowin," which he told her meant "Indian maiden." [53] All indications are that he fell in love as quickly and as deeply with her as she did with him.

By this time in his life, Long Lance wanted to marry. He

knew he was getting old, slipping into middle age. At the
Halle Brothers Book Fair in Cleveland in mid-October,
1928, he told a woman reporter that "man reaches his peak
of physical prowess at thirty-four years. At thirty-eight the
decline begins." He turned forty-one on December 1, 1931.
In a letter written to Mike Eagle Speaker in May, 1930, he
congratulated him on his marriage and added, "I am leaving
it off too long. . . ."[54] But he never asked Bessie to marry
him, probably still fearing the implications of such a commit-
ment and the constant risk of being exposed as a fraud and
an impostor. Perhaps, too, he did not want to hurt so young
and innocent a creature; there was, after all, genuine affec-
tion between them. Or perhaps he was simply too ambitious,
too selfish, to devote his life to another. In any event, he told
one further and tragic falsehood; he claimed to be engaged to
someone else. In Bessie's words, "being an Indian, he
wouldn't break his promise to her."[55]

For more than twenty years Long Lance had lived in a
world of make-believe. Cut off from any real relationship
with any living person—he had not written to Canon
Middleton for over a year—he had not a soul to rely on now
except Anita Baldwin. He wrote pleading letters and sent
her telegrams; finally, Anita agreed to help. She told him
that "if he gave up his fast cocktail-drinking New York
friends, eschewed parties and women, and left drinking
alone, his tuition would be paid at an air school and an effort
made to assist him in acquiring a plane."[56]

19

THE TRAIL ENDS

I N LATE DECEMBER, 1931, Long Lance was once again aboard the *Santa Fe Chief*, heading across the Midwest on his way to southern California. The lulling motion of the train did not calm his anxieties. Rumors that he was an impostor were circulating in New York again, and life at the Explorers Club had never been more uncomfortable. But as always he had displayed none of his inner torment. After he packed his bags the night before, he had taken the club's switchboard operator to dinner. She later reported that Long Lance had appeared happy that evening and was looking forward to his trip to the West Coast.[1] Shortly after his departure, the club secretary wrote to the commissioner of the Bureau of Indian Affairs to ask if Long Lance really was a Blackfoot and if, as another rumor had it, he had been expelled from West Point "for conduct unbecoming a cadet."[2] En route to Los Angeles he sent a note to Alice Tye, Commissioner Graham's secretary, to tell her: "I am on my way to the coast to resume my flying and get my Lockheed. My address will be just: Santa Anita, California."[3]

At Anoakia he was reunited with Anita, and any onlookers, if they did not look closely at skin coloring, might have thought it was a mother welcoming a returning son. Anita looked all of her fifty-five years, but Long Lance easily could have passed for thirty-five, the age he claimed to be. She greeted him warmly, believing that his arrival was proof of

223

reformed behavior, and later, on December 28, wrote
Baldwin: "Long Lance is here for a few days—while seeking
a place to stay in or near Glendale where he plans to finish his
[pilot] training as eastern weather delayed him too much.
He takes some scientists up 20,000 ft.—next August—to
photograph eclipse—comet or some solar event."[4]

That evening, at dinner, no doubt Anita launched into a
discussion of her favorite themes. Long Lance would try to
appear interested, but he had heard it all before, in Cannes,
Rome, Berlin and Vienna. Back in the United States, she
fretted about her country being full of racketeers, kidnap-
pers and gangsters. "At present," she said, "we are law-ed
to death and taxed to death. We have no freedom, but too
much license!" She attacked President Hoover, whom she
believed was ruining the country. "During the Hoover
administration, my holdings have shrunk in value from
$35,000,000 to about $15,000,000...." She feared that
Japan's aggression in China would eventually plunge the
United States into another world war.[5]

Long Lance stayed at a hotel in nearby Glendale but
frequently visited the Santa Anita Ranch and Anoakia.
Anita offered him "the use of my home, my collection of
books and research information, for study and for a headquarters...." She also paid his tuition for an advanced
flying course at the Glendale airfield, and visited him there.[6]

As December passed into January and then into February, time weighed heavily on Long Lance. He seemed no
closer to getting his Lockheed, and he did not hear further
about the flying expedition to Central America to find a lost
Mayan city, which he felt he had been promised.[7] Long
Lance was free to fly whenever he wanted at the Glendale
field, or to go riding at the Santa Anita Ranch, or to read the
rare books in Anita's library, but as usual he wanted something more exciting. He felt frustrated and uncertain, and
he began to drink excessively, with predictable results.

Iron Eyes Cody, the young Cherokee actor who had met
Long Lance in March, 1930, on his Hollywood publicity tour
for *The Silent Enemy*, visited Anoakia several times and
witnessed Long Lance's abusive behavior to Anita's guards.

"He'd come up drunk and push these guys around," Cody said. "He was a husky man. When he'd started drinking, boy —he'd try to break the gate down. So they said, 'Someday we're going to put one in you.' He always told me that they threatened to shoot him."[8]

There was friction, as well, between Long Lance and Anita, and it got worse when she heard he had fallen in with a fast crowd in Los Angeles. He did small things to annoy her. Soon after he returned from New York he told her, playfully, that in a single month in New York he had slept with more than a dozen women.[9] By mid-March she distrusted him so much that she hired a man to follow him and report on his movements.[10]

At the same time, Anita was obsessed with the safety of her grandchildren, for earlier in March Charles Lindbergh's infant child had been kidnapped from his isolated estate in New Jersey. Anita dispatched Ralph Tweedle, her guard, to stay at Dextra's to protect her and her daughter,[11] also named Anita. On March 7, she wrote to Baldwin in Paris:

> We are guarding Anita rather carefully — since the Lindbergh tragedy and am wondering if I should not write Nell [Baldwin's wife] to be cautious with the children. I can't afford to give them a watchman at present.
>
> Could you afford $100.00 per month for a night man? I wish Nell would move to her mother's for a while.
>
> If we could only "clean house" here—in these United States! I go about armed to the teeth like a pirate! I am wondering what awful thing will happen if this continues. We need a vigilante committee—a few lynchings, etc. God keep you, my son. . . .

By the third week in March, Long Lance became resigned to the truth that Anita's plane, his beloved Lockheed, would never be his. Then, on March 17 or 18, Bessie Clapp telephoned from New York to tell him she had married a Japanese art student, named Tom Hayakawa. The news was made no less painful by her confession that she would have married Long Lance, if only he had been free. She and her husband would be stopping in Los Angeles on their way to Japan—could she see him? Thinking fast, he replied that, regrettably, he would be leaving in three days, that he had decided to return to Canada and was heading up to Vancouver.[12]

On the evening of March 19, Long Lance finished his supper and went to a movie. It had been a pleasant March day, with the temperature that evening a mild sixty degrees. After the movie he returned to his room at the Glendale Hotel. J.H. Williams, the night clerk, brought him a special registered letter from Bessie in New York, mailed before she telephoned him.[13]

An hour later, Long Lance reported to the night clerk. Williams had warned him earlier that "his movements were being watched and that Mrs. Anita Baldwin was paying to have this done." After chatting a few minutes, Long Lance showed Williams a gun he was carrying and the police permit for it. A taxi was called, and when it arrived, Long Lance took his .45 Colt revolver, climbed in and told the driver to take him to Anoakia in neighboring Arcadia. He had been drinking.[14]

Long Lance often visited Anoakia at odd hours, day and night. When he arrived this time, about midnight, he poked his head out of the taxi and called to the guard, "It is me, Sergeant." Joseph Hannah, the watchman, nodded.[15] The gate swung open and the taxi drove up the winding driveway to the mansion.

At the entrance, the taxi stopped, and Long Lance got out and walked to the door which had an immense, three-foot peacock, the tail fully spread, etched into its glass. He rang the bell and Anita answered. Later, Anita explained that she was reading in the library when the bell rang, and that Long Lance's demeanor startled her. "He acted in a manner that I had never before seen, being quite abrupt, very depressed and non-communicative," she said. They returned to the library together. Then, as Anita described it, "I excused myself and left for my own quarters in the house, closing the doors between the library and the back hallway to the sleeping quarters." It was when she was in her room, soon after leaving Long Lance, that she heard the gunshot from the library.[16]

Sergeant Hannah, the watchman, whose room was next to Anita's, ran to the library to investigate. He testified at the subsequent inquest that after Long Lance had arrived at Anoakia, he, Hannah, went up to his room to retire for the night. He had been sleeping for an hour or two when Anita knocked on his door. "She told me she had heard a shot and for me to investigate it."

When he entered the library, Hannah saw Long Lance slumped on the leather settee by the library table, legs stretched out, head thrown back and a .45-calibre pistol in his right hand. Hannah went into a state of shock at the sight of the ugly head wound. He told Anita what he had found, then rushed to call the Los Angeles and Pasadena police, only to be told that Anoakia was not in their jurisdictions. When Anita realized that Hannah was too shaken to be of any use, she called for John Gilbert, the caretaker, to take charge. Gilbert called the chief of police of Arcadia. It was one-forty-five in the morning.

Anita left the mansion to stay with Dextra, who lived five hundred yards away, and by the time she got there she was "nervous and unstrung." Police Chief Louis Richards, a Captain Pardue and Dr. William Heidenreich arrived at about two-fifteen. Dr. Heidenreich examined Long Lance and determined that he had been dead for thirty or forty minutes. A ballistics expert arrived at the mansion at two-forty-five.

Long Lance's friends were shocked and incredulous when they heard the news. Williams, the night clerk at the Glendale Hotel, could not believe it was suicide. He wrote to Susie Curtis, who contacted the hotel when newspaper reports of the incident reached New York: "I cannot tell you all I know as it would bring the hotel into prominence and I would lose my job and gain nothing." On December 27, 1932, Elizabeth Analla, who worked at Anoakia, wrote to Chauncey Yellow Robe's daughter, Rosebud, and said Long Lance's death "surely is a mystery to the friends who knew him." She asked Rosebud, who was raising her family in

New York: "Are you coming to Dakota this coming summer? If you do let us plan to see each other. I have much I'd like to talk over with you. I have been home since May after spending six years in California. I feel sure your family are all his friends from his conversation."[17]

Jim Thorpe had received a letter from Long Lance in mid-March and, he said later, his old Carlisle friend gave "no indication of worry or despondency." The instructor at the Glendale flying school said that he appeared content in his work and very popular with his associates. Canon Middleton was convinced Long Lance had been murdered, as was Dr. Clyde Fisher, who wrote Middleton on August 14, 1933: "I do not believe that Long Lance took his own life, and none of his close friends, that I know, believe it either." Even Irvin S. Cobb—perhaps ashamed of his earlier rejection of the man—in a reply to a letter from Emma Newashe said that he did not "believe so gallant a man as he was ever deliberately took his own life." From information Cobb received, "no actual inquest was ever held, and no real investigation held, and... the so-called 'police inquiry' was a farce."[18]

Cobb was correct about the hasty nature of the investigation and inquest. Indeed, it was only because of a complaint by Irene Noonan, president of the American Indian Women's History and Art Club, and Mrs. Leta Myers Smart, an Omaha Indian, that a brief hearing was even held.[19] The inquest was conducted in Arcadia, an area carved out of Anita's father's huge estate and founded by him. Anita, who was assessed half the town's taxes, had enormous influence in Arcadia. Having been advised by her physician "to remain away from any further strain and take a complete rest," she did not even attend the inquest, nor were any steps taken to force her to testify. She merely submitted a signed statement, telling of what she knew of the events of the evening and early morning of March 19 and 20.[20]

The Arcadia and Los Angeles police reported at the hearing that no one but Long Lance himself could have fired the fatal shot. Frank Gompert, Deputy Sheriff of Los Angeles County, told the jury he had arrived at Anoakia at about 2:45 a.m. on the morning of Sunday, March 20.

After photographing the body, I removed the gun from the hands of the victim, and in removing it, the trigger was released, so that it came forward and the hammer came back to its safety position. I examined the gun and found that only one cartridge had been exploded in the gun at any recent time. This proved to me conclusively that the case was a suicide, and that the gun could only be in that condition and that position by means of a self-inflicted wound. [21]

A more thorough and complete investigation might have revealed much more of the complex and introspective Long Lance—the circumstances certainly would have justified it —but it is unlikely that the precise reasons for the act would have been brought to light. He had spent most of his life covering his tracks, lying, then lying again to cover his lies. Doubtless the rumors that circulated in New York upset him, but he had survived such gossip before. Bessie's marriage wounded him badly, probably more than anything else, for Long Lance appears to have come close to committing himself to her. Years later, when she was living in Maine, Bessie remembered how caring and affectionate he was. She added that he was "the only man I ever really loved."[22]

Another factor to consider, in addition to the loss of Bessie, was the fact that he was in his forties, well past his "peak of prowess." Throughout his life he had worked hard to keep his body in perfect shape, swimming in icy lakes, running daily on the beach, boxing at the Y. Any decline would have been hard to accept. The frustrations and boredom of living off a wealthy heiress in a mansion on a fortified estate, being denied those things which he believed were firmly promised, and followed everywhere by a hired detective would have contributed to Long Lance's unhappiness. His drinking, too, had become quite heavy. In his quest for fame and a full life, Long Lance had deliberately denied himself any close friendships. He revealed parts of himself to some, parts to others, but no one person was truly a confidant.

Shortly after his death, Anita launched an investigation into his life. She was sadly disillusioned that Long Lance was not the man he had claimed to be in his passport application or in his autobiography. She had heard all the rumors about him and they fed on her natural paranoia. In early May she bitterly told Susie Curtis that he had "kinky hair when he came to Carlisle—used grease on it to keep it down." She also said he "used make-up rouge on his cheekbones, dyed his hair, and used a straightening fluid on it." It was untrue, of course, for even his childhood friends in Winston remembered that his hair was black and straight.[23] Anita's esteem for Long Lance, for whatever reasons, had turned to hatred.

She had gone so far as to solicit information from Edgar Miller, the Bureau of Indian Affairs superintendent at the Hopi agency in Arizona. He had been the printing instructor at Carlisle twenty years earlier, and Anita had met him in the 1920s when she researched the music of the Hopi. Miller had kept track of Long Lance after leaving Carlisle, and he knew that he had fought in the Canadian army, that he called himself Chief Buffalo Child Long Lance and that he had published an autobiography. He remembered that Long Lance had registered at Carlisle as a Cherokee, although to Miller he had looked like a "half-blood [part Negro]."[24]

Anita commissioned a Pinkerton detective to investigate the Long family's racial origins. Without any qualifications or explanations the detective reported:

Subject's father full-blooded negro. Joe S. Long, 95 Brookstown Avenue, Winston-Salem, North Carolina. Mother half Indian. Two brothers, one sister respected negros. One brother negro detective. Sister divorced from negro preacher. Father was janitor at high school for 25 years; now retired. Owns property. Subject's name Sylvester.[25]

Late Wednesday night, March 23, 1932, just after the last feature, the white manager of the Carolina Theater in Winston-Salem called Abe Long to his office. In a few minutes, Abe emerged shaken, and went home. That night he wrote in his diary: Mr. U.K. Rice related to me, or conveyed the most horrible news I have ever received. It was of my poor brother's death in California Sun. Mar. 20th 1932 by his own hands. May God have Mercy on his soul."

On March 24, Joe Long sent a telegram to the Los Angeles coroner explaining that he was the dead man's father and asking that funeral arrangements be deferred until he could send further details. The family wanted to bring the body back to Winston-Salem for burial, but they could not afford the expense. Walter, curious about the circumstances of his brother's death, collected enough money to travel to Los Angeles and, in late April—one month after his brother's death—he met several of Anita's staff. He informed them that neither he nor Long Lance had any Negro blood.[26]

Walter learned from Anita's sympathetic employees that in the last year of his life Long Lance had associated with a disreputable crowd in Los Angeles, that he had been drinking too much and might even have been using drugs.[27] He was told that Long Lance had talked about suicide with his dentist the very day before his death.[28] At Anoakia, Walter observed the magnificent buildings, the lush gardens, the manicured lawns, the peacocks that ran loose on the estate. Had all this been worth the price of a man's pride and, ultimately, his very life?

At three o'clock on the afternoon of March 30, 1932, Long Lance was buried by members of the British Benevolent Society in the British Empire War Veterans' section of the Inglewood Cemetery in Los Angeles.[29]

EPILOGUE

AFTER LONG LANCE'S DEATH, it was discovered that he had spent or given away nearly all that he owned. He had lent money to his friend Jim Thorpe, given a substantial amount to the endowment fund of St. John's Military School, and sent nearly $500—a hefty sum in the early years of the Depression—to his family. When his personal effects were sold and his bank account closed, only $740 remained.[1]

On April 18, 1932, the family contested his will, but the family's poverty, and Joe's death, on November 14, defeated them. On May 18, 1933, the will produced by Canon Middleton was upheld. St. Paul's School on the Blood Reserve became Long Lance's sole beneficiary.[2] The money was used for scholarships for many years.

In 1932, Sallie Long lost Sylvester, her youngest son, her husband and her mother, Adeline, who died at the age of eighty-three.[3] Supported by Abe and Walter, Sallie lived until 1942. When Walter died in March, 1941, the Winston-Salem *Journal* published a lengthy obituary, titled: "Walter L. Long, Widely Known Negro Is Dead." Sallie's own obituary in the Winston-Salem *Twin City Sentinel* read: "The passing of Mrs. Long removes another member of one of the city's best-known Negro families." The respect in which the Long family was held is indicated by the reference to Sallie as "Mrs. Long."[4] In the South, Negro women were invariably referred to by their first names.

Through Abe's diaries one can follow his struggle. He spent the thirties and forties directing the flow of traffic up the seventy-four steps to the colored gallery of the Carolina Theater.[5] He was never reported late, never took a vacation, and only once missed a shift.[6] At work and in the community, he was constantly exposed to white bigotry. Gradually, Abe came to see and accept himself as black. In one diary entry he commented on a public issue by writing: "We the better thinking negroes . . . ."[7] Despite this, his last words on his death bed, uttered to a niece, were that the family had only white and Indian blood.[8]

Abe died in 1972, forty years after Sylvester. During a long and uneventful life, he witnessed many of the major changes that had affected blacks in the United States. He often mentioned them in his diary, as he did on Friday, September 6, 1957, when he wrote: "Miss Gwendolyn Boily admitted to Reynolds high school—first Negro to attend white city school." After shopping in a Winston-Salem store on December 3, 1958, he wrote, "a colored man waited on me, something unusual." For October 16, 1961, the entry reads: ". . . stated over television and radio tonight that 3 railroads of the South had integrated all its services. The Rev. Martin Luther King, it is said, was the cause of the action—which resulted from a talk with President Kennedy." The next year, on October 1, 1962, he recorded, "Down in Mississippi last night was a big riot caused by a negro James Meredith attempting to enter the University of Missp." Two days later, without comment, Abe wrote in his diary: "Another man flew around the earth today 6 times in 9 hours Schirra is his name."

In 1964, when Abe was eighty-three, the United States Congress passed the Civil Rights Bill. Further anti-segregationist legislation followed with the Voting Rights Act of 1965 and the Civil Rights Act of 1968. In his eighties, Abe witnessed the dismantling of the United States apartheid system.[9] He knew that if his brother Sylvester had been born in this new age he might never have left home, or, if he did, might never have had to fear coming home.

In the summer of 1930, a young Alberta teacher of Swedish origin, Lilly Sahlen, traveled to Sweden with her aunt and her sister. In London, England, Lilly met a wealthy American girl who had been studying in Paris. Her name was Bessie Clapp. The two women became friends, and after they returned to North America, they corresponded regularly. Lilly returned to teach in Alberta. Bessie settled in New York, taking an apartment in Greenwich Village and later marrying a Japanese art student in March, 1932. In the fall of that year, Lilly took a teaching job at St. Paul's Indian School on the Blood Reserve, and there she met the man she would later marry. His name was Charles Middleton, Canon Middleton's son.[10] When she heard where her friend was teaching, Bessie wrote excitedly from Japan on September 23, 1932:

> Lilly darling—
> I am so thrilled I can hardly write!. . . Oh you lucky girl, how I wish I were in your place. I always wanted to marry an Indian, and strange as it may seem, the one real love of my life (besides my husband) was a full blooded Blackfoot Indian Chief! I love him to this day, and I wanted to marry him, Lilly, but he was engaged to another girl, and being an Indian, he wouldn't break his promise to her. . . . You have heard of him, Lilly, I am sure of it, because he is quite famous throughout the United States and Canada. He wrote the most wonderful book on Indian life that was ever published, and took the leading part in an Indian movie a few years ago. His name was Chief Buffalo Child Long Lance! And I adore him Lilly—no other can ever take his place! I met him last winter in 1931, and the sweetest memories of all my life are the hours we spent together! I can never, never forget him. . . .[11]

THE REST OF THE CAST

BALDWIN, Anita. Continued to live in the Arcadia area. In 1936 she sold most of the remainder of her father's estate at Santa Anita, retaining only the property immediately around Anoakia, where she died in 1939 at the age of sixty-three.

BURDEN, Douglas. Became a noted naturalist and conservationist, and wrote two books on the subject. I met him in 1977 at his home in Vermont. He died in 1978.

CHANLER, William. Became the Corporation Counsel for the City of New York. He still kept an office in his old law firm on Wall Street when I interviewed him in 1977.

CLAPP, Bessie Randolph. Went with her husband, Tom Hayakawa, to Manchuria, and stayed there for several years. Before the outbreak of war between the United States and Japan she returned to the United States, and now lives in Maine.

COBB, Irvin S. Took severe losses in the stock market crash of 1929, and wrote few stories in the 1930s. At the age of fifty-eight he moved to Hollywood and became a movie script writer and actor. He died in 1944.

EAGLE SPEAKER, Mike. Served on the Blood Band Council for many years. I met him several times at his home. He died a respected elder of his tribe in 1979.

FISHER, Clyde. In 1933 Dr. Fisher married Te Ata, Long Lance's friend. She had left Broadway productions, and began giving recitals of Indian songs and legends (she was among the first performers to appear at the White House when Franklin D. Roosevelt became President in 1933). Dr. Fisher continued his explorations, and in 1944 a group of islands off the coast of Labrador were named in his honor. He died in 1949 during his term as president of the Explorers Club.

GOODERHAM, George. Rose to become the supervisor of all Indian reservations in Alberta and the North West Territories. On his retirement from the Department of Indian Affairs he continued working, first with the Glenbow Museum, and then with the Devonian Foundation in Calgary. When I met him at his office in 1975, he was eighty-five years old. He died in 1977.

LONG, Ray. In 1931 he resigned from *Cosmopolitan* to begin his own book-publishing firm. He later went bankrupt and tried writing for the movies, but without any great success. In 1935, at the age of fifty-seven, he committed suicide.

MIDDLETON, Canon S. H. Continued on as the Principal of St. Paul's Indian Residential School until 1949, having served for forty years in his post. He died in 1964.

SEUMAS. Continued to be active in the Explorers Club, serving as a Director and on many committees. He died at the age of eighty-one in 1961.

TOLSTOY, Ilia. During the Second World War he served as President Roosevelt's special envoy to the Dalai Lama in Tibet. In peacetime he helped Douglas Burden establish Marineland, an oceanic studio aquarium, on the east coast of Florida. He died in 1970.

ACKNOWLEDGMENTS
AND SOURCES

Abbreviations
Interview (I)
Letter (L)
Telephone Call (TC)
The asterisk indicates interviews that were taped. The tapes now
reside in the Archives of the Glenbow-Alberta Institute,
Calgary, Alberta.

My thanks to the following individuals for sharing with me their
recollections of Long Lance and the stories they have heard
about him.

Concerning Long Lance's family in Carson Town
Annie Blackburn, Carson Town, N.C. (I), 11.8.75.
Daisy Carson Blackburn, Carson Town, N.C. (I), 11.8.75*,
28.5.77.
Charles Carson, Carson Town, N.C. (I), 11.8.75*.
Kalford Carson, Lexington, N.C. (I), 12.8.75*.
Tracy Grose Caudle, Roaring River, N.C. (I), 12.8.77*.
Lillian Dalton, Mocksville, N.C. (I), 11.8.75*, 21.6.76.
Newman Dalton, Mocksville, N.C. (I), 21.8.76.
Jency Carson Gaither, Carson Town, N.C. (I), 29.5.77.
Nannie Carson Lewis, Carson Town, N.C. (I), 29.5.77.
Jaspar S. Long, Yadkinville, N.C. (I), 5.1.77*.
Mammie Carson Patterson, Carson Town, N.C. (I), 29.5.77.

Concerning Long Lance's family in Winston-Salem
Joe Bradshaw, Winston-Salem, N.C. (I), 13.7.75, 10-13.8.75*,
21.8.76, 7-8.1.77, 29.5.77.
Odell Clanton, Winston-Salem, N.C. (I), 7.1.77*.
Arthur Williams, Winston-Salem, N.C. (I), 6.1.77*.
Terrell Young, Winston-Salem, N.C. (I), 22.8.76, 7.1.77.

St. John's Military Institute
Robert Agne, New Hartford, N.Y. (L), 12.7.77.
William M. Leffingwell, Washington, D.C. (TC), 26.5.77.
Edmund C. Wall, Bronx, N.Y. (I), 22.5.77*; (L), 17.6.77.

Long Lance's Years in Calgary
Hugh Dann, Calgary, Alberta (I), 21.2.75, 12.4.78; (TC), 18.12.79.
Margaret Vahey Eakin, Vancouver, B.C. (L), 21.11.78, 15.10.80.
Maurice Fidler, Ottawa, Ontario (I), 3.6.76*; (L), 28.2.76, 4.4.76.
Harry Francis, Calgary, Alberta (I), 30.9.80.
Reg Hammond, Calgary, Alberta (I), 5.5.76; (TC), 28 and 29.10.79.
Howard Kelly, Calgary, Alberta (I), 9.3.75, 8.4.75*, 11.12.75,
4.5.76.
Paul Thompson, Calgary, Alberta (TC), 9.6.76.
Dorothy Wallace, Calgary, Alberta (I), 11.9.78.

Long Lance's Indian Visits
Earl Calf Child, Blackfoot Reserve, Gleichen, Alberta (I),
30.8.76*.
Joe Crowfoot, Blackfoot Reserve, Gleichen, Alberta (I), 30.8.76.
George Gooderham, Calgary, Alberta (I), 7.2.75*, 5.5.76.
Eli Taylor, Sioux Valley Reserve (Oak Lake Reserve), Griswold,
Manitoba (I), 14.3.80.

The Blood Indians
Sophie Allison, Waterton, Alberta (I), 9.10.75*, 15.11.75,
27.4.76, 13.20.78; (L), 27.2.79, 18.5.79, 27.1.80.
Gordon Bird, Blood Reserve, Stand Off, Alberta (I), 20.10.77.
Mike Eagle Speaker, Blood Reserve, Stand Off, Alberta (I),
16.1.76*, 18.2.76, 15.3.76, 20.4.77*.
Archdeacon Cecil Swanson, Calgary, Alberta (I), 23.9.79.
Dan Weasel Fat, Blood Reserve, Stand Off, Alberta (I), 21.10.77.

Winnipeg
Allan Bill, Calgary, Alberta (I), with Fran Fraser, 11.5.62*.
Charles L'Ami, Winnipeg, Manitoba (I), 20.10.76*.
Pearl Driscoll L'Ami, Winnipeg, Manitoba (I), 20.10.76*.
Mrs. H. O'Malley, Winnipeg, Manitoba (TC), 26.6.80; (L), 29.6.80.

West Point
R.A. Ericson, Oakland, California (L), 12.8.77.
Dorothy Fellers, Washington, D.C. (TC), 26.5.77; (L), 16.7.77,
    8.8.77, 5.9.77, 12.8.80.
F.B. Valentine, East Holden, Maine (L), 6.8.77.

The Silent Enemy
Douglas Burden, Charlotte, Vermont (I), 4-5.5.77*.
S.C. Burden, Beverly Hills, California (TC), 20.6.77.
William C. Chanler, New York, N.Y. (TC), 22.5.77; (I), 25.5.77*,
    26.5.77.
Wilfrid Eggleston, Ottawa, Ontario (L), 15.2.76, 7.1.81.
Ted Hennessy, North Bay, Ontario (I), 22.12.76*, 12.5.77; (L),
    19.5.81.
Agnes Lalonde, North Bay, Ontario (I), 2.1.76, 12.5.77.
Sheila Burden Lawrence, Charlotte, Vermont (I), 4.4.77.
George McDougall, Cochrane, Ontario (I), 11.5.77*.
Madeline Theriault, North Bay, Ontario (L), 21.9.75; (I), 2.1.76.

New York
Lee Ash, Bethany, Connecticut (TC), 28.12.75; (I), in Edmonton,
    4.3.76.
Earl Parker Hanson, Santurce, Puerto Rico (L), 13.4.76, 20.1.77.
Domenica Pallister, New York, N.Y. (TC), 25.5.77; (L), 4.7.77,
    5.8.77, 26.9.77; (I), 6.5.79*.
Elisabeth Randolph Clapp, York Village, Maine (L), 18.9.80; (TC),
    19.10.80.
Te Ata, Oklahoma City, Oklahoma (I), 12.3.76.
Lowell Thomas, Pawling, N.Y. (L), 1.11.76.

Los Angeles
Roberta Forsberg, Whittier, California (I), 10.1.76.
Ray Knisley, Boulder City, Nevada (L), 28.6.80; (TC), 26.10.80.

Lowry McCaslin, Arcadia, California (I), 16.10.80*; (L), 22.12.80.

Others helped enormously with detective work. For their assistance in supplying research information, I am indebted to the following:
The Academy of Motion Picture Arts and Sciences, Beverly Hills, Calif. (*The Silent Enemy*); H.J. Anderson, Dewitt, N.Y. (St. John's Military Academy); Elmer E. Barnes, Washington, D.C. (West Point); Eunice Baumann-Nelson, Lima, Peru (information on her sister, Molly Spotted Elk); Henry Berg (Princess Alexandra); Ted Blackmore, Eastbourne, England (the Long Lance running shoe); John Blair, Winston-Salem, N.C. (information on his father, William Blair); Michael Bliss, University of Toronto, Toronto, Ont. (information on Sir Joseph Flavelle, whom Long Lance claimed to have met in Palm Springs in 1930); Fam Brownlee, Winston-Salem, N.C. (Winston-Salem); *Calgary Herald* News Morgue, Calgary, Alta. (*Calgary Herald*); Calgary Public Library, Calgary, Alta. (Calgary); California State Library, Sacramento, Calif. (Lucky and Anita Baldwin); Anne Correll, Forsyth County Public Library, Winston-Salem, N.C. (Winston-Salem); James Crosby, Dewitt, N.Y. (St. John's); Cumberland County Historical Society, Carlisle, Penn. (Carlisle); Barbara Piattelli Dempsey, New York, N.Y. (Jack Dempsey); Hugh Dempsey, Glenbow-Alberta Institute, Calgary, Alta. (Long Lance and the Bloods); Peter Dzwonkoski, Yale University Library, New Haven, Conn. (Long Lance's correspondence with Carl Van Vechten); Joe Ellis, Mount Holyoke College, South Hadley, Mass. (West Point); John Ewers, Smithsonian Institution, Washington, D.C. (Long Lance and the Blackfoot); Evelyn Yellow Robe Feinbeiner, Wolfsburg, Germany, and Rosebud Yellow Robe Frantz, Forest Hills, N.Y. (information on their father, Chauncey Yellow Robe); Tom Flanagan, University of Calgary, Calgary, Alta. (North Carolina); Robert H. Fowler, Washington, D.C. (Carlisle); Carolyn Garner, Arcadia Public Library, Arcadia, Calif. (Anita Baldwin); Roger Graham, Queen's University, Kingston, Ont. (Arthur Meighen and Commissioner Graham); Bertha Grier, Winston-Salem, N.C. (the Long family in Winston-Salem); Lucy Griggs, Oklahoma City, Okla. (Carlisle); Stephen Grove and Kenneth Rapp, U.S. Military Academy, West Point, N.Y. (West Point); Vera Gully, Calgary, Alta. (photos of

Long Lance in Calgary); Holt, Rinehart and Winston, New York,
N.Y. (the contract for *Long Lance*); Richard Hunt, Sun Valley
Center for the Arts and Humanities, Sun Valley, Idaho
(Commissioner Charles Burke); Huntington Library, San
Marino, Calif. (Anita Baldwin); George Johnston, Vancouver,
B.C. (Long Lance in Winnipeg); Leslie Kawamura, University of
Calgary, Calgary, Alta. (for the translation of an article in
Japanese about Bessie Clapp); Homer Keever, Statesville, N.C.
(Iredell County); Georgeen Klassen, Glenbow-Alberta Institute,
Calgary, Alta. (photos of Long Lance); Nick LaTrenta, Met-
ropolitan Life Insurance Company, New York, N.Y. (Sylvester
Long's insurance policy, 1906); Omer Lavallée, Canadian Pacific
Railway, Montreal, Que. (the CPR menus with Long Lance's
Indian stories); Maurice Lewis, New York, N.Y. (St. John's); Los
Angeles Public Library, Los Angeles, Calif. (Anita Baldwin); the
daughters of Emma Newashe McAllister: Natoma Huffman,
Ramona Loman, Rita Megehee and Marcheta Thornton,
Oklahoma and California (information on their mother, Emma
Newashe); Bennett McCardle, Ottawa, Ont. (Duncan Campbell
Scott); W. A. MacIntosh, Directorate of History, Dept. of
National Defence, Ottawa, Ont. (Long Lance in the Canadian
Army); Bill McKee, Glenbow-Alberta Institute, Calgary, Alta.
(Vancouver); Les McLeod, University of Calgary, Calgary, Alta.
(Duncan Campbell Scott); David McNab, Wilfrid Laurier Univer-
sity, Waterloo, Ont. (Duncan Campbell Scott); Jean McNiven,
Department of Indian Affairs and Northern Development,
Ottawa, Ont. (biographical articles on Long Lance); Wallace
Many Fingers, Blood Reserve, Stand Off, Alta. (Long Lance and
the Blood Indians); William J. Marshall, University of Kentucky
Libraries, Lexington, Ky. (Irvin S. Cobb); Richard Maxwell,
National Archives, Washington, D.C. (Carlisle); Lilly Sahlen
Middleton, Fort Macleod, Alta. (Bessie Clapp); Walter and
Georgia Moore, Winston-Salem, N.C. (Walter Long); James L.
Murphy, Ohio Historical Center, Columbus, Ohio (Long Lance in
Ohio, 1924); Rev. Ernie Nix, United Church Archives, Toronto,
Ont. (clippings about Long Lance in Winnipeg); Thomas
Noguchi, County of Los Angeles, Calif. (the coroner's inquest
into Long Lance's death); Howard Palmer, University of
Calgary, Calgary, Alta. (Anita Baldwin and her properties on
Lake Tahoe); Roy and Mary Phillips, Winston-Salem, N.C. (the
black community in Winston-Salem); Pickaway County District

Public Library, Circleville, Ohio (Long Lance in Ohio, 1924);
Public Archives of Canada, Ottawa, Ont. (the war diary of the
38th Battalion, C.E.F., for 1917); Marie Roy, the Explorers Club,
New York, N.Y. (the Explorers Club); Edwin Scalabrino,
Biltmore Hotel, New York, N.Y. (the Biltmore Hotel); Jim
Skinner, Brandon University, Brandon, Man. (*The Silent
Enemy*); John J. Slonaker, U.S. Army Military History
Institute, Carlisle Barracks, Penn. (Carlisle); Martha Slotten,
Dickinson College Library, Carlisle, Penn. (Dickinson College);
Sandy Snider, Los Angeles State and County Arboretum,
Arcadia, Calif. (Anita Baldwin); Cynthia G. Swank, J. Walter
Thompson Company, New York, N.Y. (B.F. Goodrich ads for the
Long Lance running shoe); George F.G. Stanley, Sackville, N.B.
(Calgary in the 1920s); Elizabeth Townshend, Calgary, Alta.
(American Indian policy in the 1920s and 1930s); Bill Tye,
Calgary, Alta. (Commissioner Graham); Leon Warmski,
Archives of Ontario, Toronto, Ont. (Poetry Society of America
Annual Dinner, 1930); William B. Wharton, Department of
State, Washington, D.C. (Long Lance's passport, 1931); Keith
Wilson, Birtle, Man. (Commissioner Graham); John Wing,
Dartmouth College Library, Dartmouth, Mass. (Long Lance's
correspondence with Vilhjalmur Stefansson).

For information relating to Long Lance's career I am indebted to
Kenneth W. Porter, Professor Emeritus, Department of History
of the University of Oregon, who has been interested in the story
of Chief Buffalo Child for nearly half a century. From May, 1976,
to the present he has generously answered all my inquiries.

I am grateful to Professor Donovan Williams, Chairman of the
Department of History of the University of Calgary, 1976-81, for
his constant encouragement. I thank as well the office staff and
my colleagues in the Department for their interest and support.
Doug Cass of the Archives of the Glenbow-Alberta Institute, and
Lindsay Moir of the library both assisted. The university library's
Inter-Library Loans Office obtained dozens of microfilm reels of
Canadian and American newspapers. The photo studio of the
University's Communications Media Department reproduced
many of the illustrations, including the author's photo taken by
Bernie Dichek at the Glenbow-Alberta Museum's pioneers
exhibit. Laura and Ancet Dourado and Doreen Nordquist typed

my numerous drafts. My sister, Barbara Nair, compiled the index. Judy Abel of Calgary helped with the final corrections to the completed text. My thanks to all of the above and to all those who assisted in other ways.

Sources

The most important source is the Archives of the Glenbow-Alberta Institute in Calgary, Alberta. It contains Long Lance's two scrapbooks, and some of his papers. I have placed photocopies of Long Lance's correspondence with Mike Eagle Speaker, Bonner Fellers, Commissioner Graham and Alice Tye, Howard Kelly, Canon S.H. Middleton, and Emma Newashe McAllister, in the Archives. Long Lance's correspondence with Vilhjalmur Stefansson is located in the Stefansson Collection, Dartmouth College Library, Dartmouth, Mass. Several of Long Lance's letters are in the Carl Van Vechten Collection in the Beinecke Rare Book and Manuscript Library, Yale University Library, New Haven, Connecticut.

The National Archives in Washington, D.C., has Sylvester Long's student record (R.G. 75, Bureau of Indian Affairs, Carlisle Student Record, file 5534), and the BIA file on his true identity (R.G. 75, Bureau of Indian Affairs, General Service File, 1364-1925, 130). William Chanler's file on "Burden Pictures Inc. re—Joe S. Long (Long Lance)—Sylvester Long," 748-C10, is in the Archives of his law firm, Winthrop, Stimson, Putnam and Roberts, of New York City.

Collections of Anita Baldwin's papers are held by the Rare Book Room of the Huntington Library, San Marino, California; and by the library of the Los Angeles State and County Arboretum, Arcadia, California.

Newspapers and Periodicals Consulted
Winston-Salem *Journal*, August-September, 1909.
Carlisle *Arrow*, 1909-1913.
Calgary *Herald*, July, 1919-March, 1922.
Vancouver *Sun*, May, 1922-August, 1922.
Regina *Leader*, October, 1922-April, 1923.
Winnipeg *Tribune*, January, 1923-May, 1925.
Explorers *Journal*, 1929-1932.
Los Angeles *Times*, March 16-31, 1932.
The American Indian Magazine (Tulsa, Okla.), 1926-1931.

NOTES

CHAPTER ONE

1. New York's weather on January 5, 1931, is described on the front page of the *New York Times* the following day. For the geographic setting see the pages on "Pennsylvania Station and Vicinity" in the Federal Writers' Project, *New York City Guide* (New York: Random House, 1976), pp. 164-7. The *Guide* was first published in 1939.
2. The best physical description of Long Lance appears in Beverly Smith's feature article, "One Hundred Per Cent American," New York *Herald Tribune*, January 19, 1930. He states his height in his letter to President Woodrow Wilson, March 8, 1915, in R.G. 75, Bureau of Indian Affairs, Carlisle Student Record, file 5534, National Archives, Washington, D.C. (henceforth cited as CARLISLE FILE). The description of Walter Long is taken from Ilia Tolstoy's report to William Chanler, April 14, 1930, in file 748-C10, "Burden Pictures Inc. re—Joe S. Long (Long Lance)—Sylvester Long," Winthrop, Stimson, Putnam and Roberts, 40 Wall Street, New York City (henceforth cited as CHANLER INVESTIGATION). For biographical details see "Walter L. Long, Widely Known Negro Is Dead," Winston-Salem *Journal*, March 28, 1941.
3. Long Lance's exact words were: "Among themselves, Indians speak seldom and then only when they have something important to say." Long Lance, "My Trail Upward. I Took It Because I, a Blackfoot Indian, Wanted to Live Like a White Man," *Hearst's International-Cosmopolitan*, June, 1926, p. 138 (hereafter cited as "Trail Upward").
4. Long Lance described the incident in a letter to Walter, written the following day; see "Vester" to "My dear Brother," dated "Tuesday."

The original copy of this letter (donated by Joe Bradshaw of Winston-Salem, N.C.), as well as copies of all of Long Lance's postcards and letters from 1911 to his death in 1932, are in the Archives of the Glenbow-Alberta Institute, Calgary, Alberta (hereafter cited as GLENBOW).

CHAPTER TWO

1. Sylvester was born on "December 1"; although he changed the year of his birth, he always held to the same day and month. The year of his birth is given as 1890 in the 1900 Census, volume 25, ED 31, sheet 17, line 97, National Archives, Washington, D.C. In his diary Abe Long also cites his brother's date of birth as December 1, 1890; see entries for December 30, 1961; November 28, 1965. Abe Long (1881-1972) was the eldest of Joe and Sallie Long's sons. Abe's diaries, written when he was in his fifties, sixties, seventies, and eighties, are now in the possession of Newman Dalton, Mocksville, N.C. With the permission of Mr. Dalton, copies of the diaries can be consulted at GLENBOW.
2. Marriage of "S. D. Long" and "Lindy Carson," March 27, 1879 (both are registered as colored), Indexed Register of Marriages — Iredell County, North Carolina, L to R Males, Iredell County, N.C., p. 123. New Court House, Statesville, Iredell County, N.C. Although there are discrepancies in Joe's initials and Sallie's name, other evidence suggests that this must be the correct entry.
3. Birthdate: January 17, 1865. Sallie M. Long, Certificate of Death, February 8, 1942, Forsyth County Court House, Winston-Salem, N.C. Her full name was "Sallie Malinda Long"; see her gravestone, Silver Hill Graveyard, Buena Vista, Winston-Salem, N.C.
4. Birthdate: February 14, 1853. Joe S. Long, Certificate of Death, November 14, 1932, Forsyth County Court House, Winston-Salem, N.C. His full name was "Joseph Sylvester Long"; see his gravestone, Silver Hill Graveyard, Buena Vista, Winston-Salem, N.C. In Carson Town he was called "Vet" (from Sylvester), but in Winston he went by the name of Joe. See also "Death Claims Uncle Joe Long," Winston-Salem *Sentinel*, November 16, 1932.
5. Andrew Carson outlined his experience in the American Revolution in his application for a federal pension, August 22, 1832, in *The State Records of North Carolina*, ed. Walter Clark, vol. 22 (Goldsboro, N.C.: Nash Brothers, 1907). His family is listed in his will, Andrew Carson, April 18, 1836, and codicil, March 6, 1838, Iredell County Wills, Caldwell-Curry 1787-1890, 1915. C.R. 054 801.3, North Carolina Archives, Raleigh, N.C. Andrew Carson's tombstone is still

standing in the Young family cemetery near Houstonville. A photo of
it appears in *Iredell County Landmarks* (Statesville: Iredell County
American Revolution Bicentennial Commission, 1976), p. 61.

6. It still stands there. His gravestone states that he was born January
5, 1792, and died August 29, 1865.

7. Ilia Tolstoy's report, CHANLER INVESTIGATION.

8. The number of Robert Carson's slaves appears in the Slave Schedule,
1860 Census, Iredell County, vol. 22, pp. 291-2. North Carolina State
Archives, Raleigh, N.C.

9. Angie Debo, *The Road to Disappearance* (Norman: University of
Oklahoma Press, 1941), p. 102.

10. Tracy Grose Caudle, *Memories from My Father's Trunk* (n.p.: Alpine
Industries, 1970), p. 4. Interview with Tracy Grose Caudle, Roaring
River, Wilkes County, N.C., May 28, 1977.

11. Birthdate: January 11, 1848. Adeline Lindsy, Certificate of Death,
February 8, 1932, New Court House, Statesville, Iredell County,
N.C.

12. John Hope Franklin, *The Free Negro in North Carolina, 1790-1860*
(New York: W. W. Norton, 1971), p. 35.

13. Slave Schedule, 1860 Census, Iredell County, vol. 22, p. 291. North
Carolina State Archives, Raleigh, N.C.

14. Adeline Carson gave birth to Sallie, and Jincy Carson to Jim. Sallie
recognized Jim as her brother (half-brother). On his death certificate
Jim Carson's father is listed as Andrew Cowles. See Certificate of
Death, October 16, 1917, New Court House, Statesville, N.C. Jim
Carson was born April 20, 1860. His son, Charles Carson, remembers
him as a very fair-skinned man with blue eyes. Away from Carson
Town, where he was classified as colored, he passed racially as a
white. Interview with Charles Carson, Carson Town, August 11,
1975.

15. Andrew Carson Cowles's tombstone in the Flat Rock Cemetery,
Hamptonville, Yadkin County, N.C., reads, "born Jan. 12, 1833 died
Jan. 5, 1881." He served first as Yadkin's member in the North
Carolina House of Commons, from 1860 to 1865, and was elected to the
state senate in late 1865, where he served from 1865 to 1867, and from
1870 to 1874. John L. Cheney, ed., *North Carolina Government,
1585-1974* (Raleigh, N.C.: North Carolina Department of the Secretary of State, 1975), pp. 320, 328, 332, 334, 451, 454.

16. Colonel Calvin Duvall Cowles, *Genealogy of the Cowles Families in
America*, 2 vols. (New Haven, Connecticut: Tuttle, Morehouse and
Taylor, 1929), 1:743.

17. Andrew Carson Cowles to Calvin J. Cowles, dated Hamptonville,

April 9, 1865, Calvin J. Cowles Papers, North Carolina State Archives, Raleigh, N.C.

18. William E. Rutledge, Jr., *An Illustrated History of Yadkin County, 1850-1965* (Yadkinville, N.C.: n.p., 1965), p. 23. A photo of the home appears on p. 20.

19. His two sons by his white wife (whom he married in 1870), Hugh and Reuben, occasionally visited to see their colored first cousins. Interview with Jim Carson's daughters Daisy Blackburn, Mammie Patterson, Nannie Lewis, Carson Town, May 29, 1977.

20. Joe's sister Lindy was married to Lee Carson, a cousin of Sallie's. According to the 1880 Census (Eagle Mills Township, Iredell County, N.C., p. 198) Lindy was born in 1857, and was thus four years younger than Joe. As a young girl Lindy had been sold on a slave block. Interview with Daisy Blackburn, Carson Town, August 11, 1975.

21. Joe Long to R. H. Latham, April 9, 1930, quoted in Ilia Tolstoy's report, CHANLER INVESTIGATION; Abe Long's diary, entry for December 12, 1939.

22. "Death Claims Uncle Joe Long," Winston-Salem *Sentinel*, November 16, 1932. Joe's owner was Miles H. Long. A photo and short biography of Miles H. Long appear in Jaspar S. Long, *Long Family Records* (Winston-Salem, N.C.: Clay Printing Co., 1965), pp. 175-8. See also Miles's obituary in the *Yadkin Ripple*, September 2, 1920.

23. Joe Long to R. H. Latham, April 9, 1930, quoted in Ilia Tolstoy's report, CHANLER INVESTIGATION.

24. Caudle, *Memories*, pp. 4-5.

25. In his diaries Abe Long gives March, 1887, as the date on which the family moved to Winston; see entries of May 26, 1957, and March 1, 1970.

26. Adelaide Fries, Stuart Thurman Wright, and J. Edwin Hendricks, *Forsyth: The History of a County on the March* (Chapel Hill: The University of North Carolina, 1976), p. 170 (electric lights and streetcars); p. 191 (telephones).

27. The population statistic used here is that for Forsyth County, the county in which Winston is located. In 1900, out of a total population of 35,000, Forsyth had 10,543 blacks. Fries et al., *Forsyth*, p. 256. The effect of racial segregation was felt most after the turn of the century. In the 1890s "Jim Crow" laws were extended throughout the American South. The segregation of the races became complete in Winston in 1912 when the city council enacted an ordinance which made it unlawful for "any white person to occupy as a residence . . . any house upon any street . . . on which a greater number of houses are occupied as residences by colored than are occupied by white people." Anyone

breaking this law faced a fine of fifty dollars or thirty days in prison. Larry Edward Tise, *Winston-Salem in History. Volume 6: Government* (Winston-Salem, N.C.: Historic Winston, 1976), p. 40.

28. Abe's birthdate was August 27, 1881. Abe Miles Long, Certificate of Death, July 28, 1972, Forsyth County Court House, Winston-Salem, N.C. Walter was born on July 4, 1886. Walter Lee Long, Certificate of Death, March 27, 1941, Forsyth County Court House, Winston-Salem, N.C. Katie was born July 29, 1899; see Abe's diary entry for July 29, 1958.

29. For an understanding of the racial situation in the American South the following volumes proved extremely useful: C. Vann Woodward, *The Strange Career of Jim Crow* (New York: Oxford University Press, 1966), and John Hope Franklin, *From Slavery to Freedom: A History of Negro Americans*, 3rd ed. (New York: Vintage Books, 1967). For an understanding of the individual black's position, the two autobiographical works by black novelist Richard Wright, *Black Boy* (New York: Harper and Row, 1966, first published in 1937), and *American Hunger* (New York: Harper and Row, 1977), proved invaluable, as did white writer John Howard Griffin's *Black Like Me* (Bergenfield, N.J.: New American Library, 1976, first published in 1960). For an interesting novel about "growing up black" in Winston-Salem, North Carolina, see Alfred W. Wilkes, *Little Black Boy* (New York: Charles Scribner's, 1971).

30. The best review of Kit Carson's link with Carson Town is found in Homer M. Keever's *Iredell. Piedmont County* (Statesville, N.C.: Iredell County Bicentennial Commission, 1976), pp. 127-8. The anecdote of the oak Kit Carson topped appears in Caudle, *Memories*, p. 5. Mrs. Caudle's father, J. M. Grose, bought a portion of the old Robert Carson plantation and she grew up in the area.

31. Sallie M. Long's book, May 10, 1907. In the possession of Newman Dalton, Mocksville, N.C.

32. Affidavit prepared by William A. Blair, April 9, 1930, CHANLER INVESTIGATION.

33. Abe Long's diaries, entries for May 5, 1939, and August 18, 1959.

34. 1900 Census, National Archives, Washington, D.C. (volume 25, ED 31, sheet 17, line 97).

35. Interview with Terrell Young, Winston-Salem, N.C., August 22, 1976. Miss Young was a student at the West End School at the time, and remembers that Sylvester used to help his father clean the school.

36. Interview with Odell Clanton, Winston-Salem, N.C., January 7, 1977. Mr. Clanton was a student at the Depot School with Sylvester.

37. Sylvester Clark Long's application to Carlisle, CARLISLE FILE.

38. Abe Long's diary, entry for November 5, 1958.
39. Application to Carlisle, CARLISLE FILE.
40. George L. Chindahl, *A History of the Circus in America* (Caldwell, Idaho: Caxton Printers, 1959), p. 194.
41. The library opened in February, 1906. Fries et al., *Forsyth*, p. 199. He definitely was in Winston that year, for on May 7, 1906, he took out an insurance policy naming his mother as his beneficiary. N. D. Latrenta, Metropolitan Life Insurance Company, New York, to Donald B. Smith (hereafter cited as DBS), June 27, 1978.
42. Colonel William Blair quoted in a letter to Canon Middleton, dated December 19, 1933. Letter in the possession of Sophie Allison.
43. Charles Carson (1886-1978), Sylvester's first cousin (see footnote 14 of this chapter), told me that Sylvester and the Long family always returned to Carson Town for the Big Meeting. Interview with Charles Carson, Carson Town, August 11, 1975. This (1908) was the last year Sylvester attended.
44. Application to Carlisle, CARLISLE FILE.
45. Caudle, *Memories*, p. 4.
46. Abe married Aurelia on January 6, 1908. See his diary entry for November 4, 1940. On his fiftieth wedding anniversary in 1958 he wrote that on January 6, 1908, he had married "the prettiest girl in Winston-Salem."
47. Winston-Salem, N.C., City and Suburban City Directory, editions for 1908 and 1910. Entries for Abraham, Joe, and Walter Long.
48. Interview with Odell Clanton, Winston-Salem, N.C., January 7, 1977.
49. Interview with Tracy Grose Caudle, Roaring River, Wilkes County, N.C., May 28, 1977.
50. Carmelita S. Ryan's Ph.D. dissertation, "The Carlisle Indian Industrial School" (Ph.D. dissertation, Georgetown University, 1962), provides an excellent overview of the school. Carlisle's enrolment for 1909 is given in the *Annual Report of the United States Indian School, Carlisle, Pennsylvania, for the year ending June 30, 1910*, p. 28. Their football record is given in Gene Schoor, *The Jim Thorpe Story* (New York: Pocket Books, 1967), pp. 46, 51.
51. In early February, 1930, he told William Chanler that he had been with Robinson's Circus. See William Chanler to BIA Commissioner, February 14, 1930, CHANLER INVESTIGATION. While in Calgary, Alberta, in the early 1920s Long Lance had an excellent reputation as a rider. Interview with Howard Kelly, Calgary, March 9, 1975. He must have first learned about horses while with the Wild West Show.
52. James Henderson to BIA Commissioner, November 19, 1928, R.G. 75,

Bureau of Indian Affairs, General Service File, 1364-1925. 130, National Archives, Washington, D.C. (henceforth cited as BIA DISCOVERY FILE). Allen Whipporwill, Application for share of money appropriated for the Eastern Cherokee Indians, March 4, 1907, Number 17856, National Archives, Washington, D.C.

53. The Cherokee words are from Mary Ulmer Chiltoskey, *Cherokee Words with Pictures* (Asheville, N.C.: Gilbert Printing Co., 1972), pp. 14, 35.

54. Tise, *Winston-Salem*, p. 36.

55. Abe Long told his distant cousin, Joe Bradshaw, this story, and at the same time he gave Joe the clipping book of Long Lance's that Walter had brought back from Los Angeles (mentioned in the Preface). Joe recalls that the conversation took place shortly before Abe's death in 1972. Interview with Joe Bradshaw, Winston-Salem, July 13, 1975.

56. Application to Carlisle, CARLISLE FILE.

57. The best single volume on the mixed-blood Indian minorities in the Eastern United States is Brewton Berry's *Almost White* (Toronto: Collier Macmillan, 1969, first published 1963). For the Indian history of North Carolina see Douglas L. Rights, *The American Indian in North Carolina* (Winston-Salem: John F. Blair, 1957); on the Lumbees (formerly called Croatan) see Adolph L. Dial and David K. Eliades, *The Only Land I Know: A History of the Lumbee Indians* (San Francisco: The Indian Historian Press, 1975), and W. McKee Evans, *To Die Game* (Baton Rouge: Louisiana State University Press, 1971), pp. 19-34; on the Cherokees see Dale Van Every, *Disinherited: The Lost Birthright of the American Indian* (New York: William Morrow and Co., 1966).

58. A reference to Hamilton Willis and his school appears in Fries et al., *Forsyth*, p. 272.

59. John D. Harrison to DBS, October 2, 1976. He enclosed his grandfather's obituary.

60. Lovie Galloway is mentioned in Abe Long's diary, entry for September 21, 1959.

61. Richard B. Morris, ed., *Encyclopedia of American History* (New York: Harper & Brothers, 1953), p. 446.

62. The above scene is based on the statement of James Henderson to the Commissioner of Indian Affairs, Washington, D.C., dated Canton, N.C., November 19, 1928, BIA DISCOVERY FILE: "One thing, however, we could not reconcile was the fact that he could speak some Cherokee. This fact bothered me some although I still believed him to be an impostor. This doubt was later cleared up by finding that for a

year prior to his coming to Carlisle he had traveled with a sort of show all over the South and Cuba with a full blood longhaired Eastern Cherokee by the name of Whipporwill who taught him sufficient Cherokee to enable him to pass muster in enrolling at Carlisle." Apparently Henderson discovered in 1915 that Sylvester had learned his Cherokee from Whipporwill. See chapter 4, footnote 24.

CHAPTER THREE

1. M. Friedman, "The Carlisle Indian School: Its Foundation and Work," *The Red Man*, 3,3 (November 1910): 119. A photo of Friedman appears in *The Indian Craftsman*, 2,2 (October 1909): 34.
2. "Monthly Address to Students," *The Indian Craftsman*, 2,3 (November 1909): 37-8.
3. For information on Pratt see: Ryan, "Carlisle," pp. 1-53.
4. Ryan, "Carlisle," pp. 230-5. Good overviews of the school in the years Sylvester attended are: Edward Thomas, "As Seen by a Foreigner," *The Indian Craftsman*, 1,3 (April 1909): 39-41; New York *Sun*, "Indians as Money Makers and Students at Carlisle," *The Red Man*, 4,8 (April 1912): 330-9.
5. Charles A. Eastman, *The Indian To-day* (Garden City: Doubleday, Page & Co., 1915), p. 69. G. A. Falk, "Missionary Education Work Amongst the Prairie Indian, 1870-1914" (M.A. thesis, University of Western Ontario, 1973), p. 16, footnote 1.
6. James Henderson to BIA Commissioner, November 19, 1928, BIA DISCOVERY FILE. For an in-depth study of the Cherokees' attitudes toward blacks, see R. Halliburton, Jr., *Red over Black: Black Slavery among the Cherokee Indians* (Westport, Connecticut: Greenwood Press, 1977).
7. Emma Newashe McAllister, "Chief Buffalo Child Long Lance," *Daily Oklahoman*, March 24, 1929. She incorrectly believed that James Henderson gave him the name. Henderson himself believed that it had been "Pop" Warner, Carlisle's football coach. See James Henderson to William Chanler, February 24, 1930, CHANLER INVESTIGATION. One can speculate that Sylvester picked up the name "Chahuska" from one of the many books on Indians that he read. There was an Osage chief named Pahusca, rhyming with Chahuska, and perhaps he simply wanted to keep his initials the same. Dr. Kenneth W. Porter to DBS, dated Eugene, Oregon, November 22, 1980.
8. Emma Newashe wrote down her reminiscences of her childhood and

of Carlisle in an unpublished manuscript now in the Long Lance Papers, GLENBOW. Her comments on Sylvester at Carlisle are taken from her article, "Chief Buffalo Child Long Lance," and her Preface to *Redman Echoes*, ed. Roberta Forsberg (Los Angeles: Frank Wiggins Trade School, Department of Printing, 1933).

9. Mrs. E. H. Foster, "An Appreciation," in *Redman Echoes*, pp. 71-2 (she mentions the bird-calls); Emma Newashe, "Chief Buffalo Child Long Lance" (his defence of weaker classmates).

10. *Carlisle Arrow (The Indian Craftsman* was renamed *The Carlisle Arrow* in 1910; hereafter the newspaper is cited as CA), November 11, 1910. It appeared in *The Red Man*, 3,4 (December 1910): 173-5.

11. February 9, 1912.

12. Iva Miller's page in Sylvester Long's character book is pasted in the scrapbook donated to GLENBOW by Joe Bradshaw.

13. Elizabeth Analla to C. L. Ellis, Superintendent, Mission Agency, Riverside, California, April 9, 1932, BIA DISCOVERY FILE.

14. Fannie Keokuk, "The Croatan Indians," CA, October 29, 1909.

15. Edgar K. Miller, Superintendent, Hopi Indian Agency, to C. L. Ellis, Superintendent, Mission Agency, Riverside, California, April 9, 1932, BIA DISCOVERY FILE.

16. Edgar K. Miller, "Trade Record" of Sylvester Long, CARLISLE FILE; CA, September 15, 1911.

17. Carlisle's system of grades is explained in Ryan, "Carlisle," pp. 134-41.

18. Mrs. Foster's teaching posts are mentioned in the CA, September 5, 1913. Her reminiscences of Sylvester appear in *Redman Echoes*, pp. 71-2. For Emma Newashe's memories of Mrs. Foster see her sketch of life at Carlisle in the Long Lance Papers, GLENBOW.

19. Benjamin Franklin, *Autobiography* (Boston: The Riverside Press, 1958), p. 1.

20. New York *Evening Sun*, "Indians as Money Makers and Students at Carlisle," in *The Red Man*, 4,8 (April 1912): 331.

21. CA, November 12, 1909 (joined Invincibles); CA, December 23, 1910 (became secretary of the Invincibles); CA (mention of the debates: November 25, 1910; December 16, 1910; February 3 and 17, 1911; March 31, 1911); CA, April 7, 1911 (the hymns are listed).

22. CA, April 7, 1911 (elected club president). Two of the postcards—one to his father and one to his mother—have survived. Both are dated December 12, 1911. The originals are in the possession of Lillian Doulin, Mocksville, N.C., and copies of them are in GLENBOW.

23. CA, January 26, 1912. Interview with Ed Wall, New York, May 23,

1977. Wall was the principal musician in Sylvester's next school band, that of St. John's Military Academy.

24. See his "Outing Record" in the CARLISLE FILE. For information on Tyrone see Rev. W. H. Wilson, *Tyrone of To-day: The Gateway of the Alleghanies* (Tyrone: Herald, 1897); also Editing Committee, *Tyrone of To-day: Volume II, 1897-1976* (Tyrone: Tyrone Area Bicentennial Committee, 1976). Interview with Ed Wall, New York, May 23, 1977. Ed Wall to DBS, June 17, 1977.

25. The *Carlisle Arrow* mentioned on July 30, 1915, that he had made the track team. A photo exists of him among the intramural football players. Jim Thorpe's photograph, donated by Joe Bradshaw, Winston-Salem, N.C., is now at GLENBOW. See also Long Lance's article "Rise and Fall of Jim Thorpe," Winnipeg *Tribune*, December 1, 1923, and Thorpe's endorsement of Long Lance in Long Lance's pamphlet *How to Talk in the Indian Sign Language* (Akron, Ohio: B.F. Goodrich, 1930).

26. For information on Joe Ross consult his student file, R. G. 75, Bureau of Indian Affairs, Carlisle Student Record, file 3512, National Archives, Washington, D.C. Four years after graduation Ross wrote Carlisle asking for Sylvester Long's address as he wanted to keep in touch with him. Long Lance mentioned "Joe Ross" to Frederick Griffin, a journalist. Ross's name appears in Griffin's sketch of Long Lance in the Toronto *Star Weekly* on January 10, 1925. Long Lance referred to Wesley Two Moons in his article "The Secret of the Sioux," *Cosmopolitan*, June, 1927, p. 208. Wesley Two Moons' student file number was 1325, and his file can be consulted in the National Archives. He attended Carlisle from 1907 to 1911 (he died at the school on September 15, 1911 — pneumonia is listed as the cause of death). Robert Geronimo is mentioned as entering Carlisle in the fall of 1911; see the CA, September 22, 1911.

27. Robert Gorman, "Indian Finds Blood on Trail of Lost Child," Harrisburg *Telegraph*, May 27, 1911.

28. An excellent review of a Carlisle commencement is J. M. Oskinson's article on that of 1910 in *Collier's*, reprinted in *The Red Man*, 3, 1 (September 1910): 18-22. The students' dress at the commencement exercises is described in *The Red Man*, 4, 9 (May 1912): 428.

29. Sylvester's remarks are reprinted in the CA, April 19, 1912.

CHAPTER FOUR

1. Arthur S. Link, *Woodrow Wilson and the Progressive Era, 1910-1917* (New York: Harper and Row, 1954), pp. 63-6.

2. Sylvester's application appears in the Conway Hall Registrar, kept in the Registrar's Office, Dickinson College, Carlisle, Pennsylvania.

3. James Henderson to the BIA Commissioner, November 14, 1928, BIA DISCOVERY FILE.

4. *Students' Handbook of Conway Hall*, edited by the YMCA Cabinet, volume 6 (1912/13), p. 59. A copy of the pamphlet is in the Dickinson College Archives.

5. Long Lance (hereafter cited as LL), "Trail Upward," p. 138.

6. His marks at Dickinson are included in the CARLISLE FILE. He appears in a photo of the Hutchinson Society, and in a photo of the Conway Track Team. Dickinson College Archives.

7. CA, June 6, 1913.

8. Leigh Kimball, director, St. John's Cadet Band, to Moses Friedman, superintendent of Carlisle, July 9, 1913; Moses Friedman to Leigh Kimball, July 11, 1913, CARLISLE FILE. CA, September 19, 1913.

9. George S. Schuyler, *Black and Conservative* (New Rochelle, N.Y.: Arlington House Publishers, 1966), p. 31.

10. For information on St. John's see C. P. Hurditch, "Schools of America —St. John's, Manlius, N.Y.," *The Illustrated Sporting News* (New York), February 4, 1905, pp. 12-14, 16; Ira L. Reeves, *Military Education in the United States* (Burlington: Free Press Printing Co., 1914), pp. 175-6; Editorial, "End of a Great Tradition," Syracuse *Post-Standard*, February 24, 1973. The students' places of origin are given in the Manlius *Bulletin*, March, 1914, pp. 35-8. Kenneth S. Latourette, "Guido Herman Fridolin Verbeck," *Dictionary of American Biography*, vol. 19 (New York: Charles Scribner's Sons, 1936), pp. 248-9; H. C. Durston, "William Verbeck," Manlius *Thrift-News*, June 9, 1938.

11. Ryan, "Carlisle," pp. 220-1, 226, 238-9.

12. C. P. Hurditch, "St. John's," p. 14. The schedule is outlined in the Manlius *Bulletin*, March, 1914, p. 31. For his standing see *The Windmill* for March, 1915, April, 1915, and June, 1915. His membership in the drama society is mentioned in *The Windmill*, July, 1914, pp. 86, 87; and in the issue for September, 1915, p. 64. He is listed as a member of the track team in *The Windmill*, July, 1914, p. 101. Interview with Ed Wall, New York, May 22, 1977.

13. Interview with Ed Wall, New York, May 22, 1977; Ed Wall to DBS, June 17, 1977.

14. Syracuse *Journal*, June 10, 1914.

15. Sylvester Long to Moses Friedman, November 15, 1913. CARLISLE FILE.

16. War Department. Information Relative to the Appointment and

Admission of Cadets to the United States Military Academy, *Official Register, 1916*, p. 68.

17. "From 1802 to 1940, only four blacks were among the nearly 11,800 graduates of the Military Academy." Dr. Stephen B. Grove, USMA historian, to DBS, dated West Point, August 24, 1978. The four blacks graduated in 1877, 1887, 1889, and 1936.

18. Sylvester Long Lance to President Woodrow Wilson, March 8, 1915, CARLISLE FILE. All correspondence relating to his request is contained in this file.

19. Sylvester Long Lance to President Woodrow Wilson, dated May 14, 1915, Woodrow Wilson Papers, Series 4, no. 2281, one page. Manuscript Division, Reference Department, Library of Congress, Washington, D.C.

20. Actually David Moniac, a Creek, who graduated in 1822, was the first Indian appointed to West Point. He attained the rank of major and, ironically, was killed in battle with the Seminole Indians in 1836. Dr. Kenneth W. Porter to DBS, November 22, 1980.

21. On April 9, 1930, the Longs told R. H. Latham that Long Lance "has often sent clippings of his progress to the family." Ilia Tolstoy's report, CHANLER INVESTIGATION. For a previous reference to the postcards see chapter 3, footnote 22.

22. Winston-Salem City Directories for 1913, 1915, 1916, 1918, 1920. Gravestone of Vivian Munita Long (1909-19), Silver Hill Graveyard, Buena Vista, Winston-Salem, N.C.

23. Lovie Galloway and her husband are mentioned in Abe Long's diary, entry for September 21, 1959.

24. James Henderson to William Chanler, February 24, 1930, CHANLER INVESTIGATION: "Before Long graduated from Carlisle I went to Cherokee, North Carolina, where I was made superintendent and agent for the Eastern Band of Cherokee Indians. Soon after he was nominated by President Wilson for West Point I was called upon for the life history of this Indian. After dilligent [sic] search I could find no one on the reservation who knew anything at all in regard to his life history." Possibly, though, it was at this time that Henderson discovered Sylvester had learned Cherokee from Allen Whipporwill. See chapter 2, footnote 62.

CHAPTER FIVE

1. *New York Times*, March 21, 1916.

2. For a description of Fort Slocum and the colored recruits there see Schuyler, *Black and Conservative*, p. 33.

3. Sylvester gave details of his weight and height in his letter to President Wilson, CARLISLE FILE. For the requirements for West Point consult "War Department. Information Relative to the Appointment and Admission of Cadets to the United States Military Academy," *Official Registrar*, 1916, pp. 65-6.

4. His marks are given in "Examination of Candidates for Admission to the United States Military Academy, March 1916," United States Military Academy Archives, West Point, N.Y. His standing at St. John's is given in his reports, copies of which are in the Long Lance Papers, GLENBOW.

5. LL, "Trail Upward," p. 138.

6. We know for certain that he wrote a letter to Superintendent Lips on March 17, 1914, CARLISLE FILE; and that he was in touch with a former teacher, Adelaide Belle Reichel. Miss Reichel later told the commissioner of Indian Affairs that Long Lance had "refused an appointment to West Point." Adelaide Belle Reichel to the BIA Commissioner, dated Tulsa, Oklahoma, November 20, 1928, BIA DISCOVERY FILE.

7. James Henderson to William Chanler, February 24, 1930, CHANLER INVESTIGATION.

8. Frederick Griffin, "Redskin Extraordinary is this Indian Chief," Toronto STAR WEEKLY, January 10, 1925. "Man Mountain Dean, 63, Dies in Georgia," *New York Times*, May 30, 1953, p. 15, c. 5. Frank Leavitt's photo appears in Long Lance's large scrapbook, donated by Joe Bradshaw, GLENBOW. Who won the match? Long Lance, of course, claimed he did. Fred Griffin reports the Chief's version of the story: "In 1916, shortly before coming to Canada to enlist, he threw Frank Leavitt, heavyweight champion of the U.S. Army, four times at the West Side Athletic Club."

9. *Montreal Star*, August 5, 1916, p. 8.

10. LL, "Trail Upward," p. 138.

11. G. W. L. Nicholson, *Canadian Expeditionary Force, 1914-1919* (Ottawa: Queen's Printer, 1964), p. 154 (Sanctuary Wood), p. 218 (recruits in July 1916), p. 213 (lowering of the medical).

12. Mason Wade, *The French Canadians*, 2 vols. (Toronto: Macmillan, 1968), 2:661-7.

13. Sylvester Long Lance, Attestation Paper, Canadian Over-seas Expeditionary Force, dated August 4, 1916. I am most grateful to W. A. MacIntosh, and to the staff of the Directorate of History, National Defence Headquarters, Ottawa, for their assistance in researching Long Lance's war record. The details of his service are contained in his service record, and the "casualty form active ser-

vice." The "Particulars of Service" prepared by the Canadian Forces Record Service, July 8, 1976, was also helpful.

14. The best summary of the participation of the Canadian Indian in World War I is Duncan Campbell Scott, "The Canadian Indians and the Great World War," in *Canada in the Great World War*, vol. 3 (Toronto: United Publishers, 1919), pp. 285-328. Lance-Corporal Norwest is mentioned on p. 312.

15. The poem is in the CARLISLE FILE.

16. John Swettenham, *To Seize the Victory* (Toronto: The RyersonPress, 1965), pp. 122-3.

17. The respective positions at Vimy and the conflict itself are presented in the popular historian Ralph Allen's "The Battle of Vimy Ridge," *Ordeal by Fire: Canada, 1910-1945* (Toronto: Popular Library, 1961), pp. 143-8; and more completely and accurately in Nicholson, *Canadian Expeditionary Force*, pp. 233-68, and Swettenham, *To Seize the Victory*, pp. 145-63; see particularly pp. 146 and 161.

18. Swettenham, *To Seize the Victory*, p. 161.

19. Long Lance quoted in the New York *World*, July 22, 1917.

20. In early 1925 Long Lance told Fred Griffin, the Toronto journalist, of this injury and his narrow escape. See Griffin, "Redskin Extraordinary," Toronto *Star Weekly*, January 10, 1925.

21. The story appeared in the New York *World* on July 22 and in papers as far afield as the Washington *Post* and the Seattle *Post-Intelligencer* the following week.

22. Thomas F. Gossett, *Race: The History of an Idea in America* (Dallas: Southern Methodist University Press, 1962), pp. 269-73. John Hope Franklin, *From Slavery to Freedom*, pp. 439-41, 454, 480-3.

23. Fambrough L. Brownlee, *Winston-Salem: A Pictorial History* (Norfolk, Virginia: Donning Co., 1977), p. 148.

CHAPTER SIX

1. Long Lance's "Record of Service." W. A. B. Douglas, Directorate of History, National Defence Headquarters, Ottawa to DBS, February 28, 1980.

2. Anon., *Calgary* (London: Hodder and Stoughton, 1912), pp. 1-12. The best history of Calgary is Max Foran's *Calgary: An Illustrated History* (Toronto: James Lorimer, 1978).

3. Thorpe's batting average is given in the Calgary *Albertan*, July 12, 1919, p. 16.

4. Long Lance's style of dress is described in Walker, "Longlance," typescript of an article in the "Long Lance" file, news morgue, *Cal-*

gary Herald. "His customary garb was a Palm Beach suit and soft hat." My thanks to the *Herald* for allowing me to use their news morgue.

5. Walter McClintock, *The Old North Trail: Life, Legends and Religion of the Blackfeet Indians* (Lincoln: University of Nebraska Press, 1968), p. 11. First published in 1910.

6. The details on Calgary in the third week of July, 1919, are taken from the *Calgary Herald* (hereafter cited as CH) and the *Albertan*.

7. MacInnis is mentioned in H. G. Kennedy, *History of the 101st Regiment Edmonton Fusiliers* (1913), and is the subject of an article in the CH, August 23, 1919, p. 11. Long Lance told this story in *MacLean's* magazine on May 15, 1926, and in *McClure's* of July 1927. The text of the *McClure's* article has been used.

8. Diamond Jenness, "Canada's Indians Yesterday. What of Today?" *Canadian Journal of Economics and Political Science*, 20 (1954): 97.

9. Long Lance mentions their racial ancestry in "Indians of the Northwest and West Canada," *The Mentor*, March 1924, p. 6.

10. LL, "Trail Upward," p. 138. The Calgary Directory for 1919 mentions that the Soldiers Civil Re-establishment Office was in the Lancaster Building, p. 173.

11. LL, "Trail Upward," p. 138.

12. He is mentioned as helping coach the Calgary Canucks Football Team in October (CH, October 10 and 16, 1919). Long Lance is referred to as a reporter in the CH, April 21 and 23, 1920, and in the *Albertan*, April 23, 1920.

13. CH, November 12, 1920, p. 18.

14. Interview with Howard Kelly, Calgary, March 9, 1975. For a short biographical sketch of Howard Kelly see Bill Drever, "Personality of the Week," CH, January 8, 1955. Interview with Reg Hammond, Calgary, May 5, 1976, and October 28, 1979. In the early 1920s he worked as the *Herald*'s office boy.

15. Gerald Brawn, "A Veteran of Herald Staffers Traces Paper's Progress through the Years," CH, October 22, 1964, p. 64.

16. Margaret Vahey Eakin to DBS, November 21, 1978.

17. In 1924 he informed *The Mentor* that he was "about thirty years of age"; see the issue for March, 1924, p. 72.

18. Ralph Wilson, "The Bombing of the City Hall," file D970.2.L845, GLENBOW.

19. Walker, "Longlance" file, news morgue, *Calgary Herald*.

20. Interview with Hugh Dann, Calgary, February 21, 1975.

21. Information on the "Human Spider" appears in the CH, September 23 and 26, 1920. His militia commission as a lieutenant, dated September 1, 1921, is in GLENBOW (Long Lance papers donated by Joe Brad-

shaw). Canon Middleton's daughter, Mrs. Sophie Allison, has Long Lance's membership card in the Elks. W. B. Fraser mentions Fred McCall's flying record in *Calgary* (Montreal: Holt, Rinehart and Winston, 1967), p. 98. Maurice Fidler outlined Long Lance's boxing activities in Calgary in an interview in Ottawa, June 3, 1976. The Calgary *Eye-Opener*, October 8, 1921, commented on his "unerring judgement" as a boxing referee. His election to the Canucks' Executive is mentioned in the CH, October 22, 1920.

22. Interview with Howard Kelly, Calgary, March 9, 1975.
23. Paul Senn, *The Lawless Decade* (New York: Bonanza Books, 1957), pp. 56-60.
24. Jack Dempsey quoted in Harry Scott, "Jack Dempsey," the *Albertan*, March 24, 1921.
25. Long Lance's article on the Dempsey visit appeared in the Winnipeg *Tribune* (hereafter cited as WT), June 19, 1923. For details of Dempsey's activities in Calgary see the CH, March 23, 24, 25, 1921. Jack Dempsey's comment on Long Lance is taken from his daughter's (Barbara Piattelli Dempsey) letter to DBS, August 19, 1977.
26. Long Lance quotes Douglas Cunningham in "Coming East," *McClure's*, July, 1927, p. 122. For information on Cunningham see CH, March 13, 1926, p. 23, and CH, June 25, 1955.
27. [LL] " 'Dare Devil' Locklear Falls to his Death," CH, August 3, 1920. See also CH, June 29, 1920; CH, July 2, 1920; and Long Lance's "Ormer Locklear, Air 'Daredevil,' Gentleman and Sportsman" in Long Lance's *Aviation Annual. 1921. Devoted to Flying in Alberta* in GLENBOW.
28. "Nigger Humour," *The Beaver*, March, 1926, p. 74. My thanks to Jack Dunn of Calgary for this reference.
29. Fred Kennedy, *Alberta Was My Beat* (Calgary: The Albertan, 1975), p. 65.

CHAPTER SEVEN

1. CH, May 27, 1921.
2. Newman Dalton of Mocksville, N.C., has the originals; copies of the photos are in the Photo Library, GLENBOW.
3. My thanks to Donna Bloomfield of Calgary for her help with this description of Gleichen in the early 1920s.
4. George Gooderham, "I Remember," George Gooderham Papers, GLENBOW; George Gooderham, diary entry for Friday, May 27, 1921, Gooderham Papers, GLENBOW; interview with George Gooderham, Calgary, February 7, 1975. The Department of Indian Affairs' ruling

on school attendance is mentioned in Robert G. Moore, *The Historical Development of the Indian Act* (Ottawa: Treaties and Historical Research Centre, 1978), p. 115.

5. George Gooderham, "Twenty-Five Years as an Indian Agent to the Blackfoot Band," p. 1. Gooderham Papers, GLENBOW. S. C. Long Lance, "Blackfoot Indians," CH, June 11, 1921. L. M. Hanks and J. R. Hanks, *Tribe Under Trust* (Toronto: University of Toronto Press, 1950), p. 56.

6. George Gooderham, "Autobiography," pp. 5-14. Gooderham Papers, GLENBOW.

7. Interview with George Gooderham, Calgary, February 7, 1975.

8. Georgeen Barrass, Introduction to *Among the Blackfoot and Sarcee* by Canon H. W. Gibbon Stocken (Calgary: Glenbow Alberta Institute, 1976), pp. iii-xv.

9. Stocken, *Among the Blackfoot and Sarcee*, pp. 12-13.

10. LL, "Sarcee Indians," CH, July 23, 1921.

11. "Buffalo Child Long Lance Visits Ohio," *Ohio Archaeological and Historical Quarterly*, 33 (1924): 523.

12. CH, November 18, 1933.

13. Winnifred A. Tims, "Life on an Indian Reservation," unpublished article, p. 1, Tims Papers, GLENBOW.

14. Interview with Reginald Tims, Calgary, November 23, 1979 (son of Archdeacon Tims). CH, October 13, 1923; CH, November 18, 1933. The quotations are taken from Tims's manuscript, "Impressions Regarding Missionary Effort Amongst the Indians, January 6, 1919," Tims Papers, GLENBOW.

15. LL, "Sarcee Indians," CH, July 23, 1921. "Dr. T. F. Murray," CH, February 6, 1952. Jenness, "Canada's Indians," p. 99.

16. For information on Jim Starlight see LL, "Sarcee Indians," CH, July 23, 1921. Winnifred A. Tims, "Progressive Sarcee," CH, May 25, 1929. George Gooderham, "Northern Plains Tribes," vol. 5 (Sarcees), Gooderham Papers, GLENBOW. Stocken, *Among the Blackfoot and Sarcee*, p. 34 (Starlight's ability in chess). Long Lance to the Rev. S. H. Middleton (hereafter cited as SHM), October 12, 1924, on the loan of Jim Starlight's buckskin suit.

17. Nansi Swayze, *Canadian Portraits, Jenness, Barbeau, Wintemberg* (Toronto: Clarke, Irwin and Co., 1960), pp. 83-5. Diamond Jenness, *The Sarcee Indians of Alberta* (Ottawa: National Museum of Canada, 1938).

18. "Death of General Howard," *The Indian Craftsman*, 2,3 (November, 1909): 37.

19. Interview with George Gooderham, Calgary, February 7, 1975.

CHAPTER EIGHT

1. For biographical information on S. H. Middleton see Roberta Forsberg, *Chief Mountain: The Story of Canon Middleton* (Whittier, California: The Historical Society of Alberta, 1964); and S. H. Middleton, "Life of Service Among Indians," Lethbridge *Herald*, December 11, 1947. The Rev. S. H. Middleton became a canon in the Anglican Church in early November, 1924 (CH, November 4, 1924), and after that date is referred to as Canon Middleton.

2. For information on the Blackfoot Confederacy see Hugh A. Dempsey, *Crowfoot* (Edmonton: Hurtig, 1972), and his *Red Crow* (Saskatoon: Western Producer Prairie Books, 1980); and John C. Ewers, *The Blackfeet* (Norman: University of Oklahoma Press, 1958). In the United States, "Peigan" is spelt "Piegan."

3. James G. MacGregor, *A History of Alberta* (Edmonton: Hurtig, 1972), pp. 174, 177, 196.

4. For Canon Middleton's reminiscences of his early years on the Blood Reserve see *Kainai Chieftainship* (Lethbridge: Lethbridge Herald, 1953), particularly pp. 57 and 62; and his "Life of Service Among Indians," Lethbridge *Herald*, December 11, 1947.

5. SHM to LL, August 22, 1922.

6. Full descriptions of the school are found in Rev. Middleton's reports to the Department of Indian Affairs in the federal Sessional Papers for 1913 and 1914, and in his reports to the Anglican Church (those of 1913 and 1917 are in the Calgary Indian Mission Papers, GLENBOW).

7. Report of J. A. Markle, Inspector of Indian Agencies, Report of the Superintendent of Indian Education, Department of Indian Affairs, Annual Report 1916, p. 217.

8. Sophie Allison, "The Middleton Family," in *Fort Macleod — Our Colourful Past* (Fort Macleod: Fort Macleod History Book Committee, 1977), pp. 369-71.

9. Ken Liddell, "New Angle Found on Old School Tie," CH, December 15, 1951.

10. LL, "Alberta's Most Progressive Indian Tribe," CH, August 27, 1921.

11. SHM to Mrs. Edgar Pratt Hawkins, October 30, 1935.

12. LL, "Alberta's Most Progressive Indian Tribe," CH, August 27, 1921.

13. Canon Middleton in *Redman Echoes*, p. 185.

14. LL to SHM, dated Calgary, August 27, 1921.

15. SHM to LL, January 12, 1922.

16. My thanks to Sophie Middleton Allison (one of Canon Middleton's daughters) for confirming the details of an annual reunion of the Old Boys' and Girls' Association of St. Paul's.

17. LL to SHM, dated Calgary, January 15, 1922. The Carlisle uniform is described in Ryan, "Carlisle," p. 42.

18. Long Lance quoted in CH, February 15, 1922. Long Lance actually made these remarks in an afternoon address to the St. Paul's students, but no doubt he would have repeated the same themes to his older audience.

19. For the background of the Mountain Horse family see Mike Mountain Horse, *My People The Bloods* (Calgary: Glenbow-Alberta Institute, 1979). Chief Mountain Horse's obituary appears in the CH, October 15, 1937.

20. The *Albertan*, February 7, 1936.

21. Interview with Gordon Bird (who witnessed the ceremony), Stand Off, Blood Reserve, October 20, 1977. I have also relied on the description of the adoption ceremony given in Walter McClintock's classic, *The Old North Trail* (1910), pp. 31-5.

22. Interview with Hugh Dempsey, Calgary, April 27, 1976.

23. "Cherokee Given High Honor by Blood Indians," CH, February 14, 1922.

24. The original Buffalo Child might well have been the Blackfoot that George Catlin, the American artist, met in 1832. At the mouth of the Yellowstone River he painted the portrait of "In-ne-o-cose (the buffalo's child)." See his *Letters and Notes on the Manners, Customs, and Condition of the North American Indians* (2 vols. London: Published by the Author, 1841), 1:30.

25. "Buffalo Child Long Lance, a chief of the Bloods, in his official garb" in LL, "Before the Red Coats Came," *MacLean's* magazine, February 15, 1923, p. 12.

CHAPTER NINE

1. The *Albertan*, March 30, 1922.

2. F.G.E., "That Bogus Bomb!", the *Albertan*, March 31, 1922.

3. "Tellum Bigley," "Slaps and Slams," the *Albertan*, March 30, 1922.

4. Nicholas K. Booth, "Biographical Account of Samuel H. Adams," chapter 8, p.6, GLENBOW (D920.B725A).

5. He gives this as his address in his letter to the Rev. Middleton, dated Vancouver, May 11, 1922.

6. Eric Nicol, *Vancouver* (Toronto: Doubleday, 1978), p. 146; Walter N. Sage, "Vancouver: The Rise of a City," *Dalhousie Review*, 17 (1937): 47-54.

7. Charles Bruce, *News and the Southams* (Toronto: Macmillan, 1968), p. 181.

8. Stein was then the city editor. J. Swanson, Pacific Press Ltd., Vancouver, to DBS, December 14, 1979.
9. Patricia Roy, Introduction to *The Writing on the Wall* (Toronto: University of Toronto Press, 1974), pp. ix, xvii, xxvii. The quote from the *Sun* appears on p. vi.
10. Jenness, "Canada's Indians Yesterday. What of Today?" p. 96.
11. Franz Boas, "Diary," entry for November 6, 1886, reprinted in Ronald P. Rohner, ed., *The Ethnography of Franz Boas* (Chicago: University of Chicago Press, 1969), p. 54.
12. E. Palmer Patterson II, "Andrew Paull and Canadian Indian Resurgence" (Ph.D. dissertation, University of Washington, 1962), pp. 31-51.
13. For the background to Indian land policy in British Columbia see Robin Fisher, *Contact and Conflict: Indian-European Relations in British Columbia, 1774-1890* (Vancouver: University of British Columbia Press, 1977), pp. 146-211.
14. Wilson Duff, *The Indian History of British Columbia. Volume 1: The Impact of the White Man* (Victoria: Provincial Museum of Natural History and Anthropology, 1964), pp. 38-9. The Haidas' population dropped from an estimated 6000 in 1835 to 588 in 1915; the Bella Coola from an estimated 2000 in 1835 to 249 in 1929.
15. Patterson, "Paull," pp. 180-1.
16. Kenneth E. Kidd, *Canadians of Long Ago* (Toronto: Longmans Canada, 1951), p. 52. Nicholson, *The Canadian Expeditionary Force*, p. 218.
17. Patterson, "Paull," p. 43; E. Palmer Patterson II, "Andrew Paull (1892-1959)," *The Western Canadian Journal of Anthropology*, 6, 2 (1976): 70-1.
18. Elizabeth Bailey Price, "Magistrate Offended by Bitter Attack Sent Editor to Jail," CH, November 18, 1933.
19. LL to SHM, dated Vancouver, May 11, 1922.
20. Philip Drucker reviews the rise of native political organizations on the Pacific Coast in *The Native Brotherhoods: Modern Intertribal Organizations on the North West Coast* (Washington: United States Government Printing Office, 1958).
21. LL to SHM, dated Vancouver, May 11, 1922.
22. Forrest E. La Violette, "Missionaries and the Potlatch," *Queen's Quarterly*, 58 (1951): 237-51. Vancouver *Sun*, May 7, 1922, p. 31; Forrest E. La Violette, *The Struggle for Survival* (Toronto: University of Toronto Press, 1961), pp. 83-4, supplies slightly different figures for the total number imprisoned.
23. LL, "Squamish," Vancouver *Sun* (hereafter cited as VS), May 21, 1922.

24. In his article on the Kootenays in the VS, June 25, 1922, he cites both authorities, McLean and Boas.
25. The dates of his articles on the Indians of British Columbia are: May 21, 1922 (Squamish); May 28 (Musqueams); June 4 (Indians at Nanaimo); June 11 (Chilliwack Indians); June 18 (Haida); June 25 (Kootenays); July 2 (Lillooets); July 9 (Thompson Indians); July 16 (Shuswap); July 30 (Kwakiutl).
26. LL to SHM, dated Vancouver, June 22, 1922.
27. Alan Morley, *Roar of the Breakers: A Biography of Peter Kelly* (Toronto: The Ryerson Press, 1967).
28. Long Lance on Peter Kelly, see LL, "Name of Haida Struck Panic to Indian Heart," VS, June 18, 1922.
29. LL, "What Indian Requests to Government Really Mean," VS, July 26, 1922.
30. LL to SHM, dated Muscowpetung Indian Reserve, Saskatchewan, September 10, 1922.

CHAPTER TEN

1. J. William Brennan, ed., *Regina Before Yesterday* (Regina: Historical Committee, 1978), p. 192.
2. LL, "Where are Western Canada's Indians?" VS, June 7, 1924.
3. LL, "Before the Red Coats Came," *MacLean's* magazine, February 15, 1923, p. 13.
4. John Hawkes, "William Morris Graham," *Saskatchewan and Its People*, vol. 2 (Chicago: S. J. Clarke, 1924), pp. 1196-7. "It is Fifty Years Since a Lasting Treaty was Made with Canada's Prairie Indians," *Saturday Night*, October 18, 1924, p. 3. "William Morris Graham," a short (one-page) sketch of his life, in the possession of Bill Tye, Calgary.
5. "Indians' Friend is Dead. Wife of Former Indian Official Passes Friday," Regina *Leader-Post*, December 16, 1939.
6. W. M. Graham, "Report for South Saskatchewan Inspectorate," *Report of the Department of Indian Affairs*, 1910, pp. 416-18; *Report of the Department of Indian Affairs*, 1914, pp. 67-9. Eleanor Brass, "The File Hills Ex-Pupil Colony," *Saskatchewan History*, 6,2 (Spring 1953): 66-9.
7. Charles Stewart speaking on April 24, 1923, in the House of Commons, Ottawa, House of Commons, *Debates*, p. 2146. Commissioner Graham felt vulnerable since he owed his appointment to the Conservative Arthur Meighen, who in 1918 had acted as superintendent general of Indian Affairs. Meighen's wife was the stepdaughter of

W. H. H. Wood, one of Mrs. Graham's brothers, hence Mrs. Arthur Meighen was Mrs. Graham's niece. When Mr. Meighen served as prime minister in 1920/21, it was reported in the Ottawa *Citizen* ("Indians of the Blood Reserve Make Allegations of Scandalous Treatment by the Government," May 6, 1921) that "a public official [Commissioner Graham] is well known to be a protege and relative by marriage of the leader of the present government." My thanks to Keith Wilson, secretary treasurer, Town of Birtle, Manitoba, for helping me to establish the family tie. Keith Wilson to DBS, December 11, 1980.

8. Hugh A. Dempsey, "The Place of Indians in Western Canadian History," typed manuscript prepared in 1968, p. 12.

9. Marius Barbeau, "Our Indians—Their Disappearance," *Queen's Quarterly*, 38 (1931): 707.

10. Jenness, "Canada's Indians Yesterday. What of Today?" pp. 98-9. Charles E. Hendry, *Beyond Traplines* (Toronto: Ryerson, 1969), p. 13.

11. "Charles Stewart," Lethbridge *Herald*, December 7, 1946. Ross Hamilton, ed., *Prominent Men of Canada, 1931-32* (Montreal: National Publishing Co., 1932), p. 456.

12. LL to SHM, dated Muscowpetung Reserve, Saskatchewan, September 10, 1922.

13. E. K. Brown, "Duncan Campbell Scott," in *Responses and Evaluations*, ed. David Staines (Toronto: McClelland and Stewart, 1977), pp. 112-44.

14. Scott, "The Canadian Indians and the Great World War," pp. 325-6.

15. Charles Stewart speaking March 31, 1930, in the House of Commons, Ottawa, House of Commons, *Debates*, p. 1116.

16. Edward Ahenakew, *Voices of the Plains Cree* (Toronto: McClelland and Stewart, 1973), p. 152. Long Lance's political activities are mentioned in a note from Mike Mountain Horse to J. T. Faunt, dated Cardston, November 22, 1924, R.G. 10, vol. 3233, file 600107, Public Archives of Canada (my thanks to Bennett McCardle of Ottawa for this reference). Long Lance (presumably in early July, 1924, at the Fort Macleod Jubilee) suggested that a meeting be organized "to get the sympathy of the public, in order that pressure be brought to bear on the Government with a view to having that section of the Indian Act which authorizes the Government to lease at will any portion of an Indian Reserve without the consent of the Indians, cut out of the Indian Act." The meeting was held at Fort Macleod in mid-November, 1924, but Long Lance was not present.

17. LL to Alice Tye, dated New York, April 24, 1930.

18. Gooderham, "Twenty-Five Years as an Indian Agent," p. 2; Gooderham Papers, GLENBOW.
19. Chief Piapot's words are quoted in Long Lance's rough notes, GLENBOW.
20. Dan Kennedy, *Recollections of an Assiniboine Chief* (Toronto: McClelland and Stewart, 1972), pp. 54-6, 62.
21. LL to SHM, dated Regina, November 11, 1922.
22. Kennedy, *Recollections*, p. 87.
23. LL to SHM, dated Regina, November 11, 1922.
24. LL, *Long Lance* (New York: Cosmopolitan Book Corporation, 1928), pp. 90-1.
25. LL, "Indians of the Northwest and West Canada," *The Mentor*, 12,2 (March 1924): 7.
26. *Ibid.*
27. LL, "Red Men of the West—Yesterday and Today," Regina *Leader*, December 16, 1922.

CHAPTER ELEVEN

1. LL, "Chief Long Lance takes his readers across Broad Plain," VS, August 27, 1922.
2. "The Author in Indian Garb," WT, February 10, 1923. He later used the second photo to illustrate his article in *The Mentor*, March, 1924, p. 3.
3. Interview with Mike Eagle Speaker, Stirling, Alberta, January 16, 1976.
4. LL to SHM, dated Regina, Saskatchewan, November 11, 1922.
5. SHM to LL, February 3, 1923.
6. LL to Alice Tye, dated New York, July 12, 1930.
7. LL, "When the Indians Owned Manitoba," WT, February 12, 1923.
8. "Indian Chief at Grace Ch. Forum," WT, May 5, 1923. Garnet Clay Porter, "Long Lance, Indian Chief," *Saturday Night*, August 16, 1924. W. T. Allison, "Chief Buffalo Child Long Lance Writes Fascinating First Book," WT, October 27, 1928, magazine section, p. 6.
9. "Chief Long Lance Tells of Indian History," WT, January 16, 1923; "Indian Chief at Grace Ch. Forum," WT, May 5, 1923; "Predicts Redmen to Be Extinct in 200 Years," undated clipping about his talk to the Kiwanis Club at the Fort Garry Hotel, Winnipeg.
10. W. L. Morton, *Manitoba: A History* (2nd ed., Toronto: University of Toronto Press, 1967), pp. 300, 321. Alan Ramsay, "Winnipeg! City of Contrast and Beauty," *Canadian Geographical Journal*, 26 (1943): 44-7. Robert Craig Brown and Ramsay Cook, *Canada, 1896-1921* (Toronto: McClelland and Stewart, 1974), p. 98.

11. James H. Gray, *The Roar of the Twenties* (Toronto: Macmillan, 1975), p. 236.
12. Interview with Charles L'Ami, Winnipeg, October 20, 1976.
13. Interview with Allan Bill by Fran Fraser, May 11, 1962, a cassette of the recording is in GLENBOW.
14. See the photo of Long Lance standing on his head in F. G. Griffin, "Redskin Extraordinary is this Indian Chief," Toronto *Star Weekly*, January 10, 1925.
15. Interviews with Charles L'Ami and Pearl Driscoll L'Ami, Winnipeg, October 10, 1976.
16. Mrs. H. O'Malley to DBS, June 6, 1980.
17. Carlyle Allison, "The Corner Cupboard," WT, December 15, 1951, p. 6. Samuel Ichiye Hayakawa, a young student at the University of Manitoba, who stayed at the Allisons', met Long Lance several times. Today he is the United States senator from California. Senator Hayakawa remembers the Chief well. "In company he was perfectly charming—a good story-teller and conversationalist, gracious and flattering towards women, comradely with men." Senator Hayakawa to DBS, December 17, 1980.
18. Vernon Knowles, "Buffalo Child Long Lance is Found Shot in White Girl's Home," Toronto *Daily Mail and Empire*, March 22, 1932.
19. J. H. Cranston, *Ink on My Fingers* (Toronto: The Ryerson Press, 1953), p. 121.
20. LL, "Canadian Sioux Chief Seeks $20,000,000 from U.S. Government," Toronto *Star Weekly*, March 31, 1923. LL, "Sioux Indians to Washington to Claim $20,394,951," St. Paul *Pioneer Press*, March 18, 1923. LL, "Custer Died by Own Hand, Say Indian Braves," Chicago *Herald and Examiner*, April 8, 1923.
21. LL to SHM, dated St. Michael's Indian Boarding School, Duck Lake, May 17, 1923.
22. Interview with Howard Kelly, Calgary, March 9, 1975.
23. Mayor Webster's stampede costume is described in the CH, July 9, 1923.
24. "Calgary Captured by Indians," CH, July 12, 1923.
25. The medal with Long Lance's name on it is engraved "Calgary Exhibition and Stampede 1923," Lilly E. Middleton to DBS, November 10, 1978. LL to Mr. and Mrs. Middleton, dated Calgary, June 27, 1924.
26. LL, "How do the Indians Regard the March of Civilisation?" CH, October 13, 1923.
27. LL, "Secrets of the Forbidden Sun Dance Are Revealed," Toronto *Star Weekly*, November 17, 1923. The *Calgary Herald* also had a reporter at the Sun Dance camp, Dudley McClean. His article, "Sun Dance," appeared on August 25, 1923, in the *Herald*.

28. Interview with Hugh Dempsey, Calgary, September 10, 1980.
29. George H. Gooderham, "Chief Buffalo Child Long Lance," Northern Plains Tribes, vol. 2 (the Bloods), p. 10. Gooderham Papers, GLENBOW.
30. Interview with George H. Gooderham, Calgary, February 7, 1975.
31. Her name is given in Dudley McClean's article on the Sun Dance, CH, August 25, 1923.
32. LL, "Secrets of the Forbidden Sun Dance Are Revealed," Toronto Star Weekly, November 17, 1923.
33. LL, "The Sun Dance. A Chief of the Blackfoot Tribe Describes this Spectacular Ceremony of his People, in Which a Woman is the Central Figure," Good Housekeeping, 85 (August 1927): 64-5, 219-20. Mary's picture appears on p. 65.
34. My thanks to Omer Lavallée, supervisor, Special Projects and Corporate Archives, Canadian Pacific, Montreal, for supplying me with photocopies of four of Long Lance's menus. Omer Lavallée to DBS, April 22, 1975.
35. T. N. Campbell and H. E. Ross, "The Battle of Duck Lake, The Star's Letterbox," Saskatoon Daily Star, November 3, 1923, p. 4. When Long Lance published an article in MacLean's on Almighty Voice (February 1, 1929), his version of the facts was also contested. See "The Last Stand of Almighty Voice," MacLean's, June 15, 1929.
36. LL, "How do the Indians Regard the March of Civilisation?" CH, October 13, 1923. Grace Lee Nute, "Pierre-Esprit Radisson", Dictionary of Canadian Biography (Toronto: University of Toronto Press, 1969), vol. 2, pp. 535-40.
37. LL, "Before the Red Coats Came," MacLean's, March 1, 1923, p. 50. Fran Fraser, "Blackfoot Chief Creates Legend," CH, May 19, 1956. Interview with Earl Calf Child, Blackfoot Reserve, Gleichen, August 30, 1976. He recalls that Running Rabbit died in 1918.
38. John Hawkes, The Story of Saskatchewan and Its People (3 vols., Chicago: S. J. Clarke Pub. Co., 1924), vol. 2, p. 918.
39. Pierre Berton, "The Legend of Almighty Voice" in The Wild Frontier (Toronto: McClelland and Stewart, 1978), pp. 209-33, 239, provides a more accurate account. See his criticisms of Long Lance on pp. 215-16.
40. LL, "How Canada's Last Frontier Outlaw Died," MacLean's, January 1, 1924, pp. 19-20, 42, 44; "Indian's Stand Against Mounted Police," Family Herald and Weekly Star, January 2, 1924; "When Almighty Voice Held the Mounties at Bay," WT, January 5, 1924.
41. Here I am following Long Lance's version of the story as published in Long Lance (New York: Cosmopolitan Book Corporation, 1928), pp. 247-75.

42. Berton, "Legend of Almighty Voice," p. 215. Berton regrets this, as he claims "the Long Lance narrative is studded with so many errors, easily established from the record, that it is not possible to give credence to his account."

43. LL, *Long Lance*, pp. 264-6.

44. *Ibid.*, p. 269.

45. *Ibid.*, pp. 270, 272.

46. LL, "Right to Jaw 'Kayoes' Firpo in 2nd Round," WT, September 15, 1923. Senn, *The Lawless Decade*, p. 89.

47. LL, "Georges Carpentier Makes Poor Showing," WT, June 2, 1924. LL to SHM, dated "en route Columbus-Winnipeg," October 12, 1924. F. G. Griffin, "Redskin Extraordinary," Toronto *Star Weekly*, January 10, 1925 (on LL's style as a boxing writer).

48. Federal Writers' Project. *New York City Guide*, p. 225.

49. W. D. Moffat in an editorial note, *The Mentor*, 12,2 (March, 1924): 72.

50. Herbert Cranston quoted in Wilfrid Eggleston, *While I Still Remember: A Personal Record* (Toronto: The Ryerson Press, 1968), p. 82.

51. Ross Harkness, *J. E. Atkinson of the Star* (Toronto: University of Toronto Press, 1963), p. 179.

52. Card announcing Chief Long Lance as a judge in the City Amateur Boxing and Wrestling Championships, in LL's scrapbook, donated by Joe Bradshaw, GLENBOW. George E. Johnston to DBS, February 7 and June 15, 1976 (on Long Lance's girlfriend, the music teacher).

53. LL, "Ancient Days are Revived at Fort Macleod Festivities," WT, July 3, 1924. C. Frank Steele, "Long Lance Speaks Again," Winnipeg *Free Press*, magazine section, July 10, 1937.

54. Interview with Mike Eagle Speaker, Stirling, Alberta, March 15, 1976, and at the old St. Paul's School, Old Agency, Blood Reserve, October 20, 1977.

55. Long Lance quoted in Wilfrid Eggleston, "Fastened Sleds Under Canoe in Mushing Through Slush," Toronto *Star Weekly*, May 4, 1929.

56. "Soon I may stop writing about Indians altogether or trying to get them together for their own good; for it is the most thankless, disheartening job anyone ever tackled." LL to Mrs. Ethel T. Feathers, dated Banff Springs Hotel, August 5, 1924 (a copy of this letter is in GLENBOW, and the original in Mrs. Sophie Middleton Allison's possession). LL to SHM, dated Banff Springs Hotel, August 5, 1924. See also footnote 16, chapter 10. After suggesting that the tribes of the Blackfoot Confederacy meet together in the fall of 1924, Long Lance did not appear at the meeting that November.

57. CH, July 8, 1924, p. 11.

58. LL to SHM, dated Banff Springs Hotel, July 15, 1924.

59. John Carlisle's role is mentioned in an unidentified clipping from a Columbus, Ohio, newspaper, "City Plays Host to Indian Star of 'The Silent Enemy.'" LL scrapbook, donated by Joe Bradshaw, GLENBOW.
60. LL to SHM, dated "en route: Columbus-Winnipeg," October 12, 1924. "Buffalo Child Long Lance," *Ohio Archaeological and Historical Quarterly*, 33 (1924): 516.
61. Chief Logan quoted in *The Indian and the White Man*, ed. Wilcomb E. Washburn (Garden City, N.Y.: Anchor Books, 1964), pp. 427-8.
62. Anna Church Colley, "At Logan's Elm, Where His Famous Speech Was Uttered," *The American Indian*, March, 1929, p. 8.
63. "Ohio History Day at Logan Elm Park. Chief Buffalo Child Long Lance, Full Blooded Indian, was the Principal Orator," *The Circleville Herald*, October 6, 1924. LL to SHM, dated "en route: Columbus-Winnipeg," October 12, 1924.

CHAPTER TWELVE

1. "Full Blooded Indian Chief Takes Up Newspaper Work. Chief Buffalo Child Long Lance Exchanges Tomahawk for Typewriter," unidentified clipping in LL scrapbook, donated by Joe Bradshaw, GLENBOW.
2. LL, "Dempsey Remembers Little of Furious First Round," WT, November 6, 1923.
3. "Indian Chief on Unity of Dominion," Montreal *Gazette*, November 18, 1924. "Tells of Indian Life Before the White Man," Hamilton *Spectator*, December 3, 1924. "Says Indians Face Extinction Within Century and Half," Toronto *Daily Star*, December 11, 1924. F. G. Griffin, "Redskin Extraordinary is this Indian Chief," Toronto *Star Weekly*, January 10, 1925.
4. LL to SHM, dated Banff Springs Hotel, August 5, 1924. LL to SHM, dated Banff Winter Carnival, February 12, 1925.
5. LL to SHM, dated Winnipeg, January 7, 1925. LL to SHM, dated Banff Winter Carnival, February 12, 1925.
6. "All Blacks Get Royal Welcome," WT, February 5, 1925. "Indian Chiefs Welcome Maoris," WT, February 7, 1925. "All Blacks First Time on Ice," the *Albertan*, February 9, 1925. "All Black take Banff by Storm," CH, February 9, 1925. Maurice Fidler to DBS, April 4, 1976.
7. Eldred G. F. Walker, *Canadian Trails Re-Visited* (London: William Stevens, 1925), pp. 97-9. A photo of Eldred Walker appears opposite the book's title page.
8. Bart Robinson, *Banff Springs: The Story of a Hotel* (Banff: Summerthought, 1973), p. 80.
9. "In the ballroom he is an imposing figure. Tall and stalwart his

evening clothes seem to really belong to him. He has the ability that so many of us lack, the knack of fitting in, and is quite in demand as a dancing partner." Unidentified clipping, "Chief Buffalo Child Long Lance, Blackfoot, Carlyle graduate, press agent for the Canadian Pacific Railroad," LL scrapbook, donated by Joe Bradshaw, GLENBOW.

10. "A Chief of Indians Invited to Britain," Toronto *Daily Star*, September 5, 1924. A short biography of Paget appears in *The Dictionary of National Biography, 1951-1960* (Oxford: Oxford University Press, 1971), pp. 786-7.

11. Griffin, "Redskin Extraordinary," Toronto *Star Weekly*, January 10, 1925.

12. Fred Jones, "Earl Haig," CH, July 8, 1925.

13. Long Lance quoted in "Haig is Made Indian Chief," the *Albertan*, July 11, 1925.

14. "Chief Bull Head of Sarcees Dead; Was Their Great Leader," CH, March 15, 1911.

15. "Chief Akahtse (Field-Marshal Earl Haig) shaking hands with Chief Buffalo Child Long Lance, while Chief Big Plume of the Sarcees, stands in the left foreground," CH, July 10, 1925.

16. Providence *Sunday Journal*, October 18, 1925. LL to SHM, dated Montreal, November 22, 1925.

17. Ray Long quoted in a printed list of comments about Long Lance's lectures, prepared by the Bureau of Commercial Economics. Sophie Middleton Allison has allowed her copy to be photocopied and placed in GLENBOW.

18. LL to SHM, dated Montreal, November 22, 1925.

19. "The *Cosmopolitan* of Ray Long," *Fortune*, 3 (March, 1931): 49-55, particularly 54-55.

20. LL to SHM, dated Montreal, November 22, 1925.

21. The Bureau's objectives are outlined on the back of the Bureau's official letter-paper; see the letter of Randolph M. Boggs to LL, May 24, 1927, GLENBOW. Long Lance's nineteen railway passes are all glued in his scrapbook, donated by Joe Bradshaw, GLENBOW.

22. "American Blue Blood will Turn Red, Says Indian," Chicago *Tribune*, January 10, 1926. The comments of Dr. Bell and Charles MacConnell are listed in their printed endorsements of Long Lance's lectures, Bureau of Commercial Economics, GLENBOW.

23. List of printed endorsements, Bureau of Commercial Economics, GLENBOW.

24. LL, "I Wanted to Live Like the White Man," *MacLean's* magazine, May 15, 1926, pp. 16, 60. LL, "Coming East," *McClure's*, July, 1927, pp. 14-15, 121-2.

25. LL to SHM, dated Winnipeg, May 7, 1926.

26. LL to SHM, dated New York, November 2, 1926.
27. My thanks to Peter Mirejovsky, Calgary, for the image of the pond.
28. "Parade Notes," CH, July 5, 1926.
29. "John Jay Sheridan," *Who's Who in Chicago and Vicinity, 1931* (Chicago: A. N. Marquis Company, 1931), p. 886. Marriage Certificate of John Jay Sheridan and Florence K. Donovan, September 10, 1924. Available from Grays Harbor County Auditor, 1708 Sumner, Montesana, Washington 98563. Interviews with Hugh Dann, Calgary, February 21, 1975, and December 18, 1979.
30. Interview with Howard Kelly, Calgary, March 9, 1975.
31. A full account of the incident appears in the Banff *Crag and Canyon*, September 10, 1926. Interviews with Howard Kelly, Calgary, March 9, 1975; and Hugh Dann, Calgary, February 21, 1975, and December 18, 1979.
32. Macleod *Gazette*, March 24, 1932; *Crag and Canyon*, September 10, 1926.
33. "Victims of Banff Fray Recovering," CH, September 13, 1926. "Charge Against Long Lance First on Court Docket," CH, October 1, 1926. LL to SHM, dated Chicago, October 16, 1926.
34. Kennedy, *Alberta Was My Beat*, p. 63. I have rearranged the quote slightly. In Fred Kennedy's book the statement reads: "Although Long Lance ultimately recovered, he confessed to me later that he came close to losing his manhood, a condition [that,] so far as the gregarious Indian was concerned, would have been a fate worse than death."
35. LL to SHM, dated Chicago, October 16, 1926.
36. LL to Alice Tye, dated New York, July 17, 1930. John C. Ewers, *The Blackfeet* (Norman: University of Oklahoma Press, 1958), pp. 3-5 (on Napi, the Old Man).
37. LL, "Secret of the Sioux," *Hearst's International–Cosmopolitan*, June, 1927, p. 208. "Wesley Two Moons," R.G. 75, Bureau of Indian Affairs, Carlisle Student Record, file 1325, National Archives, Washington, D.C.
38. The comments of Bernard Clark of Didcot, Oxfordshire, England, on Long Lance's version of the Battle of Little Big Horn proved very helpful. Ted Blackmore of Eastbourne, Sussex, England, kindly forwarded them to me in early February, 1976.
39. *New York Times* Book Review Section, May 22, 1927.
40. Mrs. Custer's threatened libel action is mentioned in the CH, March 21, 1932. *New York Times*, June 19, 1927. The Frontiersmen declared that Custer was "the most gallant and bravest Indian fighter in history" and added that Long Lance's article was "nearly all fiction."

CHAPTER THIRTEEN

1. "Farrar and Rinehart Buy Cosmopolitan," *New York Times* (hereafter cited as NYT), September 24, 1931.
2. A photo of Ray Long's office appears in "The *Cosmopolitan* of Ray Long," *Fortune*, 3 (March, 1931): 50.
3. W. A. Swanberg, *Citizen Hearst: A Biography of William Randolph Hearst* (New York: Bantam Books, 1971), p. 436.
4. The contract, signed March 30, 1927, was enclosed in a letter from Ellen Datlow, Holt, Rinehart and Winston, New York, to DBS, January 17, 1977.
5. Mary Burnham, ed., *The Cumulative Book Index, 1926-1932* (New York: H. W. Wilson Co., 1933), p. 275.
6. Frazier Hunt, *One American and His Attempt at Education* (New York: Simon and Schuster, 1938), p. 293.
7. On the book's contract the typed title, "The Story of an Indian Boy," has been crossed out and "Long Lance" written above it. LL to SHM, dated New York, August 7, 1928.
8. "... he met his brothers at least, in Philadelphia and elsewhere...." Colonel William A. Blair quoted in a letter to Canon Middleton, dated Winston-Salem, January 27, 1934. Long Lance must have met Abe in Philadelphia, for he told Walter in 1931 how pleased he was to see him again—they had not met for twenty-two years. LL to Walter Long, January 6, 1931. The meeting with Abe can be dated from a letter in Lillian Doulin's possession (copy in the GLENBOW). On January 30, 1935, U. K. Rice, the white manager of the Carolina Theatre in Winston-Salem, wrote John Kirby, a distributor for Paramount. He asked Kirby to send a print of *The Silent Enemy*, and added: "Chief Buffalo Longlance, a graduate of West Point who played the lead in this film was a brother of Abe Long, the manager of the colored section and he has not seen his brother for almost eight years."
9. Vivian Munita Long (1909-19), Gravestone, Silver Hill Graveyard, Buena Vista, Winston-Salem. Interview with Joe Bradshaw, Winston-Salem, January 8, 1977.
10. Abe Long's diary, entries for December 30, 1941, and March 14 and 17, 1946.
11. "Walter L. Long, Widely Known Negro is Dead," Winston-Salem *Journal*, March 28, 1941. "Death Claims Uncle Joe Long," Winston-Salem *Sentinel*, November 16, 1932.
12. LL, "Tunney," WT, November 12, 1926. LL, "Jack Sharkey," WT, May 21, 1927.
13. Daniel J. Boorstin, *The Image* (New York: Harper Colophon, 1964),

pp. 66-8. Frederick Lewis Allen, *Only Yesterday: An Informal History of the Nineteen-Twenties* (New York: Harper and Row, 1964; first published in 1931), pp. 180-4.

14. Interview with Maurice Fidler, Ottawa, June 3, 1976, and his letters of February 28, April 4, and May 17, 1976, and February 7, 1977.

15. Interview with Maurice Fidler, Ottawa, June 3, 1976.

16. Margaret Vahey Eakin to DBS, November 21, 1978.

17. Interview with Maurice Fidler, June 3, 1976.

18. Interview with Mike Eagle Speaker, Stirling, Alberta, January 16 and February 18, 1976; and at the old St. Paul's School, Old Agency, Blood Reserve, October 20, 1977.

19. LL, *Long Lance* (New York: Cosmopolitan Book Corporation, 1928), pp. 1-3.

20. *Ibid.*, pp. 7, 11, 14, 35.

21. *Ibid.*, pp. 7-8. Long Lance comments on the practice among the Lillooets in British Columbia in the VS, July 2, 1922. Mike Eagle Speaker denied that whipping took place among the Blackfoot tribes, interview, February 18, 1976. For a summary of the "whipping complex" see Thomas R. Garth, "The Plateau Whipping Complex and its Relationship to Plateau-Southwest Contacts," *Ethnohistory*, 12 (1965): 141-70.

22. LL, *Long Lance*, p. 10. This practice was also denied by Mike Eagle Speaker, interview, February 18, 1976.

23. *The Scotsman*, quoted on the back cover of the latest paperback British edition of *Long Lance* (London: Abacus, 1976).

24. LL, *Long Lance*, p. 11.

25. *Ibid.*, pp. 209, 243.

26. *Ibid.*, p. 277.

27. *Ibid.*, p. 247. See Hugh A. Dempsey, *Crowfoot* (Edmonton: Hurtig, 1972).

28. LL to SHM, dated Calgary, November 21, 1927. LL to SHM, dated New York, February 11, 1928.

29. Publicity circular prepared by Cosmopolitan Book Corporation, August 24, 1928, a photocopy is in GLENBOW. The book was published on that day.

30. LL to Howard Kelly, dated New York, February 2, 1928.

31. The quotations from the *Public Ledger* and *Times-Picayune* are taken from the advertisement for *Long Lance* published in the book section of the New York *Herald Tribune*, October 28, 1928. *The New Statesman*, quoted on the back cover of the latest British paperback edition of *Long Lance* (London: Abacus, 1976). Ernest Thompson

Seton, ed., *Famous Animal Stories* (New York: Brentano's Publishers, 1932), p. 327.

32. Paul Radin, "An Indian's Own Story: *Long Lance* by Chief Buffalo Child Long Lance," New York *Herald Tribune*, October 14, 1928, p. 7. For information about Radin consult Harry Hoijer, "Paul Radin, 1883-1959," *American Anthropologist*, n.s. 61 (1959): 839-43.

33. The translations of *Long Lance* and the various editions of the book are listed in *The National Union Catalog, Pre-1956 Imprints* (London, England: Mansell Information, 1970), vol. 83, p. 258, under "Buffalo Child Long Lance."

CHAPTER FOURTEEN

1. Long Lance describes the luncheon in a letter to Howard Kelly, dated New York, February 2, 1928. Ludwig's *Napoleon* was the number two non-fiction book in 1927, and number four in 1928. Alice Payne Hackett and James Henry Burke, *80 Years of Best Sellers* (New York: R. R. Bowker Company, 1977), pp. 103, 105.

2. Fred Gus Neuman, *Irvin S. Cobb: His Life and Achievements* (New York: Beekman Publishers, 1974; first published in 1934), p. 194. A picture of the house appears on p. 191.

3. Irvin S. Cobb, quoted in the Indianapolis *Times*, May 14, 1942.

4. Neuman, *Cobb*, p. 107. A shorter account of Cobb's life is Irving Dilliard's sketch in the *Dictionary of American Biography, Supplement Three, 1941-1945* (New York: Charles Scribner's Sons, 1973): 170-1.

5. "Bob Davis Recalls," WT, October 17, 1928.

6. "Irvin S. Cobb to Receive File American Indian," *The American Indian*, November 1927, p. 16.

7. Neuman, *Cobb*, pp. 50, 206, 225-8, 261; Elisabeth Cobb, *My Wayward Parent: A Book About Irvin S. Cobb* (Indianapolis: Bobbs-Merrill Company, 1945), p. 17; Leo Fox, Oct. 16, 1981.

8. Irvin S. Cobb, "Foreword," *Long Lance*, pp. vii-viii.

9. LL to Howard Kelly, dated New York, February 2, 1928.

10. A Norwegian journalist, Theodor Findahl, was present. He described Cobb's party in his book *Manhattan Babylon, en bok om New York idag* (Oslo, Norway: Gyldendal, 1928), pp. 42-50. He gave Long Lance an English version of a draft of his chapter "An Indian Chief on Park Avenue." This is now at GLENBOW. Long Lance also describes the party in his letters to Howard Kelly (February 10, 1928) and to Canon Middleton (February 11, 1928). My thanks to Elise Corbet of Calgary for her comments on the dress of the late 1920s.

11. The direct quotes have been taken from Long Lance's address to the Ohio State Archaeological and Historical Society on October 2, 1924. See "Buffalo Child Long Lance Visits Ohio," *Ohio Archaeological and Historical Society*, 33 (1924): 519.

12. *Ibid.*, 518.

13. *Ibid.*, 520.

14. *Ibid.*, 521-2.

15. Findahl, "An Indian Chief," p. 4.

16. For information on black New York in the 1920s see Gilbert Osofsky, *Harlem: The Making of a Ghetto: Negro New York, 1890-1930* (New York: Harper and Row, 1966); and the chapter "Africa" in Konrad Bercovici's *Around the World in New York* (New York: The Century Co., 1924), pp. 211-48.

17. Interview with Maurice Fidler, Ottawa, June 3, 1976.

18. Findahl, "An Indian Chief," p. 7.

19. LL to Howard Kelly, dated New York, June 8, 1928.

20. O. O. McIntyre, a New York columnist, called Long Lance "a sepia edition of the late Valentino." O. O. McIntyre, "New York Day by Day," Washington *Herald*, May 22, 1928.

21. Each woman gave him her photograph. Mildred wrote on hers, "To Long Lance the Maker of Dreams," and Vivian, "To Chief Longlance with every good wish, Vivian Hart 1928." For press references to Vivian Hart see the NYT, December 6, 1929, p. 26, c. 7; and to Mildred McCoy, NYT, August 4, 1929, section 8, p. 1.

22. Interview with Howard Kelly, Calgary, March 9, 1975. Long Lance wrote Howard telling him that Irvin S. Cobb had termed him "the Beau Brummel of Broadway."

23. Frederick Cunliffe-Owen, "Royalty in Jobs Doing Well," NYT, October 21, 1923, section 9, p.4; "Princess Alexandra Seeks Citizenship Here," NYT, January 31, 1929, p. 27. Her sketch of Long Lance is dated 1930.

24. O. O. McIntyre, "New York Day by Day," Washington *Herald*, May 22, 1928. For his readership see Charles B. Driscoll, *The Life of O. O. McIntyre* (New York: Beekman Publishers, 1974; first published 1938), pp. 20, 35; "O. O. McIntyre is Dead," NYT, February 15, 1938, p. 25.

25. Interview (by telephone) with Dorothy Fellers, Washington, D.C., May 26, 1977. For a short biography of General Bonner Fellers consult *Association of Graduates* (United States Military Academy), 23,3 (December 1974): 104-5.

26. "Cadet W. D. Moore" quoted in LL to Howard Kelly, dated New York, February 2, 1928. Kenneth W. Rapp, assistant archivist, USMA Archives to DBS, dated West Point, June 30, 1977.

27. LL to Howard Kelly, dated New York, February 2, 1928.
28. Gladys Baker, "Blackfeet Chief is Polished Man," Birmingham *News-Age-Herald. "The South's Greatest Newspaper,"* October 7, 1928. On Gladys Baker see Lily May Caldwell, "An Interviewer Who Understands," Birmingham *News-Age-Herald*, September 29, 1929.
29. LL to Howard Kelly, dated New York, February 10 and June 8, 1928. LL to Canon Middleton, dated New York, February 11 and August 7, 1928. LL to Bonner and Dorothy Fellers, dated New York, February 9 and June 4, 1928. Bonner Fellers Papers, Hoover Institute on War, Revolution and Peace, Stanford University, California (hereafter cited as HOOVER).
30. "Original Americans' First Vote," *Literary Digest*, September 22, 1928.
31. Long Lance mentions his lecture fee in a letter to Vilhjalmur Stefansson, dated Calgary, July 5, 1927. Presumably his expenses were also paid. Stefansson Collection, Dartmouth College, Dartmouth, N.H. (hereafter cited as DARTMOUTH). "According to the Brookings estimates, even in this banner year of 1929 no less than seventy-eight per cent of the American population have family incomes of less than $3,000 or individual incomes of less than $1,500, and something like forty per cent have family incomes of less than $1,500 or individual incomes of less than $750." Frederick Lewis Allen, *Since Yesterday, 1929-1939* (New York: Bantam, 1965; first published 1940), p. 11.
32. LL to Bonner and Dorothy Fellers dated New York, September 13, 1928, and dated Cleveland, October 18, 1928, HOOVER.
33. Kenneth Williams quoted in the "Editor's Introduction," *How to Talk in the Indian Sign Language* (Akron, Ohio: The B. F. Goodrich Rubber Co., 1930).
34. Untitled manuscript written by Long Lance, GLENBOW (file AL856B f5). For a short review of American Indian Policy in the twentieth century see James Wilson, *The Original Americans: U.S. Indians* (London, England: Minority Rights Group, 1976).
35. The quotations are taken from Long Lance's untitled manuscript, pp. 11, 13, 19, 23.
36. Charles Burke quoted in Herbert Corey, "He Carries the White Man's Burden," *Colliers*, May 12, 1923.
37. Margaret Garretson Szasz, "Indian Reform in a Decade of Prosperity," *Montana: The Magazine of Western History*, 20,1 (January 1970): 20-1.
38. Institute for Government Research. *The Problem of Indian Administration* (Baltimore: Johns Hopkins Press, 1928), termed the Meriam

Report. D'Arcy McNickle, *Indian Man: A Life of Oliver LaFarge* (Bloomington: Indiana University Press, 1971), pp. 50, 76.

39. Bowles's letter (and all other correspondence relating to the inquiry) is in the BIA DISCOVERY FILE.
40. "Indian from Blood Reserve Shakes Hand of President. Also Meets Lindbergh, Dempsey and Ford," Lethbridge *Herald*, November 17, 1927.
41. LL to Vilhjalmur Stefansson, dated New York, September 5, 1928, DARTMOUTH. ". . . my publishers want another book — an Indian novel of pre-white vintage; that is, a novel dealing entirely with Indians before the coming of European stock."
42. LL to SHM, dated Rabbit Chutes, Temagami, December 24, 1928. "Do you know that you have written me a letter and I have not received it? Just before I left New York in late October I received a four line note from you, saying; 'Here are the letters that I mentioned in my letter.' Well, I never received that letter, and had been wondering all along why you had not answered my last letter nor written to tell me what you thought of the book which I sent you in August. And, if you will remember, I wired you from Cheyenne, Wyoming, asking you why you did not write."
43. Interview (by telephone) with S. C. Burden, Los Angeles, June 20, 1977.

CHAPTER FIFTEEN

1. Interview with Douglas Burden, Charlotte, Vermont, May 4-5, 1977; *Who's Who in America, 1976-1977* (Chicago: Marquis Who's Who, 1976), vol. 1, p. 446.
2. Douglas Burden, "Autobiography. 'The Silent Enemy,'" p. 1. Manuscript shown to me, Charlotte, Vermont, May 4, 1977.
3. Interview with William Chanler, New York, May 25, 1977.
4. Douglas Burden quoted in William L. Laurence, "A Camera Record of the Indian," New York *World*, May 11, 1930. Hearne's book is entitled *A Journey from Prince of Wales's Fort in Hudson's Bay to the Northern Ocean 1769, 1770, 1771, 1772*.
5. Douglas Burden quoted in Kevin Brownlow, *The War, The West and The Wilderness* (New York: Alfred A. Knopf, 1979), p. 550.
6. Interview with Douglas Burden, Charlotte, Vermont, May 4-5, 1977. "Film Depicts Tribal Life of the Ojibways," *Christian Science Monitor*, May 19, 1930. Interview with Madeline Theriault, an Ojibwa who appeared in the film, North Bay, Ontario, January 2, 1976. Interviews with Ted Hennessy, who supplied the camps with wood,

North Bay, Ontario, December 22, 1976, and May 12, 1977; and a visit with him to Rabbit Chutes, August 5, 1977. For information on the decline of the beaver in Northern Ontario and Quebec in the late 1920s see Grey Owl, *Pilgrims of the Wild* (Toronto: Macmillan, 1935), pp. 47-8.

7. John J. Rowlands, *Cache Lake Country* (New York: W. W. Norton, 1947), pp. 211, 220.

8. "Long Lance in Thrilling Movie," unidentified clipping, LL scrapbook, donated by Joe Bradshaw, GLENBOW. Interview with Douglas Burden, Charlotte, Vermont, May 4, 1977.

9. For details on the film and those who made it, see the film's programme, *How The Silent Enemy Was Made*, souvenir edition. The theme of the movie is outlined in Betty Shannon's article "The Silent Enemy," *Moving Picture Stories*, August 12, 1930, pp. 10-11, 25-6.

10. Interview with George McDougall, Cochrane, Ontario, May 11, 1977. Interview with Douglas Burden, Charlotte, Vermont, May 4-5, 1977. Barbara Johnson, "Maine Indian Princess of Many Talents Wins Fame in Motion Pictures," Portland (Maine) *Telegram*, June 8, 1930.

11. The sketch of Chauncey Yellow Robe is taken from three sources: his obituary in the NYT, April 8, 1930; his article in *How The Silent Enemy Was Made*, pp. 4, 17; Mildred Fielder, "Chauncey Yellow Robe, Bridge Between Two Cultures," *Sioux Indian Leaders* (Seattle: Superior Publishing Company, 1975), pp. 112-26.

12. William Chanler, an expert archer, shot the arrows, but Douglas Burden was actually the one who killed the animal with a high-powered rifle. Interview with Ted Hennessy, North Bay, Ontario, December 12, 1976. Long Lance mentions the slashes in his letter to Bonner Fellers, dated Rabbit Chutes, Temagami, January 27, 1929, HOOVER.

13. LL to SHM, dated Rabbit Chutes, Temagami, January 24, 1929.

14. LL to Bonner Fellers, dated Rabbit Chutes, Temagami, January 27, 1929, HOOVER.

15. Brownlow, *The War*, p. 556.

16. Interview with Douglas Burden, Charlotte, Vermont, May 4, 1977. Douglas Burden, "Autobiography. 'The Silent Enemy,'" manuscript shown to me May 4, 1977, Charlotte, Vermont. Interview (by telephone) with S. C. Burden, Los Angeles, July 14, 1978. Interview with Ted Hennessy, North Bay, Ontario, December 22, 1976.

17. Interview with Agnes Belaney Lalonde, Temagami, Ontario, May 12, 1977.

18. Grey Owl, *Men of the Last Frontier* (Toronto: Macmillan, 1972; first published in 1931), p. 210.

19. LL to SHM, dated Rabbit Chutes, Temagami, December 24, 1928.
20. Interview with Odell Clanton, Winston-Salem, January 7, 1977.
21. Ted Hennessy to DBS, May 19, 1981. Long Lance did not kill it. Off-camera the moose was shot with the rifle — although it looks in the cleverly spliced film as if Long Lance killed it with his spear.
22. County of Los Angeles, County Clerk's Office, Archives, Probate of Will, No. 126691, Longlance.
23. The description of the funeral-pyre sequence appears in *How the Silent Enemy Was Made*, souvenir edition, p. 7.
24. Chauncey Yellow Robe quoted in Fielder, *Sioux Indian Leaders*, p. 118.
25. William Chanler to Ilia Tolstoy, dated New York, March 26, 1930, CHANLER INVESTIGATION. Chanler mentions that Yellow Robe has told him that Long Lance "does not know the sign language as well as he pretends."
26. Interview with Mike Eagle Speaker, Stirling, Alberta, January 16, 1976. He recalls that the Indians at Fort Macleod's Jubilee in 1924 were interested in watching Long Lance dance, as he danced so "differently" from them.
27. "Another Place for Burke," NYT, March 14, 1929, p. 17.
28. Fielder, *Sioux Indian Leaders*, p. 124, mentions that he returned to Rapid City briefly in 1929.
29. *How The Silent Enemy Was Made*, p. 5.
30. Chauncey Yellow Robe quoted in *How The Silent Enemy Was Made*, p. 2.
31. "Indians as Linguists," *Variety*, June 11, 1930.
32. "Society to Attend Indian Epic," New York *World*, May 19, 1930. General Verbeck to LL, telegram, dated Manlius, May 19, 1930, in LL scrapbook, donated by Joe Bradshaw, GLENBOW. LL to W. M. Graham, dated New York, November 8, 1929. Anne Morgan to LL, dated New York, May 12, 1930, GLENBOW. LL to Vilhjalmur Stefansson, dated New York, May 24, 1930, DARTMOUTH.
33. Robert E. Sherwood, "Motion Picture Album," New York *Post*, May 17, 1930; *Time*, May 26, 1930; *New Republic*, June 4, 1930, p. 73; *Wall Street Journal*, May 20, 1930.
34. Irene Thirer, "'Silent Enemy,' Realistic Indian Epic," *Daily News*, May 19, 1930; Regina Crewe, "'The Silent Enemy' Indian Epic Movie, Of Much Interest," New York *American*, May 20, 1930, second section, p. 15; "The Silent Enemy," *Variety*, May 21, 1930.
35. For details on Grant's life see Fairfield Osborn, "Madison Grant (1865-1937)," *Dictionary of American Biography*, vol. 22, supple-

ment 2 (New York: Charles Scribner's Sons, 1958), p. 256, and Thomas F. Gossett, *Race: The History of an Idea in America* (Dallas: Southern Methodist University Press, 1963), pp. 353-64, 389-90, 396-8.

36. Interview with Douglas Burden, Charlotte, Vermont, May 4, 1977.
37. Madison Grant, *The Conquest of a Continent* (New York: Charles Scribner's, 1933), pp. 37, 285, 288.
38. Grant's letter is printed in *How The Silent Enemy Was Made*, p. 5.
39. Robert E. Sherwood, "Motion Picture Album," New York *Post*, May 17, 1930.
40. Brownlow, *The West*, pp. 559-60.
41. Kevin Brownlow in "The Silent Enemy: An Epic of the American Indian," *Blackhawk Films. Bulletin B-264* (June 1975), p. 2.

CHAPTER SIXTEEN

1. Wilfrid Eggleston, "Fastened Sleds under Canoe in Mushing through Slush," Toronto *Star Weekly*, May 4, 1929.
2. Interview with Douglas Burden, Charlotte, Vermont, May 4-5, 1977.
3. SHM to LL, dated St. Paul's School, Blood Reserve, February 18, 1928.
4. Long Lance quoted in *JWT Co. News Letter*, 11,33 (April 15, 1929):1. Cynthia G. Swank, archivist, J. Walter Thompson Company, to DBS, dated June 13, 1980. She listed the publications in which the ads appeared.
5. "Long Lance Frequent Visitor to N.Y. Office," *J.W.T. News*, 11, 48 (March 1930): 2. Roland Cole, "Consumer's Suggestion Is Adopted as New Design for Product," *Printers' Ink*, August 29, 1929, pp. 79-80.
6. Gene Schoor, *The Jim Thorpe Story* (New York: Pocket Books, 1967; first published 1951), pp. 160-4. Two of Thorpe's letters to Long Lance (in which he mentions his financial problems) are held in the U.S. Army Military History Research Collection, Carlisle, Pennsylvania. After Long Lance's death they were donated to the museum by his friend Clyde Fisher. The first letter is dated Las Vegas, Nevada, December 30, 1929, and the second, Hawthorne, California, January 3, 1930.
7. Federal Writers' Project. *New York City Guide* (New York: Random House, 1976; first published 1939), p. 321.
8. William Tomkins, *Universal American Indian Sign Language* (San Diego: Published by William Tomkins, 1970; first edition 1926). Seton's "Sign Talk," with about 1700 signs, appeared in 1918. See Tomkins, *Universal*, p. 7.

9. LL, "West Point's Predicament. Why are there more than two hundred vacancies in its Corps of Cadets?"*Century*, 117 (January 1929): 375-83.

10. Interview (by telephone) with Dorothy Fellers, Washington, D.C., May 26, 1977; Dorothy Fellers to DBS, August 12, 1980.

11. *About the Explorers*, a recent booklet (eight pages long) which contains a short sketch of the club today and its past history (available from the club headquarters, 46 East 70 Street, New York, N.Y. 10021). The price of the rooms is mentioned in the *Explorers Journal*, 9,3 (1930): 67.

12. "Clyde Fisher," *Explorers Journal*, 27 (1949): 29-30. Fisher's visit to, and his induction into, the Sioux tribe is mentioned in *Explorers Journal*, 6,3 (1927): 13.

13. On Seumas see "Chief Seumas is Dead," NYT, March 28, 1961; "Clan Chief's Death Sparks Will Dispute," New York *Post*, September 8, 1961, also "Descendant of Royal Scots Dwells in N.Y.," Brooklyn *Daily Eagle*, December 13, 1931. My thanks to Marie E. Roy, executive secretary of the Explorers Club, for kindly allowing me to see Seumas's entrance form to the Explorers Club, dated 1921.

14. Sergius Martin Riis, "In Memory. Seumas, The Chief of Clannfhearghuis of Stra-chur, C.M. etc.," *Explorers Journal*, 39,2 (1961): 50.

15. Clyde Fisher's letter is dated October 2, 1929, and E. W. Deming's, September 28, 1929. My thanks to Marie Roy for allowing me to examine Long Lance's file at the Explorers Club. E. W. Deming quoted in "High Ideals of American Indian Win Esteem of Author-Painter," *Christian Science Monitor*, March 20, 1931 (his comment on the Blackfoot). Clark Wissler quoted in Therese O. Deming, *E. W. Deming: His Work* (n.p.: T. O. Deming, 1925), p. 31.

16. *Explorers Journal*, 8,3 (1929): 72. Minutes of the Membership Committee, October 11, 1929, Explorers Club.

17. Federal Writers' Project. *New York City Guide*, pp. 257, 266.

18. For information on Hodge's life consult Cole Fay-Cooper, "Frederick Webb Hodge, 1864-1956," *American Anthropologist*, n.s. 59 (1957): 517-20. Lee Ash, who worked in the Explorers Club Library in 1929 and in the early 1930s, recalls that Dr. Hodge "always said good things about Long Lance." A short biography of George Heye appears in *Who Was Who in America*, vol. 3, 1951-1960 (Chicago: Marquis, 1960), p. 397. Long Lance claimed in a letter to Canon Middleton (January 10, 1930) that George Hyde wanted him "to teach him a little of the sign language." Clark Wissler's life is summarized in George Peter Murdoch's "Clark Wissler, 1870-1947," in the *American Anthropologist*, n.s. 50 (1948): 292-304; and in George W. Stocking,

Jr., "Clark Wissler," *Dictionary of American Biography, Supplement Four, 1946-1950* (New York: Charles Scribner's Sons, 1974), pp. 906-9. Clyde Fisher's widow, Te Ata, has Long Lance's copy of *The American Indian* with the inscription, "With the compliments of Clark Wissler to Buffalo Child Long Lance." At the bottom Dr. Fisher wrote, "To Chief Buffalo Child Long Lance in appreciation of his writing *Long Lance*, Clyde Fisher, American Museum of Natural History, Sept. 12, 1929." She showed the book to me in Oklahoma City, March 13, 1976.

19. Clyde Fisher mentioned that Dr. Wissler had read the book, and noted Wissler's comment on it in his review of *Long Lance* in the *Explorers Journal*, 8,3 (1929): 74.

20. As historian Ralph K. Andrist has written of Clark Wissler in his introduction to a re-edition of Wissler's *Red Man Reservations* (New York: Collier Books, 1971), p. viii: ". . . he was a fairer, more detached observer of the scene than most of his contemporaries. He saw Indians as human beings, in a time when far too many people still looked on them as little better than vermin."

21. Jim Thorpe quoted in Schoor, *Thorpe*, p. 6. Etha Lawrence, "Mrs. Iva Thorpe Has Lived a Very Picturesque Life," *The American Indian*, November 1926, p. 4. Ewers, *The Blackfeet*, p. 326. Hugh A. Dempsey, "Black White Man," *Alberta Historical Review*, 6,3 (1958): 7-11.

22. Kathleen Jamieson, *Indian Women and the Law in Canada: Citizens Minus* (Ottawa: Ministry of Supply and Services, 1978).

23. Allen, *Only Yesterday*, pp. 266-81.

24. Circular advertising Chief Buffalo Child Long Lance's talk "An Indian's Story of his People," American Museum of Natural History, November 21, 1929, LL scrapbook, donated by Joe Bradshaw, GLENBOW. *Explorers Journal*, 8,4 (1929): 97.

25. "Fannie Hurst," NYT, February 24, 1968, pp. 1,29. Fannie Hurst to LL, December 30, 1929, GLENBOW.

26. LL to SHM, dated New York, January 10, 1930.

27. LL to Howard Kelly, dated New York, June 8, 1928. LL to Bonner and Dorothy Fellers, dated New York, October 5, 1929, HOOVER. On W. R. Edrington, see *Who Was Who in America*, vol. 1, 1897-1942 (Chicago: Marquis Who's Who, 1966), p. 359.

28. LL to Carl Van Vechten, letter postmarked November 30, 1929, in Carl Van Vechten Papers, Beinecke Rare Book and Manuscript Library, Yale University, New Haven, Connecticut. Bruce Kellner, *Carl Van Vechten and the Irreverent Decades* (Norman: University of Oklahoma Press, 1968), p. 200.

29. "Walter Winchell on Broadway," New York *Daily Mirror*, December 24, 1929, p. 16.

30. Mrs. Domenica Pallister to DBS, dated New York, July 4, 1977. Mrs. Pallister's father was a close friend of Seumas's and she served as his secretary in the 1940s and '50s.

31. Eleanor Ruggles, *The West-Going Heart: A Life of Vachel Lindsay* (New York: W. W. Norton, 1959), pp. 398-9.

32. Katharine Hale, "About Canadian Writers, Chief Buffalo Child Long Lance," *The Canadian Countryman*, June 14, 1930, pp. 8, 15. For a sketch of Katharine Hale's life consult Lotta Dempsey, "Katharine Hale," in *Leading Canadian Poets*, ed. W. P. Percival (Toronto: The Ryerson Press, 1948), pp. 79-87.

33. The evening is described in *Poetry: A Magazine of Verse*, 36,1 (1930): 53. The description of the Biltmore's ballroom is taken from the article "Open Big Biltmore on New Year's Eve," NYT, December 26, 1913, and from the pamphlet *The Biltmore* forwarded to me by Edwin Scalabrino, general manager, April 1, 1980.

34. "The Death Song of Long Lance" printed in *Scholastic*, 22, 1 (February 4, 1933): 11.

35. "Yellow Robe called on me about three months ago and told me that he had just discovered that Long Lance was not a Blackfoot and that he understood he was really a negro." William Chanler to Ilia Tolstoy, dated March 26, 1930, CHANLER INVESTIGATION.

CHAPTER SEVENTEEN

1. William Chanler to SHM, February 6, 1930, CHANLER INVESTIGATION.

2. NYT, February 5, 1930. Lindbergh's birthday on the fourth was reported on the fifth.

3. Interviews with William Chanler, New York, May 22 (by telephone), May 25-26, 1977. William Chanler to Ilia Tolstoy, dated March 26, 1930, CHANLER INVESTIGATION.

4. William Chanler to the commissioner of Indian Affairs, February 14, 1930, CHANLER INVESTIGATION.

5. William Chanler to Ilia Tolstoy, dated March 26, 1930, CHANLER INVESTIGATION.

6. William Chanler to the commissioner of Indian Affairs, February 14, 1930, CHANLER INVESTIGATION.

7. Interview with William Chanler, New York, May 26, 1977. William Chanler to Mr. Campbell, Blackfoot Indian Agency, Browning, Montana, February 14, 1930, CHANLER INVESTIGATION.

8. James Mooney, "Croatan Indians" in *Handbook of American Indians North of Mexico*, ed. by Frederick Webb Hodge (2 vols., Washington, D.C.: Government Printing Office, 1907), 1:365.

9. William Chanler to Ilia Tolstoy, March 26, 1930, CHANLER INVESTIGA-TION. "Jules S. Brulatour Dies in Hospital, 75," NYT, October 27, 1946, p. 62.

10. SHM to William Chanler, March 3, 1930, CHANLER INVESTIGATION.

11. William Chanler to Ilia Tolstoy, March 26, 1930, CHANLER INVESTIGA-TION.

12. Earl Parker Hanson to DBS, April 13, 1976, enclosing an excerpt from chapter nine of his projected autobiography. In the late 1920s and early '30s Mr. Hanson was acting executive secretary of the Explorers Club. He heard this story about Cobb from E. W. Deming's eldest daughter.

13. Mrs. Domenica Pallister to DBS, August 5, 1977.

14. I have no documentary proof that Long Lance actually confessed to Yellow Robe. Some reconciliation, though, must have taken place as Yellow Robe acquiesced in the decision to send Long Lance on the Hollywood trip. See Chauncey Yellow Robe to William Chanler, dated March 31, 1930 (in the "Chauncey Yellow Robe" file, Winthrop, Stimson, Putnam and Roberts, 40 Wall Street, New York City). After Yellow Robe's death Long Lance mailed his letter to Rosebud Yellow Robe on April 23, 1930 (who kindly sent me a copy which is now in GLENBOW). I learned that Long Lance offered to pay for Evelyn Yellow Robe's education in a letter from her, November 17, 1976.

15. LL to Alice Tye, dated New York, April 24, 1930. Senn, *The Lawless Decade*, p. 136.

16. LL to SHM, dated New York, April 23, 1930. LL to Alice Tye, dated New York, April 24, 1930.

17. Lee Shippey, "The Lee Side o'L.A." Los Angeles *Times*, March 27, 1930.

18. Anita Baldwin signed the sheet music for *My Blossom Bride (Hopi Indian Love Song). Text and Music by Anita Baldwin (Composer of "Omar—The Tentmaker") from The Romantic Play of the Southwest "His Blossom Bride" by Richard Walton Tully*. This is now in GLENBOW. The inscription reads, "For Chief Long Lance from Anita M. Baldwin, March 22 '30." The physical description of Anita Baldwin is from her passport issued January 22, 1926, Anita M. Baldwin Collection, Box 1, Huntington Library, San Marino, California.

19. Details on Ilia Tolstoy's life are taken from his obituary in the NYT, October 30, 1970; a memorial address given at the Explorers Club; and his application for membership in the club, dated April 29, 1931.

My thanks to Marie Roy of the Explorers Club for copies of these last two items.

20. My thanks to Tom Flanagan of Calgary for the description of North Carolina in April.

21. "Camels of Winston-Salem," *Fortune*, 3,1 (January, 1931): 45, 48, 54.

22. Ilia Tolstoy's report to William Chanler, April 14, 1930, CHANLER INVESTIGATION. The information on the Longs' home on Brookstown Avenue is taken from Abe's diaries, entries for August 28, 1946; March 11, 1959; April 15, 1959; September 1, 1959; November 17, 1964; March 9, 1965.

23. Circular distributed by Abe Long, Carolina Theater, apparently prepared about 1930, in the volume of his diary for the years 1937-46.

24. For a short biography of Latham, consult, "R. H. Latham, Educator, Dies at 67," Winston-Salem *Journal*, April 3, 1948.

25. Ilia wrote in his report that his name was "John Weston" but he heard the name incorrectly. On Joe Long's death certificate, Walter Long lists his father's parents as "John Vestal" and "Mary Long." Standard Certificate of Death, Forsyth County Court House, Winston-Salem, N.C., November 14, 1932.

26. From 1913 to 1953 the North Carolina State Legislature re-designated the "Croatans" as "Cherokees." Finally, in 1953, the Legislature changed their name to "Lumbees." Brewton Berry, *Almost White* (Toronto: Collier-Macmillan, 1969; first published 1963), p. 156.

27. "Colonel William Allen Blair," in *North Carolina: The Old North State and the New*, vol. 3 (Chicago: The Lewis Publishing Company, 1941), pp. 49-51. "Animate and Inanimate," Winston-Salem *Journal*, August 12, 1909, p. 6.

28. "Pushkin... Negro according to American standards, i.e. has ancestor with mixture of Negro blood." M. N. Work, *A Bibliography of the Negro in Africa and America* (New York: H. W. Wilson, 1928), p. 456.

29. William Blair's affidavit, dated April 9, 1930, CHANLER INVESTIGATION.

30. Arlene Edwards, "First Poindexter Arrived 200 Years Ago. Man Married Granddaughter of Indian Chief," Winston-Salem *Journal*, August 11, 1975.

31. Edith Bolling Wilson, *My Memoir* (Indianapolis: Bobbs-Merrill Company, 1938), p. 230.

32. Colonel William A. Blair to SHM, dated Winston-Salem, January 27, 1934. Letter in the possession of Mrs. Sophie Middleton Allison, Fort Macleod, Alberta. Copy in GLENBOW.

33. Colonel William A. Blair to SHM, dated Winston-Salem, December 19,

1933, letter in the possession of Mrs. Sophie Middleton Allison, Fort Macleod, Alberta. Copy in GLENBOW.

34. They were married on March 27, 1879. New Court House, Statesville, Iredell County, N.C.

35. William Chanler to Ilia Tolstoy, April 17, 1930; to R. H. Latham, April 17, 1930; to William A. Blair, April 17, 1930. CHANLER INVESTIGATION.

36. In "Longlance-ese" this last word, "Hanka-wanzi," is his highest compliment. In his article on "The Secret of the Sioux," *Hearst's International-Cosmopolitan*, June, 1927, p. 41, he wrote of the "Weh-hunka-wanzi" or blood-brother relationship: "When an Indian declares another man his *Weh-hunka-wanzi* it brings that man closer to him than his own consanguineous brother. On reaching manhood every Indian forms a 'blood brother' relationship with some particular member of his tribe whom he likes more than anyone else, and there can be no secrets between himself and this person. In battle and in peace they are Damon and Pythias for the rest of their mortal lives, and no one can come between them." "Netawa" simply means "your" in Sioux (Dakota). Long Lance then would translate "Netawa Hanka-wanzi" as "your blood brother."

CHAPTER EIGHTEEN

1. LL to Alice Tye, dated New York, July 17, 1930.
2. *Liberty*, September 20, 1930. Rose Reilly, "Long Lance, Chief of Heart-Breakers," *Screenland*, October 1930, p. 114.
3. "A Reporter meets Long Lance, Chief of the Blackfoot Indians, Writer, Actor, Explorer, a Modern Version of the American Tradition," *The Great Outdoors*, August 1930.
4. "Has Great Faith in Medicine Man," NYT, October 3, 1930.
5. Dan Arapaho, student file, R.G. 75, Bureau of Indian Affairs, Carlisle Student Record, file 1325, National Archives, Washington, D.C. LL to Emma Newashe McAllister, dated New York, July 13, 1930. Ramona Loman, daughter of Emma Newashe McAllister, kindly allowed me to make copies of her mother's letters from, and about, Long Lance. These are now in GLENBOW.
6. Interview with Te Ata, Oklahoma City, March 13, 1976.
7. Interview with Lee Ash, Edmonton, March 4, 1976.
8. Mrs. Domenica Pallister to DBS, July 4, 1977.
9. "Indian is Entered in Air Race Jump," Trenton *Evening Times*, October 16, 1930. "Indian Takes Course at Roosevelt Field," Bridgehampton (N.Y.) *News*, October 10, 1930.

10. "Jersey Guard Wins Roebling Air Race Prize," Trenton *Times-Advertiser*, October 19, 1930.
11. "Indian Loops on First Solo Hop," New York *Sun*, October 29, 1930, p. 13.
12. Interview with Te Ata, Oklahoma City, March 13, 1976. C. R. Roseberry, *The Challenging Skies: The Colorful Story of Aviation's Most Exciting Years, 1919-1939* (Garden City, N.Y.: Doubleday, 1966), p. 244. "Buck and Woman Flier Set New Coast-to-Coast Records," Trenton Sunday *Times-Advertiser*, October 19, 1930.
13. LL to Mike Eagle Speaker, sent from Roosevelt Field, no date (probably sent in March, 1931). LL to Isabel Fellers Bush, dated Roosevelt Field, December 18, 1930 (a copy of the letter is now in GLENBOW, supplied by Dorothy Fellers).
14. Abe Long's diary, entries for January 11, July 26, November 3, 15, 23, 26, 1930 (about his parents' illnesses). On January 10, 1931, he recorded that Walter had left for New York on December 31 and had just returned that day.
15. "Vester" to "My dear Brother," dated "Tuesday" (January 5, 1931).
16. The amounts sent home are listed in Abe Long's ledger, 1928-32, in the possession of Lillian Doulin, Mocksville, N.C. Long Lance's letter to Abe is also in Mrs. Doulin's possession, a copy of it and the ledger book are at GLENBOW.
17. New Hyde Park (N.Y.) *Herald*, January 16, 1931. "Labor Secretary to Speak at National Board Luncheon Next Saturday," unidentified clipping, LL scrapbook, donated by Joe Bradshaw, GLENBOW. "Doak Hails Movies as Force for Good," NYT, January 25, 1931, p. 19.
18. Copy of a letter from Anita Baldwin to Susie B. Curtis, dated Santa Anita, California, May 10, 1932, enclosed in a letter from Susie B. Curtis to SHM, no date (probably late May, 1932). This letter from Anita Baldwin is hereafter cited as BALDWIN-LETTER. Copies of all of the correspondence between Susie B. Curtis and Canon Middleton are in GLENBOW. Statement of Anita Baldwin, dated March 23, 1932, read at the "Coroner's Inquest into death of Sylvester Long (also known as Sylvester Long Lance)," March 24, 1932, State of California, County of Los Angeles, no. 40150 (hereafter cited as BALDWIN-STATEMENT).
19. New York *Daily News*, May 14, 1931. LL to Alice Tye, dated *The Santa Fe Chief* en route to California, May 19, 1931.
20. Susie B. Curtis to SHM, dated Elmira, N.Y., May 8, 1932; Susie B. Curtis to SHM, no date (probably late May, 1932).
21. The information on Anoakia is taken from several sources: interview with Lowry McCaslin, Arcadia, October 16, 1980. Mr. McCaslin was

Anita Baldwin's business manager in the early 1930s. Interview (by telephone) with Raymond Knisley, Logandale, Nevada, October 26, 1980. Mr. Knisley was the manager of Anita Baldwin's ranches in the early 1930s. Lavinia Griffin Graham, "Peacock used as Motif of Home of Mrs. M'Claughry," Los Angeles *Examiner*, June 30, 1913. Anon., "Unique Among Homes of America's Rich," Los Angeles *Times*, September 21, 1913. The Editor, "The Building up of an Ideal California Ranch," *Outwest*, May-June, 1914. Porter Garnett, "Anoakia: Stately Homes of California," *Sunset-The Pacific Monthly*, January, 1914, pp. 145-8. C. B. Glasscock, *Lucky Baldwin: The Story of an Unconventional Success* (Indianapolis: Bobbs-Merrill Company, 1933), p. 221. The value of Anoakia is given on a note in Box 1, Anita M. Baldwin Collection, Huntington Library, San Marino, California.

22. "Tour Guide of Anoakia," prepared by Russell Chandler in 1976, p. 14. My thanks to Lowry McCaslin for giving me a tour of Anoakia, October 16, 1980.

23. Edward B. Scott, "Tallac," *The Saga of Lake Tahoe* (Crystal Bay, Lake Tahoe, Nevada: Sierra-Tahoe Publishing Co., 1957), pp. 151-65. Interview (by telephone) with Raymond Knisley, Logandale, Nevada, October 26, 1980.

24. Notes of an interview with Ralph Tweedle, Sierra Madre, California, May 26, 1976, conducted by Lucette Fogwill, volunteer, History Section, Los Angeles State and County Arboretum, Arcadia, California (hereafter cited as LASCA). Ralph Tweedle was a guard at Anoakia and Anita's home at Tallac from January 11, 1931, to February 28, 1933. The interview is in the Archives, LASCA.

25. Glasscock, *Lucky Baldwin*, pp. 15, 74, 100, 115, 206, 305.

26. *Ibid.*, p. 221.

27. *Ibid.*, p. 136.

28. Sandra Lee Snider, "Elias 'Lucky' Baldwin: Southern California Rancher and Town Builder, 1875-1909," M.A. thesis, California State University, Los Angeles, 1979, pp. 31-2.

29. "A Millionaire's Third Marriage," NYT, June 1, 1884, p. 4. "Mrs. Lily Howard Coast," NYT, November 10, 1938, p. 27. Genealogy of Anita Baldwin, Anita M. Baldwin Collection, Box 2, Huntington Library, San Marino, California.

30. "Divorced in Twelve Hours," NYT, October 8, 1900, p. 1. "Anita Baldwin, Heiress of 'Lucky'," NYT, October 26, 1939, p. 23. For a short biography of Anita Baldwin see John Steven McGroarty, *The California Plutarch* (2 vols. Los Angeles: J. R. Finnell, 1938), 2: 241-5.

31. "Denial by Mrs. McClaughrey," NYT, May 6, 1914, p. 5. "Dogs More

Constant than Men Says Anita Baldwin," San Francisco *Chronicle*, April 27, 1916.

32. Anita M. Baldwin to C. L. Lowman, Letterman Hospital, San Francisco, May 23, 1919, LASCA. Interview with Sandy Snider, historian, LASCA, October 17, 1980. As the arboretum is located on Lucky Baldwin's old Rancho Santa Anita, LASCA has collected a considerable amount of material on the history of the Baldwin family.

33. Anita M. Baldwin Collection, LASCA. See Anita's letters to her son of April 4, May 20, December 16, 1930; the undated letter written in the spring of 1931; and the letter of July 6, 1931.

34. Notes of an interview with Ralph Tweedle, May 26, 1976, LASCA. Anita Baldwin's letter to Baldwin, April 7, 1931, provides a good example of her fear of communists. "She'll Devote Life to Music," Los Angeles *Examiner*, December 23, 1929.

35. Notes of an interview with Ralph Tweedle, May 26, 1976, LASCA.

36. Passport Application (Form for Native Citizen). Edition of 1930, United States of America, State of California, County of San Francisco. The following quotations are all taken from the passport application, and its supporting documents.

37. LL to Emma Newashe McAllister, undated letter from Tallac, probably mailed in early June, and his second letter from Tallac, dated June 28, 1931.

38. Elizabeth Analla to Rosebud Yellow Robe, dated Wagner, South Dakota, December 27, 1932. Copy in GLENBOW.

39. LL to Emma Newashe McAllister, dated Tallac, June 28, 1931. Anita Baldwin to Susie B. Curtis, May 12, 1932, BALDWIN-LETTER. Anita Baldwin to Baldwin M. Baldwin, postmarked March 7, 1931, LASCA.

40. Interview with Lowry McCaslin, Arcadia, October 16, 1980. The itinerary of the trip enclosed in a letter from Anita Baldwin to Baldwin M. Baldwin, early 1930, LASCA. LL to Alice Tye, dated Chicago-California, December 10, 1931.

41. "Young Baldwin Goes to Work," Hollywood *Citizen*, August 28, 1930, clipping in LASCA. "Baldwin's Grandson Succumbs," Arcadia *Tribune*, September 27, 1970, clipping in LASCA.

42. Wilfrid Eggleston, "Fastened Sleds under Canoe in Mushing through Slush," Toronto *Star Weekly*, May 4, 1929.

43. The itinerary of the trip enclosed in a letter from Anita Baldwin to Baldwin M. Baldwin, early 1930, LASCA. LL to Alice Tye, dated Chicago-California, December 10, 1931.

44. John Toland, *Adolf Hitler* (New York: Ballantine Books, 1976), p. 329. NYT, June 18, 1931, p. 5.

45. Statement of Anita Baldwin, March 23, 1932, BALDWIN-STATEMENT. Anita Baldwin to Susie B. Curtis, May 10, 1932, BALDWIN-LETTER.

46. Interview with Lowry McCaslin, Arcadia, October 16, 1980.

47. Anita Baldwin to Susie B. Curtis, May 10, 1932, BALDWIN-LETTER.

48. "N.Y. Society Girl Weds Japanese," New York *Sunday News*, March 6, 1932. "N.Y. Society Girl, Forced to Leave U.S. for Wedding Japanese, Arrives Here," *The Japan Times and Mail* (Tokyo), June 20, 1932. "Japanese-American Couple Here Describe Their Romance and Troubles in New York," *The Japan Advertiser* (Tokyo), June 19, 1932. Interview (by telephone) with Elisabeth Randolph Clapp, York Village, Maine, October 19, 1980.

49. Bessie Randolph Clapp Hayakawa to Lilly Sahlen, dated Osaka, Japan, September 23, 1932. Copies of this correspondence are in GLENBOW. As Elisabeth used the name "Bessie" in her letters to Lilly, this is the form followed in the text.

50. Her uncle was C. E. Clapp. Through his obituary in the NYT on January 4, 1957, I was able to locate his widow in Virginia (Anne Robinson, Research Librarian of the University of Virginia, Charlottesville, helped me locate her). Mrs. C. E. Clapp wrote back with the address of Bessie's stepmother, Mrs. Harold Clapp, in Oregon, who put me in touch with Bessie, who is now living in Maine.

51. Philip B. McDonald, "Henry Clay Frick," *Dictionary of American Biography* (New York: Charles Scribner's, 1931), vol. 7, pp. 29-31; and Oliver Jensen, "Essay: Filial Piety and the First Amendment," *American Heritage*, 18,6 (October 1967): 2-4.

52. Bessie Randolph Clapp Hayakawa quoted in *The Japan Times and Mail*, June 20, 1932.

53. Bessie Randolph Clapp Hayakawa to Lilly Sahlen, dated Osaka, September 23, 1932.

54. "Mary Rennels Says," Cleveland *Press*, October 16, 1928, 2nd section, p. 25. LL to Mike Eagle Speaker dated New York, May 26, 1930. Copies of Long Lance's letters to Mike Eagle Speaker are in GLENBOW.

55. Bessie Randolph Clapp Hayakawa to Lilly Sahlen, dated Osaka, September 23, 1932.

56. Anita Baldwin to Susie B. Curtis, May 10, 1932, BALDWIN-LETTER.

CHAPTER NINETEEN

1. Susie B. Curtis to SHM, dated Elmira, N.Y., April 17, 1932.

2. Louis Schellbach, assistant secretary, Explorers Club, to the commissioner of the BIA, dated New York, December 7, 1931. BIA Records, R.G. 75, file no. 1364-1925, 130 General Service, National Archives, Washington, D.C.

3. LL to Alice Tye, dated *The Santa Fe Chief* en route to California, May 19, 1931.

4. Anita Baldwin to Baldwin M. Baldwin, postmarked December 28, 1931, Santa Anita, LASCA.

5. "Mrs. Baldwin Quitting U.S.; Raps Regime," Los Angeles *Examiner*, August 5, 1932, section 1, p. 3. Interview with Lowry McCaslin, Arcadia, October 16, 1980.

6. Statement of Anita Baldwin, March 23, 1932, BALDWIN-STATEMENT. "Indian Chief Suicide on Eve of Air Survey," Los Angeles *Examiner*, March 22, 1932.

7. Interview (by telephone) with Raymond Knisley, Logandale, Nevada, October 26, 1980.

8. Iron Eyes Cody quoted in Kevin Brownlow, *The War, The West and the Wilderness* (New York: Alfred A. Knopf, 1979), p. 553. For a biographical sketch of Cody consult Bill Richards, "A Couple of Old Timers' Slings and Arrows for the New Westerns," Washington *Post*, July 6, 1976, p. B1, B6.

9. Anita Baldwin to Susie B. Curtis, May 10, 1932, BALDWIN-LETTER.

10. A copy of a letter sent by J. H. Williams, night clerk of the Glendale Hotel, to Susie B. Curtis, dated May 12, 1932, enclosed in letter of Susie B. Curtis to SHM, dated Elmira, N.Y., and probably sent in late May (hereafter cited as WILLIAMS-LETTER).

11. Notes of an interview with Ralph Tweedle, May 26, 1976, LASCA.

12. Bessie Randolph Clapp Hayakawa to Lilly Sahlen, dated Osaka, September 23, 1932.

13. G. C. Harrington to Edgar K. Miller, dated Los Angeles, April 15, 1932, BIA DISCOVERY FILE. Harrington was an employee of Anita Baldwin. He reported to Edgar Miller at the Hopi Reservation in Arizona the "further information" that they had obtained about Long Lance's activities (immediately before the evening of March 19). The weather for March 19 is reported in the Los Angeles *Times* March 19, 1932.

14. J. H. Williams to Susie B. Curtis, dated May 12, 1932, WILLIAMS-LETTER.

15. Testimony of Joseph Hanna given at the "Coroner's Inquest into death of Sylvester Long (also known as Sylvester Long Lance)," March 24, 1932, State of California, County of Los Angeles, no. 40150, p. 15. The subsequent information is taken from the minutes of the inquest.

16. Statement of Anita Baldwin, March 23, 1932, BALDWIN-STATEMENT.

17. J. H. Williams to Susie B. Curtis, dated May 12, 1932, WILLIAMS-LETTER. Mrs. Elizabeth Analla to Rosebud Yellow Robe, dated Wagner, South Dakota, December 27, 1932.

18. "Chief Long Lance Ends His Life in California," NYT, March 22, 1932 (Jim Thorpe quoted). The manager of the Glendale Airport told Susie Curtis that Long Lance "was happy in his work and every one liked him." Susie B. Curtis to SHM, dated Elmira, N.Y., May 8, 1932. SHM to Mrs. Edgar M. Hawkins, dated October 30, 1935. Irvin S. Cobb to Emma Newashe McAllister, dated New York, April 4, 1932.

19. "Indian's Death Calls Inquest," Los Angeles *Times*, March 24, 1932.

20. Glasscock, *Baldwin*, p. 242. "Anita Baldwin Pays Half Town's Taxes," San Francisco *News*, September 2, 1932, clipping in LASCA. Statement of Anita Baldwin, March 23, 1932, BALDWIN-STATEMENT.

21. Testimony of Frank Gompert given at the "Coroner's Inquest," March 24, 1932, p. 10.

22. Interview (by telephone) with Bessie Randolph Clapp Hayakawa, York Village, Maine, October 19, 1980.

23. Anita Baldwin to Susie B. Curtis, May 10, 1932, BALDWIN-LETTER. Interview with Odell Clanton, Winston-Salem, January 7, 1977. Interview with Charles Carson, Carson Town, August 11, 1975.

24. Miller told Emma Newashe McAllister in a letter dated May 19, 1932, that he knew Mrs. Baldwin "very well," and "there is no finer or better woman." Edgar K. Miller to C. L. Ellis, Mission Agency, Riverside, California, dated Hopi Indian Agency, April 9, 1932, BIA DISCOVERY FILE.

25. Pinkerton report enclosed in letter of Edgar K. Miller to Superintendent Ellis, dated Hopi Agency, April 26, 1932, BIA DISCOVERY FILE. Anita Baldwin told Susie B. Curtis that she "requested information" from the Pinkerton Agency. See Susie B. Curtis to SHM, no date, probably sent in late May, 1932.

26. The family's wish to bring the body back to Winston is mentioned in "Sylvester Long Dies a Suicide. Native of this City Found Dead at Santa Anita, Calif. Well Known," Winston-Salem *Journal*, March 25, 1932. In his diary Abe mentions that Walter left for Los Angeles on April 24, 1932, returning on May 16, 1932. Walter's statement disclaiming negro blood is mentioned in a letter from Susie Curtis to SHM, no date, probably sent in late May, 1932. She quotes from one of Anita Baldwin's letters to her: "This brother Walter denies negro blood but the Pinkertons', of whom I requested information gave me an entirely different story."

27. Raymond Knisley to DBS, January 28, 1980.

28. G. C. Harrington to Edgar K. Miller, dated April 15, 1932, BIA DISCOVERY FILE.

29. Frank A. Nance, coroner, Los Angeles County, to Emma Newashe McAllister, dated March 30, 1932. Interview with Roberta Forsberg,

Whittier, California, January 10, 1976. Although she had never met Long Lance, Miss Forsberg was very fond of his writings, and with her mother's help printed a number of his articles and testimonials from his friends. This beautifully produced book, *Redman Echoes* (1933), is very useful for any study of Long Lance's life and writings. Miss Forsberg was just completing high school when she finished the book.

EPILOGUE

1. Jim Thorpe thanked Long Lance for a loan of $100 in his letter of January 3, 1930. Original in the U.S. Army Military History Research Collection, Carlisle, Pennsylvania. The gift of $100 to St. John's (Manlius) was acknowledged by Walter R. Stone, December 24, 1928, GLENBOW. The value of Long Lance's estate is mentioned in County of Los Angeles County Clerk's Office Archives, Probate of Will, no. 126691, Longlance.

2. The County of Los Angeles County Clerk's Office Archives, Probate of Will, no. 126691, Longlance. This file contains the judgment in favor of St. Paul's School, May 18, 1933, as well as Joe Long's affidavit of heirship, dated April 18, 1932.

3. "Death Claims Uncle Joe Long," Winston-Salem *Journal*, November 16, 1932. Adeline died, according to her death certificate in the New Court House, Statesville, Iredell County, N.C., on February 8, 1932.

4. "Walter L. Long, Widely Known Negro is Dead," Winston-Salem *Journal*, March 28, 1941, p. 4. A. A. Mayfield, "Activities of Colored People," Winston-Salem *Twin City Sentinel*, February 9, 1942.

5. Abe Long diary, entry for August 24, 1938.

6. Abe Long diary, entry for April 1, 1939.

7. Abe Long diary, entry for August 1, 1941.

8. Interview with Annie Blackburn, Carson Town, August 11, 1975.

9. A good review of racial legislation in the United States is Louis Claiborne, *Race and Law in Britain and the United States* (London: Minority Rights Group, 1974).

10. Interview with Mrs. Lilly Sahlen Middleton, Fort Macleod, February 18, 1976.

11. A copy of this letter is now in GLENBOW.

A SELECTED BIBLIOGRAPHY

ALLEN, FREDERICK LEWIS, *Only Yesterday: An Informal History of the Nineteen-Twenties*. New York: Harper and Row, 1964. First published in 1931.

BERRY, BREWTON. *Almost White*. New York: Macmillan, 1963.

BERTON, PIERRE, "The Legend of Almighty Voice," Chapter 7 in *The Wild Frontier*. Toronto: McClelland and Stewart, 1978.

BROWNLEE, FAMBROUGH L., *Winston-Salem: A Pictorial History*. Norfolk, Virginia: Donning Co., 1977.

BROWNLOW, KEVIN, "The Silent Enemy" in *The War, the West and the Wilderness*. New York: Alfred A. Knopf, 1979.

"Buffalo Child Long Lance Visits Ohio," *Ohio Archaeological and Historical Society*, 33 (1924): 516-26.

CAUDLE, TRACY GROSE, *Memories From My Father's Trunk*. N.p.: Alpine Industries, 1970.

DEMPSEY, HUGH, *Crowfoot*. Edmonton: Hurtig, 1972.

EWERS, JOHN C., *The Blackfeet*. Norman: University of Oklahoma Press, 1958.

Federal Writers' Project, *New York City Guide*. New York: Random House, 1976. First published in 1939.

FORAN, MAX. *Calgary: An Illustrated History*. Toronto: James Lorimer, 1978.

FORSBERG, ROBERTA, ed., *Redman Echoes. Comprising the Writings of Chief Buffalo Child Long Lance and Biographical Sketches by His Friends*. Los Angeles: Frank Wiggins Trade School, Department of Printing, 1933.

FORSBERG, ROBERTA, *Chief Mountain: The Story of Canon Middleton*. Whittier, California: The Historical Society of Alberta, 1964.

FRANKLIN, JOHN HOPE, *From Slavery to Freedom: A History of Negro Americans*. Third Edition. New York: Vintage Books, 1967.

GRIFFIN, JOHN HOWARD, *Black Like Me*. New York: New American Library, 1976. First published 1960.

JENNESS, DIAMOND, "Canada's Indians Yesterday. What of Today?" *Canadian Journal of Economics and Political Science*, 20 (1954): 95-100.

KENNEDY, DAN, *Recollections of an Assiniboine Chief*. Toronto: McClelland and Stewart, 1972.

KENNEDY, FRED, *Alberta Was My Beat*. Calgary: The Albertan, 1975.

LONG LANCE, *Long Lance*. New York: Cosmopolitan Book Corporation, 1928.

McCLINTOCK, WALTER, *The Old North Trail: Life, Legends and Religion of the Blackfeet Indians*. Lincoln: University of Nebraska Press, 1968. First published in 1910.

MOORE, ROBERT G., *The Historical Development of the Indian Act*. Ottawa: Treaties and Historical Research Centre, 1978.

MOUNTAIN HORSE, MIKE. *My People, the Bloods*. Calgary: Glenbow-Alberta Institute, 1979.

PATTERSON, E. PALMER, II, "Andrew Paull and Canadian Indian Resurgence," Ph.D. dissertation, University of Washington, 1962.

RYAN, CARMELITA S., "The Carlisle Indian Industrial School," Ph.D. dissertation, Georgetown University, 1962.

SANN, PAUL, *The Lawless Decade. A Pictorial History of a Great American Transition: From the World War I Armistice and Prohibition to Repeal and the New Deal*. New York: Bonanza Books, 1957.

WILKES, ALFRED W., *Little Boy Black*. New York: Charles Scribner's Sons, 1971.

WRIGHT, RICHARD, *Black Boy: A Record of Childhood and Youth*. New York: Harper and Row, 1966. First published in 1937.

INDEX

Radin, Dr. Paul, 147
Rambova, Natacha, 154
Red Gun, Harry, 59
Red Man, The, 20, 21
Regina, 90
Regina Leader, 90, 99, 105, 114
Reynolds, R. J. 4, 199
Rhoads, Charles, 193, 194
Rice, Grantland, 177
Robeson County, N.C., 202
Robinson's Circus, 12
Roosevelt Kermit, 176
Roosevelt Field, N.Y., 207
Ross, Joe, 24
Running Rabbit, 107, 111

Sahlen, Lilly, 234
St. John's Military
    Academy, 29-31, 36, 232
St. Paul Pioneer Press, 105
St. Paul's Blood Indian School, 67,
    70, 74, 75, 232, 234
Santa Anita, Calif., 211
Sarcee Indians, 48, 61-4
Saskatchewan Indians, 91
Saskatoon Daily Star, 111, 114
Scott, Duncan Campbell, 88, 89,
    94, 146, 187
Screenland, 205
"Secret of the Sioux, The," 134-5
Seton, Ernest Thompson, 147, 182
Seumas, Chief of Clann
    Fhearghuis of Stra-chur and
    Clann Ailpein, 184, 189, 197,
    206, 236
Shelby, Mont., 106
Sheridan, Florence, 131, 132
Sherwood, George, 176
Shuswap Reserve, 87
Silent Enemy, The, 1, 164-78, 191,
    198, 204, 205, 210
Sitting Bull, 134, 135
Smart, Mrs. Leta Myers, 228
Smith, Beverly, 189
Smith, C. O., 80
Soldiers Civil Re-establishment
    Office, 48
Spotted Elk, Molly, 168
Squamish Indians, 85, 86
Starlight, Chief Jim, 64

Stefansson, Vilhjalmur, 125
Stein, Bert, 81
Stewart, Charles, 88, 89, 93, 94,
    95
Stocken, Canon, 60, 61
Stoney Reserve, 107, 111
Strother, Bill, 52
Sun Dance, 60, 63, 68, 108-10
Syracuse Journal, 31

Tallac, Calif., 213
Te Ata, 206, 235
Tem-Kip Camp, 166, 172
Thirer, Irene, 176
Thompson, J. Walter, Advertising
    Agency, 181
Thompson, Mary, 206
Thorpe, Jim, 12, 21, 24, 45, 181-2,
    187, 228, 232
Thunder Dance, 64
Time, 176
Tims, Archdeacon John, 61-3
Tims, Winnifred, 63
Tolstoy, Ilia, 169, 170, 172, 180,
    196, 198-204, 236
Toronto Mail and Empire, 190
Toronto Star Weekly, 105, 114,
    120, 122, 125, 139, 179
Tweedle, Ralph, 213, 216, 225
Twin City Daily Sentinel, 34
Two Moons, Wesley, 24, 134
Tye, Alice, 91, 96, 223

Underwood, Katherine, 71
United Farmers of Alberta, 61

Vahey family, 51, 78, 141
Van Vechten, Carl, 189
Vancouver, 80
Vancouver Sun, 81, 86, 87, 88, 89,
    100
Vanderbilt, William K., 176
Variety, 176
Verbeck, General William, 29, 32,
    176
Vimy Ridge, 41, 42
"Virginia Dare, or the White
    Fawn," 20

Wahl, Major General, 160